Intimate Enemies

AARON BOBROW-STRAIN

Intimate Enemies

Landowners, Power, and Violence in Chiapas

Duke University Press   Durham & London   2007

© 2007 Duke University Press

All rights reserved

Printed in the United States of America

on acid-free paper ∞

Designed by C. H. Westmoreland

Typeset in Carter & Cone Galliard with Quadraat Sans

display by Keystone Typesetting, Inc.

Library of Congress Cataloging-in-Publication Data

appear on the last printed page

of this book.

Contents

Illustrations and Maps

Illustrations

Maps

Acknowledgments

This book owes a great deal to a great many people. Roberto Trujillo welcomed me to Chilón and embraced my project with enthusiasm. He provided many of my initial contacts, spent long hours answering my endless questions, and, along with Gloria Trujillo, gave me a place to live in Chilón and a place at their table in the Restaurant Susy. The willingness of many landowners and former landowners in Chilón, Sitalá, Yajalón, and elsewhere to talk with me about their lives and troubles made this project possible. I especially thank Delio Ballinas del Carpio, Alejandro Díaz, Oscar and María Franz, Wenceslao and Deyanira López, Israel Gutiérrez, Samuel Rodríguez Sr. and Jr., Carlos and Amparo Setzer, and Miguel Utrilla for long conversations and countless cups of coffee. Alí Reyes, a schoolteacher and town historian, offered many critical insights and served as a great sounding board for my ideas. I am also grateful to the staff at Chilón's Centro de Derechos Indígenas for their openness to my project.

Hubert Cartón de Grammont and Sara María Lara Flores played key roles in the early stages of my work. Hubert generously offered institutional affiliation with the Universidad Nacional Autónoma de México's Proyecto Interinstitucional de Investigaciones sobre el Campo en México. Hubert and Sara also introduced me to Jorge Martínez, my first contact with a Chiapan landowner. During my first research trip, Jorge picked up the phone and set up meetings for me with landowner relatives and friends all over north and north-central Chiapas. Jorge told me that he engaged with my project on both emotional and intellectual levels, seeing it as part of his process of working through the loss of his family's estate to land invaders. I fear I may have taken my research in directions that Jorge and many of the other landowners cited above, may not approve of, but I believe my work remains true to their desire to understand how and why their worlds came unglued in 1994.

The Chiapas scholars María Eugenia Reyes, Daniel Villafuerte, Sonia Toledo, Anna Garza, Richard Stahler-Sholk and Neil Harvey were sources of invaluable support and encouragement. Jan Rus provided detailed comments on the book manuscript and was available, above and beyond the call of duty, to gently correct my errors, steer me toward key archival sources, and generously share his rich historical knowledge of Chiapas. Jan's great enthusiasm for the study of Chiapas is contagious and his advice priceless. Jan also shared photocopies of Thomas Benjamin's notes on documents related to nineteenth-century Chiapas in the Colección General Porfirio Díaz. I thank Thomas Benjamin for making these notes public. Although we met only once, June Nash offered a critical bit of encouragement over lunch at her house during a low point in my research. Tomás Johnson and Teresa Ortiz opened their homes and hearts to Kate and me in San Cristóbal de Las Casas.

At the University of California, Berkeley, my dissertation committee — Jonathan Fox, Gillian Hart, Nancy Peluso, and Michael Watts — struck a perfect balance between rigor and support, direction and independence. Michael Watts was both a careful adviser and a constant source of inspiration for me. I marvel at the breadth of his expertise and the depth of his insights, and I feel lucky to have been his student. Thanks are also due to Laura Enriquez, Gastón Gordillo, Donald Moore, Joe Nevins, and Peter Rosset for their input at key points in the development of this project.

I had the good fortune to work and play with an incredible group of graduate students at Berkeley. I especially thank Joe Bryan, Jennifer Casolo, Sharad Chari, Rachel Cleaves, Rebecca Dolhinow, Ben Gardner, Greig Guthey, Julie Guthman, Jake Kosek, Claudia Leal, María Elena Martínez, James McCarthy, Nitasha Sharma, Susan Shepler, Shawn Van Ausdale, and Wendy Wolford. Each influenced this work in important ways. Throughout my studies I have also learned a great deal from Leslie Gates and Nathan Sayre. Since leaving Berkeley I have found friendship and new sources of intellectual challenge in my colleagues at Whitman College. The support and encouragement of Paul Apostolidis, Shampa Biswas, Phil Brick, Tim Kaufman-Osborn, Bruce Magnusson, Jeanne Morefield, and Jason Pribilsky helped make this book possible.

Scholarship is not possible without money, so I am most grateful for the generous support of the Social Science Research Council's International Dissertation Research Fellowship, the National Science Foundation's Geography and Regional Science Dissertation Improvement Grant, the University of California Humanities Research Grant, the University of California Human Rights Center, and Whitman College's International Teaching and Research Award.

Chad Johnson, Christine Fade, and Natalie Hanemann produced the maps. Valerie Millholland at Duke guided me through the world of publishing with great skill and patience.

Jim and Pat Corbett, Rick Ufford-Chase, John Ostermann, and many others affiliated with BorderLinks in Tucson, Arizona, challenged me to engage with the lived experiences of "bad guys" while not losing sight of my sense of social justice. But if I have managed to do this at all, it is thanks to the love and tireless efforts of my parents, Charles and Dianne. From their roots in civil rights struggles to their eagerness to confront new challenges from Chicago to Latin America, they are my constant anchors and inspirations. My brother Daniel challenges me at every turn to write well and engage an audience outside of the social sciences.

I thank Hana Ruth Bobrow-Strain (who learned to say "thank you" as I completed this book's first draft) and Samuel Bobrow-Strain (who is learning to say "thank you" as the book goes to press) for gracing my life. They keep me happy, laughing, and on my toes. Finally, my deepest thanks go to Kate Bobrow-Strain for supporting me through this long process. I apologize for all the stressful days and nights when I was over my head in teaching, writing, and attendant anxieties. Oh, and also for taking that dangerous, bumpy six-hour "short cut" through Cancuc and Tenejapa when you were pregnant and suffering morning sickness around the clock (even if we thought it was just giardia at the time). As an editor you grounded my worst flights of fancy and gave flight to my best ones. As a friend and partner you are beyond compare.

Abbreviations and Acronyms

AMDH   Academia Mexicana de Derechos Humanos (Mexican Academy of Human Rights)

CAM   Comisión Agraria Mixta (Mixed Agrarian Comission)

CDHFBLC   Centro de Derechos Humanos "Fray Bartolomé de Las Casas" (Fray Bartolomé de Las Casas Human Rights Center)

CEDIAC   Centro de Derechos Indígenas, A.C. (Center for Indigenous Rights, A.C.)

CENCOS   Centro Nacional de Comunicación Social (National Center of Social Communication)

CEOIC   Consejo Estatal de Organizaciones Indígenas y Campesinas (State Council of Indigenous and Peasant Organizations)

CESMECA   Centro de Estudios Superiores de México y Centroamérica (Center for Advanced Studies of Mexico and Central America)

CIESAS   Centro de Investigaciones y Estudios Superiores en Antropología Social (Center for Research and Advanced Studies in Social Anthropology)

CIOAC   Central Independiente de Obreros Agrícolas y Campesinos (Independent Union of Agricultural Workers and Peasants)

CNC   Confederación Nacional Campesina (National Peasant Confederation)

CNG   Confederación Nacional Ganadera (National Cattlemen's Confederation)

CNPI   Coordinadora Nacional de Pueblos Indígenas (National Coordinating Body of Indigenous Peoples)

CONPAZ   Coordinación de Organismos No Gubernamentales por la Paz (Association of Nongovernmental Organizations for Peace)

DAAC   Departmento de Asuntos Agrarios y Colonización (Department of Agrarian and Colonization Affairs)

EZLN   Ejército Zapatista de Liberación Nacional (Zapatista Army of National Liberation; Zapatistas)

FONAES   Fondo Nacional de Apoyo para las Empresas de Solidaridad (National Support Fund for Solidarity Enterprises)

IADB   Inter-American Development Bank

INAREMAC   Instituto de Asesoría Antropológica para la Región Maya, A.C. (Institute of Anthropological Consultation for the Maya Region)

INEGI   Instituto Nacional de Estadística Geografía e Informática (National Institute of Geography and Statistics)

INI   Instituto Nacional Indigenista (National Indigenous Institute)

IRC   institutionalized revolutionary community

NAFTA   North American Free Trade Agreement

PAN   Partido Acción Nacional (National Action Party)

PRA   Programa de Rehabilitación Agraria (Rural Restitution Program)

PRD   Partido de la Revolución Democrática (Party of the Democratic Revolution)

PRI   Partido Revolucionario Institucional (Institutional Revolutionary Party)

PROCAMPO   Programa de Apoyos Directos al Campo (Program of Direct Aid to the Countryside)

PRODESCH   Programa de Desarrollo Socio-económico de los Altos de Chiapas (Chiapas Highlands Socioeconomic Development Program)

PRONASOL   Programa Nacional de Solidaridad (National Solidarity Program)

PST   Partido Socialista de los Trabajadores (Socialist Workers' Party)

SAIIC   South and Meso American Indian Rights Center

SIC   Sistema de Información Campesina

SOCAMA   Solidaridad Campesina Magisterial (Peasant-Teacher Solidarity)

SRA	Secretaría de Reforma Agraria (Secretariat of Land Reform)
UCIAF	Unión de Comunidades Indígenas, Agropecuarias y Forestales (Union of Indigenous, Agricultural, and Forestry Communities)
UCPFV	Unión Campesina Popular Francisco Villa (Francisco Villa People's Peasant Union)
UGRCH	Unión Ganadera Regional de Chiapas (Regional Cattlemen's Association of Chiapas)
UNAM	Universidad Nacional Autónoma de México (National Autonomous University of Mexico)
UNRISD	United Nations Research Institute for Social Development
USAID	United States Agency for International Development
WTO	World Trade Organization

Rethinking Thuggery

Introduction

This is a story of village tyrants come to grief; of men and women whose carefully defended world of racial privilege, political power, and landed monopoly has come unglued. It examines the experiences of relatively powerful landowners confronted with a dramatic reordering of space and social relations in north-central Chiapas, Mexico.

From about 1930 on, a handful of ladino landowners and thousands of indigenous peasants have fought a pitched multifront battle for political, economic, and cultural dominion over a large part of north-central Chiapas.[1] The outcomes of this struggle remain unclear, but one thing can be said for certain. Ladino landowners, once the sole heirs to vast stretches of rich agricultural land and the nearly undisputed source of moral and political authority in the region, have suffered a phenomenal reversal of fortune. In the *municipios* of Chilón and Sitalá, where much of this story is set, the insurrectionary years at the end of the twentieth century augured the end of a way of life.[2] The uprising of the Ejército Zapatista de Liberación Nacional (EZLN, or Zapatistas) in 1994, followed by the invasion of more than 100,000 hectares of private property across the state and subsequent redistribution of nearly a half-million hectares of land, constituted a challenge that landowners in Chilón could not or would not defend themselves against. Acting between February 1994 and late 1998, the invaders stepped into a political opening left in the wake of the EZLN uprising, but their groups spanned the entire spectrum of Mexican politics and most were not directly affiliated with the Zapatistas.

As invasions mounted through the spring and summer of 1994, landowners screamed for justice. "We're giving the government until April 20. If there's no positive solution we'll adopt other means," one declared to a reporter (D. Scott 1994). The image of landowners "adopting other means" required no elaboration. The threat fit neatly into enduring representations of Chiapan landed elites as a violent and powerful class of modern *latifundistas*. Influential books by Luís M. Fernández Ortiz and María Tarrío García (1983) and Antonio García de León (1998 [1985]) exemplified and helped reproduce this powerful set of representations. These portrayals, in turn, seemed to confirm Barrington Moore's (1966) classic depiction of the connection between landed elites, labor-repressive production regimes, and violence. In the end, however, most landowners in this southern Mexican state, fabled for its violent agrarian politics and powerful landed oligarchy, responded to these invasions with quiescence and resignation instead of thugs and guns.

As of 2000, only 28 percent of the almost 1,300 invasions had been evicted—as opposed to an 82 percent eviction rate in the ten years leading up to 1994.[3] Instead, attempts by government mediators to resolve the disputes nonviolently culminated in March 1996 with the signing of the historic Agrarian Accords (Acuerdos Agrarios) that paved the way for unprecedented state-subsidized purchases and redistribution of land. From 1996 through 2000, peasant groups, landowners, and state officials negotiated the transfer of 244,000 hectares — 13 percent of the state's private agricultural property — and the swift resolution of outstanding land reform petitions covering an additional 242,000 hectares of private and public lands in favor of the claimants. Coming only three years after President Carlos Salinas declared the definitive end of land reform and two years after he championed changes to the Mexican Constitution that allowed for the eventual privatization of land reform institutions, the invasions in Chiapas dramatically forced agrarian demands back to center stage, leveraging massive redistributions with unprecedented speed. Contrary to both the plans of neoliberal policy makers and the fears of critics on the left, land tenure in Chiapas underwent a rapid repeasantization and reindigenization rather than privatization and concentration. After decades of inchmeal change, 1994–2001 saw the rapid and, for many rural ladinos, intolerable triumph of indigenous political leaders, monumental steps toward the destruction of land concentration, and accelerated ladino out-migration.

What most observers gloss as "the Chiapas conflict" is in fact a constellation of temporally and spatially differentiated conflicts. This book focuses on one slice of that shifting "warscape" (Nordstrom 1997): struggles between landowners and peasants in the north-central Chiapan municipios of Chilón and Sitalá, which I refer to with

Headquarters of the Olga Isabel Zapatista Autonomous Municipio in
Rebellion on a former cattle ranch outside Chilón. The sign reads: "You
are in Zapatista territory. Here the people rule and the government
obeys." *(Photo by author.)*

the shorthand label "Chilón" (see Map 1).[4] Thus, while most people
know of Chiapas only in association with the 1994 Zapatista rebellion,
this book tells a different story about different actors: it is the first
English-language study of the state's 1994–1998 agrarian mobilizations and the only fine-grained ethnography of ladino landowners,
critical but largely ignored actors in the Chiapan warscape.[5]

In Chilón, land invasions commenced in the early-morning hours
of February 14, 1994. Within two weeks, indigenous peasants from the
ejidos of San Sebastián Bachajón and San Jerónimo Bachajón, led by
the Coordinadora Nacional de Pueblos Indígenas (CNPI, or National
Coordinating Body of Indigenous Peoples), had seized more than
2,000 hectares of coffee and ranch land. By the spring and summer, a
diverse collection of organizations, from the pro-government Municipal Solidarity Committee to the Centro de Derechos Indígenas, A.C.
(CEDIAC, or Center for Indigenous Rights), an opposition group
grounded in Catholic liberation theology, followed CNPI into the fray.

Chilón's landscape mirrored these upheavals, as young corn shoots

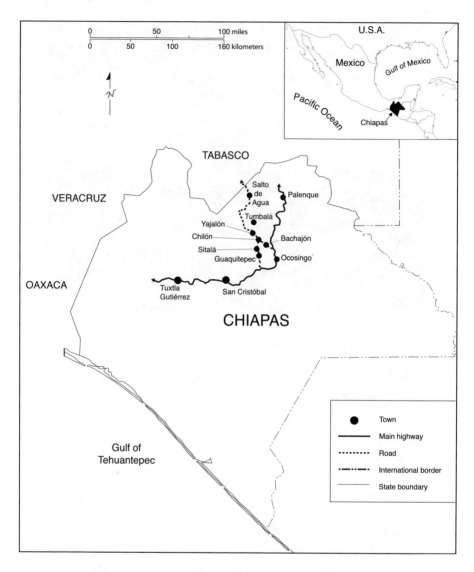

Map 1. Chiapas

appeared in hastily burned pastures and makeshift settlements grew up in what were once the region's most productive fields. Shocked ranchers watched the invasions from a distance, intervened to save livestock, and organized emergency meetings of the Asociación Ganadera Local (AGL), the Local Cattlemen's Association. That March, the ladino municipal government under Roberto Trujillo resigned under duress and was replaced by one headed by Manuel Jiménez Navarro, an indigenous land invasion leader.

Chilón's AGL pressed for evictions and threatened violence into the summer of 1994, but its demands went largely unheeded, as state and federal officials distanced themselves from landowners. By Christmas the AGL had relaxed its demands, calling for only eleven evictions and volunteering to sell thirty-six properties to land invaders.[6] With rare exceptions, Chilón's landowners eventually cooperated with a state-wide program designed to purchase and redistribute land for peasant claimants. Ultimately, according to government records, only one property was evicted in Chilón and Sitalá, and by 1999 state officials had brokered the purchase and transfer of more than 7,000 hectares to land claimants.[7]

Why would coffee planters and cattle ranchers with a long and storied history of violent responses to agrarian conflict react to these recent invasions with quiescence and resignation instead of thugs and guns? In addressing this puzzle, I rethink conceptual frameworks that have long guided the study of landowners and landed production. This analysis remains firmly rooted in agrarian political economy, highlighting the importance of what David Ricardo, Karl Marx, and generations of political economists have understood as the rentier logic of landed production. Yet I reject economic determinism, posing landed production as a social and spatial relation; not a thing, but rather a set of relational practices operating on multiple material and discursive levels that order space in particular ways. Thus, building on the work of Marxist agrarian studies, poststructural understandings of power, and critical human geography, I trace the dialectical connections between estate agriculture, cultural politics, and the ordering of space and territory.

In broad strokes, I argue that the nature and character of landed production in Chilón has always been shaped by struggles over the territoriality of estate agriculture—diverse constellations of social-spatial practices that produce the bounded spaces of estate production. These struggles constantly reshaped landed production in Chilón, generating a succession of new unstable forms over time. Each of these forms in turn conditioned subsequent struggles and shaped the channels, constraints, and opportunities for landowners' defense of territory. Thus, understanding landowners' responses to the invasions of 1994–1998 requires understanding landed production both historically and in the immediate conjuncture surrounding contemporary conflicts.

Contrary to the prevailing tendency to treat Chiapan landowners as a "divine caste" (García de León 1978:31) exercising a "perfectly coordinated" (Fernández Ortiz and Tarrío García 1983:152) and "incontestable hegemony" (García de León 1998:103) over the Chiapan countryside that remains "constant through time" (Tejera Gaona 1997:46),[8] my perspective emphasizes the incongruities and contradictions of landowners' hegemony. Thus, while the invasions of 1994 achieved an epochal reordering of social and spatial relations in Chilón, they also formed part of an ongoing process of struggle through which landed production was continually contested and remade through time. Although the acclaimed Mexican political analyst Enrique Krauze (1997:780) declared that Chiapas "was a place that . . . Agrarian Reform had ignored," the opposite is true. Agrarian reform has, in fact, effected major transformations of the state, reshaping both the material landscapes of landed production and the social relations of landowner domination. Understanding landowners' responses to the radical upending of their world in 1994 requires us to understand this broader historical geography of land conflict in Chilón.

Tacking between past and present, I conclude that Chiloneros' responses to land invasions after 1994 must be seen as the result of both broad historical shifts in the configuration of regional hegemony and conjunctural formations of landowners' identities and interests. In the years leading up to 1994, I argue, landowners already found themselves squeezed between indígenas' increasingly organized struggles for territory and declining political and economic support from the neoliberal Mexican state. Caught between these two flames, landowners found their ability to define and defend the spaces of landed production eroded in important ways. Critically, as part of these historical changes, shifting patterns of political mediation displaced landowners from their positions as the sole nexus between countryside and nation, indigenous peasants and the state—positions that had long been central to the construction and maintenance of landowners' territorial claims.

In this historical context, two conjunctural formations of identity and interests profoundly shaped landowners' calculations of the costs and benefits of violent territorial defense after 1994. First, the changing way landowners were positioned and positioned themselves in the larger nation — a complex process worked out through struggles over the meaning of nature, race, and neoliberal development — produced a strong sense of limits and constraints on their use of violence. Second, landowners' displacement from their historical role as paternal mediators between peasants and the larger polity radically upended their sense of physical security. Over many years, but explosively after 1994, indigenous people, once "known" to landowners through myriad intimate relations, have become increasingly unintelligible and unpredictable to landowners. Experienced by landowners as the unraveling of the *respeto* (respect) indígenas once accorded them, shifting hegemony kindled a geographic imaginary of fear — a palpable and territorialized terror of indigenous "savagery" — that pushed landowners toward quiescence after 1994.

This historically and geographically specific rethinking of the Chiapas case has broad implications for understanding transformations of landed production around the world. From Chiapas to Brazil, South Africa to El Salvador, traditional landed elites — often depicted as superannuated artifacts of a distant past — survive and even thrive in new political and economic contexts. The upheavals of globalization, economic restructuring, and peasant mobilizations test these actors in different ways — sometimes threatening their very existence, sometimes creating unexpected new opportunities. But, as recent developments in each of these countries suggest, landed elites continue to play critical roles shaping the trajectories of political reform — even in such highly urban nations as Mexico and Brazil. Nowhere is this more clear than in landowners' responses to a wave of new land reform movements and initiatives that emerged around the world in the early 1990s.

After two decades of declining international support for land reform, landowners today increasingly find themselves sandwiched between, on one hand, powerful new peasant movements calling for land redistribution and, on the other, states and multilateral institutions that have rediscovered land reform as a central policy tool. In this context, the transformation of landed production has taken a variety of forms and trajectories, from the União Democrática Rural's successful "uncivil movement" against redistribution in Brazil to more ambiguous outcomes in Colombia, Zimbabwe, and the Philippines.[9] Nevertheless, studies specifically focused on contemporary landed elites are few and far between, with most appraisals of recent land struggles centered on public policy and peasant movements.[10]

While studies of contemporary landed elites are rare, research that attempts to interpret the everyday lived experiences of landowners — of actors typically constructed as the bad guys — is even rarer. Despite the ongoing transformations and metamorphoses of landed production, the basic theoretical tool kit used to understand this category of political economy has not changed much since the late nineteenth century. With this book I seek to breathe new life into the study of landed elites by treating "landed production" and "landed elite" as categories without fixed meanings, categories that are everywhere constructed through contingent processes of social struggle. Centrally, I argue that landowners (as complex subjects) and landed production (as particular configurations of space and social relations) are constituted through processes of struggle over hegemony.

A Note on Fieldwork and Method

Research on agrarian conflict in Chiapas requires filtering through the attics of memory, gutted archives, rat-eaten memos, incomplete and contradictory reports issued by competing government agencies, the fragmented minutes of sham court proceedings, reports of "on-site inspections" conducted by men who never left their offices, outright lies by actors at all levels of society, and a menagerie of land titles issued by more than a half-dozen bodies over the past two hundred years. The history of agrarian conflict in Chiapas is the story of an overdetermined convergence of monumental bureaucratic incompetence, high-stakes class conflict, intimate race relations, and struggles over the meaning of gender, class, and nation. It is the story of secret meetings, under-the-table favors, deliberate misinterpretation of legal rulings, lost papers, burned archives, and late-night ambushes on lonely roads. It was the kind of process in which 1,200-acre estates could be, and were, lost by bureaucrats in the Secretariat of Agrarian Reform.[11]

Despite these difficulties, I made the decision to center my research on the causes of change in Chiapas in full awareness of the many strong criticisms of social scientific understandings of causality that have emerged out of poststructural social theory. My work represents an explicit attempt to hold in tension two seemingly incompatible leanings: on one hand, the desire to provide adequate best-guess explanations of social change and the belief that it is possible to do so, and on the other, recognition of the inescapably socially constructed nature of knowledge and its entanglements with power. Andrew Sayer's (2000, 1992) reflections on critical realism provided a powerful guide for this effort.

I made three research trips to Mexico over four years (1998–2001), one stretching out over twelve months and the others lasting two months each. In 2005 and 2006 I returned to the region for a month of follow-up research in San Cristóbal and Chilón. During each of the longer trips I split my time between interviewing various actors in Mexico City, Chilón, and San Cristóbal and conducting research at nine local, state, and national archives.

In Chilón I interviewed more than fifty current and former landowners spanning four generations. These conversations ranged between thirty minutes and six hours, although most lasted around two hours. In most cases I conducted one or more follow-up interviews. Of that group of fifty landowners, I became close to and spent considerable time drinking coffee, driving around, visiting ranches, and talking with a core group of about eight. I chose not to tape-record my interviews. Given the sensitive nature of many of my discussions and landowners' well-founded suspicions of foreign academics, this choice made sense. I grew quite proficient at scrawling nearly word-for-word transcriptions of conversations into a handheld notebook. Many of my subjects laughed and marveled at my ability to maintain eye contact and the thread of conversation while writing almost nonstop. Within a few hours of each conversation, I reconstructed the dialogue from those notes in long interview reports. Thus the quotes I present are the products of careful and disciplined efforts to produce records of long conversations as accurate as possible, but they are not mechanical reproductions. And in translating Spanish words, I balanced the demands of accuracy with the need to maintain fidelity to the immediacy and intensity of the speakers' language.

In addition to interviewing landowners, I spoke with leaders of land invasions; priests, nuns, and lay religious activists; human rights workers; government officials; and other people closely associated with peasant movements in Chilón. These interviews, however, were conducted primarily to check landowners' stories and in no way represent an ethnographic perspective on indigenous peasant mobilizations.

In assembling all this data into a set of causal arguments, I made important narrative choices. This is a *story* that makes claims about causality while striving to convey the tone and texture of social relations. It draws characters into conflicts and moves toward resolution of those conflicts. It begins and ends according to a plan. In short, it is structured not to mimic life but rather to provide convincing answers to particular questions. While I respect many efforts in this direction, I avoid the nontotalizing aesthetic of poststructural narrative, choosing instead to impose explicitly artificial closures on my material in the interest of communication, argument, and movement. At the same time, this is in no way an objective narrative. I situate myself, my motives, and my interactions with others in the text, often admitting my own ambivalence and uncertainty. "Storytelling does not aim to convey the pure essence of the thing," Walter Benjamin (1969:93) reminds us, "it sinks the thing into the life of the storyteller, in order to bring it out of him again. . . . Traces of the storyteller cling to the story the way the hand prints of a potter cling to the clay vessel."

With some exceptions, the names of people, places, and estates used in this book are real. My break with the ethnographic tradition of anonymity reflects the explicit wishes of my subjects. An overwhelming majority of landowners urged me to use their real names and laughed at the idea of concocting a pseudonym for Chilón (some would love to rename their municipio, but that's another story). This break with ethnographic tradition also reflects my interest in the workings of power. For the purposes of understanding power in the Chiapan countryside, it matters greatly that Carlos Setzer's brother Elmar served as the governor of Chiapas or that Alejandro Díaz Díaz is related to the Manuel Díaz Cancino whose name appears repeatedly in public historical documents. Short of creating an entirely fictional Chiapas, I could not have conveyed these critical dynamics of power, these articulations of land and family, and these interweavings of public and private by using pseudonyms.

I make several exceptions to this rule: First, at the beginning of every interview I asked subjects whether they wanted anonymity, and I have gone to great lengths to disguise the identity of those who answered affirmatively. Second, when using quotes from chance conversations or from people with whom I had a limited relationship, I refer to the speaker with a pseudonym or as "anonymous." Finally, when I judge that a subject's words might harm the speaker's relations, reputation, or safety, I refer to the speaker anonymously regardless of his or her wishes. These choices are, of course, subjective and difficult, so I have erred on the side of caution.

Throughout this book I use "landed elite," "landowner," and at times Chilonero interchangeably in an effort to stave off the mind-numbing repetition of a key term. For the same reasons, I also rotate between "estate agriculture" and "landed production." No analytical difference is intended.

Organization of the Book

Part I (chapters 1–3) introduces the ethnography of landed elite hegemony in Chilón and situates me as an embodied and often conflicted actor within the narrative that follows. Chapter 2 poses a series of ethical, methodological, and theoretical questions about studying elites, while chapter 3 lays out the theoretical frameworks through which I understand the connections between hegemony, space, and landowners' interests and identities.

Part II (chapters 4–6) situates the events of 1994–2000 in the larger historical context of one hundred fifty years of estate agriculture and agrarian conflict. Chapter 4 begins with the transformation of the Chiapan countryside in the late nineteenth century. Millions of acres of land were surveyed and privatized during the second half of the nineteenth century, and almost overnight, more than half the state's indigenous population found themselves dispossessed of customary land rights and put to work as debt-bound workers on coffee estates. Chapter 3 shows how, through the complex workings of overlapping scales of enforced isolation, through the twin coercions of debt servitude and carefully cultivated alcoholism, and through elaborate rituals of paternalism and respect, estates made subjects. It argues that central to this process of subject formation was the construction of a multiscalar set of social-spatial relations that constructed estates around boundaries of insidedness and outsideness and placed landowners as the sole mediators between inside and outside. Landowners' position as the sole nexus between estates and the larger world would stand as one of the most important means by which landowners' hegemony operated and, in the years to come, one of the central arenas of struggle between landowners, indigenous peasants, and the state.

Chapter 5 examines the articulations of postrevolutionary state projects aimed at subordinating the countryside. It argues that new and more effective forms of indigenous territoriality emerged out of this articulation, even as landowners appropriated many elements of post-revolutionary rule to buttress their defense against peasants' claims.

Chapter 6 continues this examination of challenges to landowners' hegemony by focusing on a massacre that took place on Sitalá's Golonchán estate in 1980. On the surface, this massacre—committed during the eviction of land invaders—seemed like another violent victory for landowners, but this chapter contends that it should be seen as evidence of a major reorientation in the relations between landowners, *indígenas*, and the state. To make this argument, the chapter examines three key factors that shaped agrarian conflict in the late 1970s and early 1980s: first, dramatic spatial, economic, and political shifts in estate agriculture associated with the transition to livestock production; second, the appearance of new actors—proponents of liberation theology in the Catholic Church and leftist opposition political parties—that fomented indígenas' radical territorial claims and further undermined landowners' ability to materially and symbolically police the boundaries of their estates; and third, conflicts among rival peasant groups that increasingly drew the state's attention away from more traditional antagonisms between landowners and peasants and led to a decline in state support for landowners.

Finally, Part III (chapters 7–9) focuses on the invasions between 1994 and 1998. Chapter 7 provides both a detailed examination of the invasions in Chilón and a broad statewide analysis of the invasions and their resolution. It is centrally concerned with, first, establishing the contours of Chiloneros' quiescence and resignation—their inability to defend the territoriality of estate agriculture. Second, it examines indígenas' invasions of estates, arguing that they must be seen as far more complex and diverse than simple land grabs aimed at securing scarce land for production.

Chapters 8 and 9 provide a two-part ethnographic explanation for landowners' responses to the invasions. Chapter 8 relates how landowners constructed their identities around racialized understandings of the meaning of "production," and how this field of meaning shaped their calculations of the possibilities for violent defense of their territory. By the 1980s, and acutely after 1994, it argues, landowners' attempts to leverage state support for estate agriculture by articulating their importance to the nation *as producers* rang increasingly hollow. Worked through the cultural field of production, this change appeared to landowners as a complete upending of the way the world worked—

a change that left landowners flailing for new ways to position themselves in the nation, and deeply endowed with a strong sense of limits on the use of violence.

Chapter 9 shows how changes in landowners' intimate relations with their indigenous neighbors intensified landowners' wariness about the use of violence. It traces how landowners' identity in Chilón has been deeply shaped by an ontological (and ultimately spatial) awareness of existing as a tiny minority surrounded by a large and frequently hostile indigenous population. This chapter explores landowners' fear of indigenous "savagery" and its role in shaping the spaces of landed production. It argues that a geographic imaginary of fear, whose formative power has ebbed and flowed and taken on new meanings over time, has always been part of landowners' taken-for-granted lived experience. After 1994, chapter 9 argues, the combination of land invasions and abandonment by the state pushed this consciousness from the realm of the habitual into the realm of immediate danger. The sheer magnitude and many layers of indígenas' transgressions of Chilón's partitioned geographies after 1994 fundamentally shaped landowners' calculations of risk and pushed them toward quiescence. Finally, in chapter 10 I outline broader implications of the Chiapas case and speculate on the ways in which landed elites in Chilón continue to remake landed production in the new circumstances.

2

Honest Shadows

Ethnography and Ordinary Tyrants

> I tell you my good friend, the chief enemy in our business [estate agriculture] is not the hare, not the cockchafer, nor the frost, but the stranger. — Anton Chekhov, "The Black Monk"

> An ability to affirm what is contingent and incoherent in oneself may allow one to affirm others who may or may not "mirror" one's own constitution. — Judith Butler, *Giving an Account of Oneself*

As I rode out of town in the back of a pickup truck carrying passengers across the mountains to Ocosingo at the end of my first stay in Chilón, an old indigenous man caught my eye. Lurching with the bounce of the truck, the man leaned toward me on the brink of an important confidence. "You," he declared with a conspiratorial jab at my pressed white shirt and wire-rim glasses, "are with the priests."

I smiled at the recurrent confusion over my clean-cut appearance and calculated my response. "No," I said, hoping that I sounded convincing enough to reassure the man if he was one of the area's many indigenous peasants violently opposed to the liberation theology church, but not so convincing as to appear apostate if he sided with the priests. The Mexican government had just expelled several foreign priests from the country, including one accused of supporting guerrilla activities in the nearby town of Yajalón. I did not want to be associated with them, but I really wanted an impromptu interview with this outgoing man.

"Ahh, so you must be with human rights!" he deduced. The man spoke fluent Spanish — all but unheard of in a Tzeltal Mayan of his age. I looked around the overflowing pickup truck to see who else might understand our conversation. Even non-Spanish-speaking Tzel-tals would recognize the phrase "human rights," and this public political situating made me uncomfortable.

I responded honestly that I wasn't "with human rights," but the man no longer put any faith in my denials.

"Yes, you are!" he said triumphantly, practically winking at me.

"No," I insisted, still unsure of his allegiances or those of any of the dozen or so other ears aboard the truck. And then, almost swallowing my words, I tried out the generic cover story I had prepared for tricky political situations: "Actually, I'm doing research on cattle production in the region. Interviewing the ranchers." This wiped the smile from the man's face.

"Oh," he said, no longer a co-conspirator, "so you're with the haves, then."

"Well . . . I don't know," I stammered stupidly.

"Yes, you do know. You're with the powerful, the rich." Disgusted, he looked away, spied a convenient spot along the road, and pounded the truck bed to signal the driver to stop. Wordlessly he climbed over me, banging his can of Ranger herbicide behind him, and disappeared into the forest.

For decades the fields of anthropology and geography contained little room for research among the haves. As Renato Rosaldo (1993:199) noted, "In Mexico, Indians have culture and 'ladinos' . . . do not. . . . To the ethnographic gaze, 'civilized' people appear too transparent for study; they seem just like 'us'—materialistic, greedy, and prejudiced." Today, thanks to changing conceptions of fieldwork within anthropology and other disciplines, research that listens closely to the powerful has slowly been recognized as a legitimate, even necessary subject of ethnography.[1] Nevertheless, when carried out in a manner that truly embraces the possibility of even momentary seduction by the attitudes and actions of one's subjects, this kind of ethnography presents significant hazards to the ethnographer. For me these dangers took two forms. First, engaged and, for all intents and purposes, complicit (at least tactically and temporarily) in landowners' often reactionary practices, I drifted in limbo, unable to connect with my subjects' sense of justice and estranged from my own; unwilling to join in landowners' politics but alienated from people who, like the indigenous stranger and his liberation theology priests, might have been natural allies under different circumstances. Second, and worse, I feared that my work might unintentionally undermine efforts to transform relations of domination and repression in the Chiapan countryside. Like scholars of whiteness within critical race studies, I wondered whether focusing on relatively powerful landowners would only further marginalize indigenous people whose voices had for so long been left out of academic analysis.

Like many U.S. and Mexican researchers, I entered the study of Chiapas through activism. When the Zapatista uprising electrified the world on January 1, 1994, I was working with a small nongovernmental organization (NGO) on the U.S.-Mexico border. For someone with a background in Central American solidarity activism and a long interest in Mexico, it was an easy leap down to Chiapas, on Mexico's southern border. As I began to visit Chiapas and got involved in various Zapatista solidarity organizations, however, I grew increasingly unsatisfied by the dualism of "good" indigenous peasants and "bad" ladino landowners around which much discussion of Chiapas revolved. What would it mean, I wondered, to take seriously—in an ethnographic and theoretical way—the lived experiences of the bad guys? How would this commitment change the ways we think about how power works in the Chiapan countryside? How would it change understandings of how positions of privilege and domination are created in general? And, most important, how would it change understandings of the politics of challenging those positions?

Following Laura Nader's (1999) classic work, I believe that "studying the colonizers" holds enormous promise for reframing debates around the formation of power, privilege, and domination. In doing this, I challenge a sustaining discourse—found in Chiapas and elsewhere—that collapses the diversity of landowners, glosses their historical mutability, and invests them with almost superhuman powers of class unity, political domination, and resistance to change. Prevailing representations of landowners that condense complex social relations and histories into essentialized visions resonate powerfully in the Chiapan countryside because the motifs and imagery of these representations reflect real histories of domination and exploitation. Yet these processes of simplification are analytically weak and empirically untenable. Facilely drawn causal connections between contemporary conflicts and Chiapas's long history of oligarchy and inequality gloss decades of political and economic transformation that have substantially altered the contours of landowners' hegemony.[2]

By focusing on Chilón's landed elites, I radically flip the story of contemporary Chiapan history and politics constructed by journalists, activists, and academics. I do not, however, suggest that ladino landowners and their allies played noble or heroic roles in seventy years of struggle. Nor should the frequent assertion that ladino landowners have suffered tremendous physical and psychological damage as a result of the battle over rural space be read as an effort to diminish the oppression and repression of indigenous participants in the struggle. Simply put, I argue that if we are to understand and perhaps move toward resolving conflict in Chiapas, research on landowners' domination must begin, as Michel Foucault (2003:30) suggests with respect to power in general, "with [power's] infinitesimal mechanisms, which have their own history, their own trajectory, their own techniques and tactics," and only then track the ways they converge — often in unpredictable and unintended ways — into more general forms of domination. Only in this way can the incongruities and instabilities of landowners' domination be seen, the unexpected trajectories of agrarian change understood, and potential leverage points for social change identified.

My introduction to Chiapan landowners came through two men who embodied the group's complex entanglements. Jorge Martínez, husband of an anthropologist friend of my principal academic sponsors in Mexico, grew up on a large estate in Chilón, left his birthplace to study biology, and then dabbled in leftist student politics in Mexico City in the 1960s. Like a number of other landowners I encountered in Chiapas, he surprised me by moving fluidly between the language of his Marxist student years and nostalgia for a harmonious rural past fractured by the incursion of the left's foreign ideas. With the family estate lost to indigenous land invaders, Martínez lived in Villahermosa, Tabasco, where he administered community development projects as the state director of the Fondo Nacional de Apoyo para las Empresas de Solidaridad (FONAES, or National Support Fund for Solidarity Enterprises).[3] In 1998 Martínez made phone calls introducing me to landowners throughout northern Chiapas and hoped that his close friends Fausto Trujillo and Gustavo Utrilla would serve as my guides in Chilón. I managed to interview Utrilla once that summer before he died of a heart attack, purportedly induced by post-1994 stress. Later I met Fausto, a novelist and retired electrical worker, but for a variety of reasons I grew closer to Fausto's brother Roberto.

Waddling like Charlie Chaplin in a camouflage fedora, Roberto

Roberto Trujillo Vera in Chilón's plaza. *(Photo by author.)*

Trujillo Vera walked just ahead of me, inspecting the progress of work-ers who had cleared undergrowth around his coffee plants. In his late sixties, Don Roberto had enjoyed retirement after juggling a career as a fieldworker in the federal malaria eradication program, in positions in the municipal government (including the post of municipal presi-dent during the Zapatista uprising), and as manager of his family's coffee estate, El Carmen Tzajalá. Things changed in the spring of 1994. Like the majority of ladino landowning families in Chilón, the Tru-jillos lost their 155-hectare estate to indigenous land invaders in Febru-ary. In March, Manuel Jiménez Navarro, leader of the largest group of land invaders, unseated Don Roberto and his ladino municipal coun-cil, replacing them with an indigenous municipal government. Today, thanks to his federal pension and income from a small restaurant and hotel, Don Roberto farms for enjoyment — "hobby farms," as he says — on fourteen hectares purchased after 1994 from loyal indigenous peasants who had been given title to land in the 1950s in return for labor on El Carmen.

From time to time as we walked through the coffee grove, Don Roberto stabbed at a plant with the ceremonial *charro* sword he affects instead of a machete. With each stab he explained why the plant hadn't been weeded: one makes a nice tea, another is used for tamale wrappers, another helps maintain proper moisture balance around young coffee plants. Through frequent drives into the countryside to visit Don Roberto's ranch at different points in coffee's annual cycle, I grasped a small piece of the ecology and business of shade-grown coffee. More important, I toured the topography of Don Roberto's childhood, watched his interactions with indigenous workers, and saw how he looked at Chilón's changing landscape.

From the top of a knoll, Don Roberto pointed through a break in the shade trees at a long hillside rising in the distance. The treeless slope stands out brightly against a background of mountains covered in dark green forest. Before 1994, Elí Rodríguez, Chilón's most prominent cattleman, owned the hillside, known as Xixontonil, and had converted it into a broad pasture. Don Roberto continued, "That used to be one of the most productive pastures in Chilón. You'd look over there and just see the green filled with brown dots — with cattle. Then [in February 1994] indígenas from Piquinteel — on the other side of the hill — invaded it. Now look at it. It has a handful of milpas over there on one side and the rest of it is just overgrown with weeds."

Don Roberto's perspective on changes in land use after 1994 is remarkably mild. For many of his friends, the conversion of pasture to vast stretches of "unproductive" wild land (*monte*) "planted only with corn" symbolize the waste and devastation wrought by the transfer of land to indigenous communities after the 1994 invasions. Images such as this one of Xixontonil overgrown with weeds serve as touchstones for the phenomenal anger that grips the ladino world. Don Roberto, however, tries to maintain a more positive outlook and stronger relations with his indigenous neighbors, so he only shakes his head and directs my attention to the sounds of a basketball game and Tzeltal cheers floating up through the forest below.

In 1902 Don Roberto's grandfather, a skilled mason, came to Chilón with a contract to restore the town's eighteenth-century church. Riding a wave of commercial expansion that accompanied the spread of coffee production into the region, he stayed in Chilón to marry into a landowning family. Don Roberto's father, Benjamin, helped found the Local Cattlemen's Association in 1962, served three terms as municipal president, expanded El Carmen Tzajalá, and struggled to ensure that his children received the education he never received. In 1988, when

Benjamin divided the estate among his nine children, most of them had successful careers outside Chiapas. Only Roberto, Fausto, and Eugenia remained nearby to manage the estate.

When Benjamin Trujillo donated sixteen hectares to his favorite debt-bound workers, he secured a stable, grateful labor force and a tactical buffer against land reform demands (see chapter 5). His actions should not, however, be read merely as an instrumental expression of objective economic interest. Asymmetrical relations of paternalism — constituting and constituted by benevolent landowner and loyal peasant subjects — saturated the pores of life in Chilón's coffee estates and were, to use Raymond Williams's (1980:37) language, "lived at such a depth . . . [that they] even constitute[d] the substance and limit of common sense for most people under [their] sway." Half a century and several waves of peasant mobilization later, these complicated ties of affection and exploitation endure in Benjamin Trujillo's children and the children of his former peons.

The sounds of basketball — a wildly popular sport in Chiapan indigenous communities — rose from a court that Don Roberto had constructed for La Providencia during his term as municipal president. In December 2000, residents of La Providencia — the name given by El Carmen's former peons to their land — insisted that Don Roberto's wife, Doña Gloria, attend their celebration of the feast of the Virgin of Guadalupe. When Doña Gloria demurred, claiming that her poor health would not allow her to climb the path to La Providencia, the men of La Providencia offered to convey her from the road to their fiesta on a palanquin, a gesture deeply inscribed with symbols of racial domination and submission.[4]

Despite the close connections between the Trujillo family and its former workers, the residents of La Providencia have fought a twenty-five-year running battle with Don Roberto's closest friend, Carlos Setzer, a powerful German-Mexican landowner and merchant. The dispute, over nearly seventy hectares claimed by both parties, erupted in violence numerous times over the years, including an October 1997 shootout between masked men from La Providencia and Setzer's employees that left a young boy dead and many wounded. Don Roberto explained that the people of La Providencia "would never touch *us*, but Carlos is another story." The complications in the relation between La Providencia and the Trujillos run even deeper. At one point Don Roberto casually remarks that "many of the people in La Providencia are *catequistas*," trained by Jesuits at the mission to teach Christian doctrine to other indígenas. With most landowners holding the progressive Catholic Church and its corps of indigenous catequistas in large part responsible for the Zapatista uprising and subsequent mobilizations, "catequista" is nearly synonymous with "guerrilla" in Don Roberto's world.[5]

Don Roberto holds these contradictions lightly. Many older landowners in Chilón, stripped of their lives' work by the insurrection, have nothing left to do but contemplate the sedimentary decline of their houses, the slow dying of everything they knew. Abandonment by the state, homilies preached against them by their priests, betrayal by formerly loyal workers — they take all these inside themselves and die of diabetes, high blood pressure, heart attacks, of *coraje* — rage. Don Roberto suffers from diabetes, but it long predates the smoke and fury of 1994. Sometimes pensive and reserved but typically outgoing and prone to long humorous anecdotes, Don Roberto serves as a bridge between factions in Chilón. As an active volunteer on the municipio's public health committee, he maintains close relations with members of the indigenous municipal governments that have formed since 1994. Although I sought subjects through avenues other than Don Roberto in order to avoid limiting myself to his circle, his circle has a broad reach. Early in my fieldwork, he even introduced me to Manuel Jiménez Navarro, the man who led the invasion of El Carmen Tzajalá and unseated Don Roberto as municipal president. Don Roberto maintains cool but cordial relations with him.

As the person who most frequently presented me to new subjects, Don Roberto helped craft the external face of my work in Chilón, emphasizing my academic purpose, listing the various landowners who had already talked with me, and interpreting my commitment to "telling the world that we are not to blame for all the problems here." Despite this introduction, my true purpose and affiliations remained subject to debate.

The signs of affluence that surrounded my North American body suggested that I should be a natural ally. I had brought a newish used Nissan Pathfinder from California to negotiate Chilón's battered roads, thinking that the made-in-Mexico Nissan would fade anonymously into the background. Unbeknownst to me, a luxury model of the Pathfinder had only that year debuted in the Mexican market and was considered the vehicle of choice among young elites. With only a handful in the entire state, mine didn't fade into the background; it became a focal point of conversations with landowners and, ironically, helped establish my trustworthiness. Leftist agitators don't drive Pathfinders.

My whiteness and foreignness also had contradictory effects. On one hand, without any intention on my part, I benefited from Chiloneros' profound belief in racial hierarchies. "You Americans are smarter, more broad-minded, and more scientific. More *chingón* [badass], as we say," one landowner informed me at the very start of an interview. "We Mexicans are more mediocre, not as capable compared to the Americans. But the indígenas are even worse. They're not motivated to do anything. Yes, they have a spirit of acquisition. We have seen that, but not a spirit of production or commerce. They have no culture of production."

At the same time, many landowners I interviewed saw foreign priests and academics as having, in one man's words, "poisoned the minds of the indígenas against ranchers." As Barrington Moore (1966:491) observed, "contempt for 'decadent' foreigners and anti-intellectualism" have for centuries characterized the attitudes of landed upper classes threatened by political mobilizations and "new and strange sources of economic power." In Chiapas, blame for the peasant uprising fell squarely on the shoulders of outside agitators. In the words of the son of a prominent merchant and landowner: "Anthropologists, sociologists, historians, priests, nuns, monks, teachers, human rights workers, missionaries from Mexico, from Europe, from the United States come here and make us out to be the exploiters. They tell the indígenas, 'This land is yours, you work it, take it from them.'"

More often than not, however, the desire to speak and be heard overwhelmed landowners' hesitation to talk with a foreigner. Interviews were often charged with emotion; rough hard men choked down tears, raised their voices in anger, or fell into long dispirited silences. Often my subjects spoke of the great relief they felt after speaking with me and thanked me for listening — something that, in Carlos Cañas's words, "no one in Tuxtla [the state capital] ever does." The more time I spent in Chilón, the more landowners took my presence for granted, but questions remained. What tactical advantage could be gained from my research? What dangers risked? I was both a likely ally and an instant suspect.

This tension played itself out disturbingly one afternoon in Yajalón. Don Roberto had introduced me to an eighty-year-old man who had lost his land in 1994, and I was following up with an interview. The man had opened up his rich memory of days spent as a traveling merchant walking from estate to estate in the 1940s, and his wife recounted in painful detail violent events surrounding the invasion of their property. Together they offered me free access to an old suitcase full of historical documents. As I sat at the kitchen table chatting, eating cookies, and taking notes on the wealth of documents, the couple's daughter appeared. Her eyes darted from me to the papers to her parents, and when her father offered pleading explanations of my presence, she exploded in an angry diatribe. The daughter accused me of working with "an organization," of using the documents to plan a new round of land invasions, of taking advantage of the elderly. She accused me of trying to steal documents and made veiled threats against my life. I had left my letters of introduction from Berkeley in Chilón, and a long recitation of local landowners who supported my work failed to impress her. I offered to show her my hard-won official permission to conduct research in Chiapas, but her mother screamed that that would be an affront to their hospitality. Her father insisted that I was there to help them, and the daughter and I found our only point of agreement: my work was not going to get the family ranch back.

Rolling her eyes at her parents' naiveté, the daughter stormed out the door with a final warning: "If we don't see a copy of your book soon, there's going to be an investigation of who you really are and what you're really doing here." Her father sat at the table a moment staring at the pile of papers between us, visibly shaken by his daughter's reaction and silently questioning his own judgment. Finally he looked up and asked directly, "Will your work help me get my ranch back?"

"No," I replied, repeating the stock phrase with which I began every interview, including this one: "At the very most, my work will raise awareness that landowners are not as bad as they're made out to be in the press." The man stood up, wiped his glasses, and walked out of the room. Mortified, almost convinced that I *had* done something wrong and wanting to escape the daughter in case she returned, I stood to leave, but her mother blocked my way, indicating that I should continue examining the documents. Fifteen minutes later, the man returned to the table and watched silently while I made my way uneasily through the pile.

Even as I shared family celebrations, rode with the local charros, and formed friendships with a handful of landowners, I knew that my relationships rested on tactical withholding. There were few outright lies among us, at least from my end and at least as far as I could discern through aggressive checking of what landowners shared with me. Instead, we omitted. We dissimulated, "drawing a veil composed of honest shadows, which does not constitute falsehood, but allows truth some respite" (Eco 1995:112). I cultivated a neutral demeanor and frequently deployed a psychologist's noncommittal "hmmm" against a steady stream of racist right-wing discourse. I never mentioned my support for many aspects of the Zapatista movement and hid my wife's involvement with EZLN women's cooperatives. Landowners, in turn, glossed their involvement in unseemly or illegal activities. When I returned to Don Roberto's restaurant after an interview with a land-owner and apparel merchant, for example, Don Roberto asked me whether the man had told me about being the major arms trafficker in town. No, of course he had not mentioned that.

Landowners maintained secret lives, and the chasm between dis-course and practice often seemed unbridgeable. Israel Gutiérrez, a merchant and former municipal president of Sitalá, for example, served as my primary informant there. In my presence Israel appeared mild and thoughtful, exuding a rare kind of quiet, self-conscious analysis of the decades of exploitation exercised by landowners in Sitalá. But here is how Don Roberto prefaced my first meeting with the former mayor: "Sitalá has a tradition of getting rid of its [municipal] presidents, if you know what I mean. Shooting them, throwing them off bridges, that kind of thing. But Israel . . . he stayed in power through his whole term because every day at noon he would charge out onto the porch of the town hall, shoot off a few rounds of his pistol into the air, and scream, 'Who's the biggest fucker in Sitalá!' [¡Quién es el más chingón de Sitalá!]."

I chose not to jeopardize my long and rich conversations with Israel by questioning him about the contradiction between his mild be-havior in my presence and this story. On other occasions, I challenged landowners' words with contradictory material from archival docu-ments or other interviews. In the end, I exercised stealthy listening, participant observation, interrogation of landowners' discourse, and interviews with peasant leaders to ensure that the contents of land-owners' secret lives did not undercut the conclusions I drew from my fieldwork.

The existence of secret lives concealed from me does not mean that landowners operated within the bounds of a fixed culture or that I could eventually cross a threshold beyond which all would be revealed. Landowners themselves did not entirely understand their predica-ment. From the mysterious architectures of imperialist conspiracy and economic globalization — shadowy forces, as insubstantial as TV waves, existing beyond landowners' will and controlled by unknown powers — to the lived, concrete but equally inexplicable emergence of peasant political consciousness, landowners cast about for ways to make sense out of a world of change and betrayal. Like me, landowners urgently craved comprehension, and it was this common search for explanation that provided the basis for my work in Chilón, a basis that transcended the obstacles of political differences, dissimulation, and the mutual exploitation on which almost any ethnography rests. In the end, while I was sometimes considered part of the external threat to landowners' livelihoods and at other times an element of symbolic capital that landowners might deploy against their enemies, my presence and endless questions served primarily as a forum through which landowners worked out their own memories and uncertainties.

One evening in the summer of 1998, after a long conversation at the home of a prominent merchant about the origins of the Zapatista uprising, Carlos Setzer's brother Hans took me aside and presented me with a folder. Shaking his head skeptically, he urged me to "take a look and see what you think — draw your own conclusions." Clipped in the folder I found a thick photocopied report on the Zapatista uprising titled "Shining Path North Rises in Chiapas: The Narcoterrorist Plot to Annihilate the Nations of Iberoamerica Advances." A "special report" from *Executive Intelligence Review* (1994), a monthly journal published in almost a dozen languages by Lyndon LaRouche, the document charted a striking bestiary of strange bedfellows purportedly responsible for the 1994 uprising: Fidel Castro; the former CIA director William Colby; "the armies of the Catholic Church"; "ex-narcotrafficker Rigoberta Menchú"; and "Nazi anthropologists" affiliated with the Harvard Chiapas project. Strangely, the report presented traditional notions of the Marxist left — imperialist plots to seize Chiapas's strategic mineral and petroleum reserves, the social costs of the Latin American debt crisis, and the threat of free trade to national sovereignty — refracted through the carnival mirror of right-wing conspiracy theory. This evocation of shadowy outside forces aligned powerfully against law and progress in Chiapas resonated strongly with landowners I met all over Chiapas during my first period of fieldwork. An Ocosingo cattleman and veterinarian explained the origins of the 1994 uprising this way: "[Bishop] Samuel Ruiz and his commando catequistas did deep sociological and psychological work in indigenous communities for decades, sowing hatred of mestizos and the idea that the indígenas were the original owners of the land and that they should start taking the land . . . [but] *behind all this are interests.* Lots of people want Chiapas's uranium—especially our neighbors. The U.S. is trying to get Chiapas to secede from Mexico . . . so it would be more vulnerable and easier to exploit. It would be easier for a foreign power to negotiate with an independent country."

This kind of discourse arises from landowners' restless sense of unmanageable change, but it also performs important ideological work. Global conspiracy explains peasant uprisings without requiring any reference to decades of unequal power relations between peasants and landowners. The landowner from Ocosingo continued: "This is just a hypothesis, but I'll tell you there was never poverty in Chiapas. Don't believe what the clergy say about social backwardness and abandonment. . . . When a foreigner like you sees the indígenas all dirty and ragged, you may think they're poor, but that's just the way they live their lives. No shoes, no education. They have their own style of health care."[6]

By the summer of 2000, when I returned to Chiapas for a second and longer period of fieldwork, fantastical rationalizations of the 1994 uprising and ensuing land struggles had largely faded. Time and distance from the events of 1994 allowed for the emergence of more worldly and ultimately more compelling accounts. The common architecture of these explanations depicted the breakdown of a system in which ladinos exercised benevolent and nearly unchallenged paternalist hegemony in the region. Shifting state allegiances, the rise of new indigenous political mediators, and the cultivation of indígenas' political consciousness by priests who promoted liberation theology and opposition political parties served as the reagents of this decomposition. One afternoon, over chess and pastries, the notorious former municipal president Israel Gutiérrez offered this subtle account of recent changes grounded in histories of landowners' exploitation, patterns of state formation, and the rise of ethnic consciousness among the indígenas:

Gutiérrez: [Years ago] the peons weren't free at all. They needed the patrón's [boss's] permission to leave. Or, for example, if they had a pig that they had fattened and they wanted to sell it, they had to pay an *alcabala*—a tax to the patrón for permission to sell the pig. . . . They worked five days for the patrón and two days for themselves.

The patrón dealt out harsh punishments and some fincas even had jails. The *finquero* punished workers for mistakes with fines to keep the worker on the finca. Many also had stills and used the liquor to keep the worker there.

Bobrow-Strain: When did this start to change?

Gutiérrez: This system began to fall apart . . . when the people began to form associations. . . . The first associations were the coffee associations formed by the INI [Instituto Nacional Indigenista, or National Indigenous Institute]. The INI came and began to train and orient [*capacitar y orientar*] the people, tell them they didn't have to work for one patrón. They could buy the land instead.

Bobrow-Strain: When was this?

Gutiérrez: The INI started . . . in 1976 and the clergy started before that . . . around 1963, I think.[7] The INI mostly focused on helping with production. The clergy . . . focused on consciousness raising. The INI would sponsor an assistance program, but the indígenas would have to go to meetings to get the benefits. They'd have assemblies and out of these assemblies grew a sense of unity. The church and the INI seemed to work together because the church gave the indígenas the idea that they should take over land and the INI gave them the money to buy the land. That was in the 1980s [when the indígenas invaded dozens of estates and then leveraged state subsidies to buy them]. The clergy taught the value of conquest and the INI gave the money. . . . [In 1994] the invasions were more difficult. The peasants had the idea of finishing everything off. . . . The indígenas don't want a little or half, they want everything. They want all the mestizos to leave.

Bobrow-Strain: Why is that?

Gutiérrez: Because that's how they've been indoctrinated by the clergy, the Agrarians [Agrarian Reform officials], and other branches of the government.

Unconsciously, my own working assumptions and research priorities morphed in tandem with landowners' changing perspectives. At first I located metanarratives of globalization and neoliberal agricultural restructuring at the heart of transformations in Chilón. By 2000, however, my focus had shifted toward the micropolitics of relations between landowners, peasants, and state actors. In fact, with some exceptions, my arguments mirror almost exactly those of landowners with whom I share a common urge to understand the sources of change. Our differences lie in how we interpret the meanings of change.

Asked to reflect on the changes he had seen in his lifetime, Oscar Cruz, a young Chilonero whose father had been tortured and almost killed by indigenous land invaders in 1994, blurted out a cryptic phrase: "Before there was more innocence. Now there's more ignorance." Oscar turned the words over in his mouth a few times — "Innocence. Ignorance. Innocence. Ignorance" — before elaborating: "There was innocence because there was more respect, more morality. That innocence is lost and now there's much less respect. People are more liberal. There's more conflict now because there's no respect for the law."[8]

In the end, those two words stuck with me. This book tells the story of landowners who believe that they have lived through the end of respect and innocence and the dawn of insecurity and ignorance. James Ferguson (1999:20), in his account of the splintering lives of urban residents of the Zambian Copperbelt, reflects on "the ethnography of decline": "The tragic course that so many people's lives were taking was not only an anthropological fact of some theoretical interest; it raised ethical and methodological difficulties of a sort that I was not well prepared to deal with. My fieldwork left me a terrible sense of sadness, and a recognition of the profound inability of scholarship to address the sorts of demands that people brought me every day. . . ." Landowners in Chilón counted on significantly more resources and cultural capital with which to confront a world spun out of control than Zambia's urban poor, but — particularly older landowners — had lives equally defined by "decline, confusion, and fear."

These men and women fit themselves within crumbling adobe walls, lived their lives in a narrow town and under mossy tile roofs. They built modest coffee farms, wore pressed white suits on Sundays, and shuffled the same few last names like playing cards. Their sons went to school in the big provincial town and wrote patriotic odes on national holidays. Sometimes they married well. One became governor. Now they sit at home and contemplate the decay of respect and production, or they leave in search of new bases for prosperity. They are the sad and dangerous strata of people who feel as run over themselves as the others they have run over. Those older Chiloneros who insisted that their children put their faith in higher education — not agriculture — receive solace and critical financial support from their children's careers. Yet even these children — veterinarians, lawyers, teachers, and truck drivers — express a longing for something lost.

As with Ferguson, my engagement with Chiloneros and their losses produced sadness. Born in human connections made around kitchen tables and coffee fields, my sadness rose from appreciation of the pain of loss and decline. Unlike Ferguson, however, I could never accept landowners' decline as wholly unfortunate. A growing realization that most forms of indigenous authority emerging through the cracks of landowners' declining hegemony have been cut from the same fabric of corrupt and violent clientelism as those of their ladino predecessors deepened my ambivalence about the changes in Chilón. These feelings, however, never blurred into longing for the simpler days of the paternal *casa grande* and its happy peons. While my research challenges many facets of landowners' thuggish reputation, time spent with landowners reminded me at every turn that they were, and in large part continue to be, the millstone of a grinding racist violence of everyday life.

What follows then, is a story of a past that was not as innocent and a present that is not as ignorant as landowners contend. Nevertheless, to replace landowners' unmediated tale of innocence lost with a reiterated discourse of sweeping condemnation would substitute caricature for caricature. Instead, twisting Umberto Eco's evocation of dissimulation, I seek to replace the sharp dualisms of evil and good, landowner and peasant, with "honest shadows."

Landed Relations,

Landowner Identities

Race, Space, Power, and Political Economy

> The rural bourgeoisie . . . [is the] small and medium landowner who
> is not a peasant, who does not work the land, . . . but who wants to
> extract a convenient life from the little land that he owns. . . . [The rural
> bourgeoisie] desires to send its sons to university . . . [and exhibits]
> an atavistic and instinctive fear of the peasant and his destructive
> violence. — Antonio Gramsci, *The Southern Question*

Enrique Díaz laid out family photos as we sat together on a plank
bench in his shabby grocery shop. One photo from the 1920s caught
my eye immediately. It was a formal family portrait, a photo of stiff
people in starched collars.[1]

Enrique's mother and father stood at the rear. He wore a high-
collared shirt, white suit, and tie, she a white dress and brooch. In
the foreground, Enrique and his brothers, sporting linen pants and
starched shirts, mirrored their father — at least from the knees up. As
my eyes moved down the photo, however, their linen pants ended
abruptly in bare feet; dark, swollen, mud-cracked *peasant* feet.

Landowners in Chilón and Sitalá often comment on the similarities
between indigenous peasants and themselves. Enrique's relative Alejandro Díaz offered this very common insistence: "I spent my whole
life on a ranch surrounded by *campesinos* [peasants]. . . . Even though I
live in a more civilized place now [the town of Chilón], I still have a
lot of Tzeltal customs and mannerisms." Another rancher's son, now
an urbanized leftist journalist, added to this image: "I call them the
'bourgeoisie' but they don't come anywhere near our [urban] middle-

class life. You and I have our cell phones, our cable [TV]. These people live with burlap sacks of coffee stacked in their living room. They like their little tortillas handmade with their little country beans."

During World War II, although he came from one of the most powerful families in Sitalá, Enrique Díaz left home to work as a bracero picking garlic in Texas. When we spoke in 2000, Díaz could not contain the sense of superiority this cosmopolitan experience instilled in him. His recently removed and slightly furry prostate floated in a jar of cane liquor on the bench beside us as we talked. It is critical to save these artifacts of modern medical science, the octogenarian farmer told me, "in order to show the *naturales* that their witchcraft and superstitions are things of the past."[2]

Enrique Díaz is part of a backwater landed oligarchy, a strange hybrid of cosmopolitan suits and peasant feet. Chilón's landowners are a group that defies easy classification on the axes of class, race, and gender. What matters is how the categories of class (landowner, peasant), race (ladino, indígena), and gender (machismo and masculinity) come to mean something to landowners as they struggle to define themselves in relation to each other, their indigenous neighbors, and the state.

Nearly all the men and a few women who populate this study identify themselves as *propietarios* (landowners)[3] or *comerciantes y propietarios* (merchant-landowners). These labels, however, mask considerable diversity. All "landowners" I encountered derived income from landed production, almost always in the form of coffee cultivation and cattle ranching (at least before 1994), but most also had off-farm sources of income. Some, such as Miguel Utrilla and Carlos Setzer, fit the image of wealthy *caciques* (political bosses), influencing regional politics from behind the scenes, producing substantial quantities of coffee on large tracts of land, and engaging in large-scale commercial activity. Others, such as Gabino Vera, who was accidentally arrested and convicted of belonging to an illegal peasant organization, are at first glance barely distinguishable — in manner, dress, speech, and wealth — from prosperous peasants.

Roberto and Fausto Trujillo both combined employment in low-level but comfortably unionized government jobs (the Ministry of Health and the Federal Electrical Commission, respectively) with the administration of their family estate. The income of a third Trujillo brother, who was in the upper management of PEMEX, the national petroleum company, sustained all the family's holdings through hard

Prominent ladinos outside Chilón's town hall, c. 1920.
(From the private collection of Alí Reyes.)

times. Thanks to the gendered politics of educational and professional opportunities, only Roberto and Fausto's sister Eugenia truly fit the pure category of landowner. While her brothers balanced landowner-ship with careers that took them away from Chilón, Eugenia remained to serve as the primary estate manager after their father's death.[4]

Other landowners survive peasant-style by cobbling a living out of farming and meager incomes earned as tradesmen or small-time merchants. Before losing his land in 1994 and taking up full-time work as a small-time merchant, another landowner relied heavily on remittances sent by a son who worked as a service employee in Cancún. After the invasions of 1994–1998, these differences grew even larger, as wealth and status enjoyed before 1994 strongly determined the degree to which landowners could negotiate settlements from the state and recover from the loss of landed livelihoods.

Landowners frequently used the language of class and production to distinguish among themselves, often differentiating between "real" and "false" landowners. As Eulalio Hernández insisted, "I am a landowner . . . ranching is my vocation, but there are some landowners who have the money to own ranches but don't live on them. They just visit them from time to time. They don't have a passion for production." Nevertheless, despite these very real differences, the category of landowner has come to mean something to those who use it. While this meaning is constantly debated, it retains a certain coherence in the minds of most people who position themselves as landowners. Perhaps even more remarkably, as chapter 7 indicates, landowners' responses to land invasions after 1994 defied predictions based solely on individual actors' positions in relation to land, labor, and capital. Indeed, in chapters 8 and 9 I argue that landowners' relatively unified response to invasions turned on the ways in which they, as a group, were positioned in larger discourses of Mexican national development, neoliberal citizenship, and race violence that ignored differences within the group.

Like the classed elements of landowner identity, race serves as an axis of both difference and unity. Going against common usage in Mexico, where the label "mestizo" is typically used to indicate people of mixed European and indigenous origins, I refer to landowners as ladinos throughout this book. Although Latin American notions of *mestizaje* (the fusion of races) have their origins in revolts against Spanish colonial privileging of racial purity (de la Cadena 2000, Mallon 1996), the term itself continues to evoke biology and bloodlines. "Ladino," on the other hand, although also a deeply contradictory category (Nelson 1999 and 2003, Gould 1998, Hale 1996), is widely understood in Chilón as a category lived out in practice. Alí Reyes, a young schoolteacher and landowner's son, reflected: "'Mestizo' isn't very precise, because everyone has mixed blood here. You have Tzeltals with blond hair and blue eyes, but who identify as Tzeltal. . . . When you use 'ladino' it indicates that the difference is more a style of life, how people dress and act."

Faced with this complexity, biology and phenotype provide little purchase in defining landowners. Alí's grandfather, Oscar Franz, whose parents were German, is married to an indigenous woman. Their dark-skinned son, Alí's father, was an active member of the Cattlemen's Association and lost land to indigenous invaders in 1994. Alí, on the other hand, is lighter-skinned than his father, but actively engaged in local indigenous politics.

Despite this imprecision, landowners make frequent and deliberate use of biologically based racial hierarchies as they position themselves in relation to others. This positioning took multiple forms, from frank deployment of racial hierarchies to subtle rituals of domination and subordination to frequent self-deprecating wordplay, as in an encounter at the Restaurant Susy that revealed deep anxieties about whiteness:

> Gloria: Aaron, how do you like your steak à la mexicana?
> Aaron: It's delicious, thanks.
> Nango: But wouldn't it be better with a Rubia [a brand of lager; lit. Blonde Woman]?
> Gloria (*A relatively light-skinned ladina*): Sorry, Aaron, we're all Negras Modelos [a brand of dark beer; lit. Black Female Models] here!

Thus while German-descended Carlos Setzer openly disparaged ladinos' impure bloodlines and light-skinned ladinos differentiated themselves from their darker-skinned compatriots, the broad category of ladino still meant something. It clearly distinguished "people like us" from indígenas (even when I could see no outward differences between poor ladinos and their indigenous neighbors [cf. Nelson 1999:75]). For landowners, rich and poor, the term operates primarily to define and confirm a binary opposition between "us" and "them." Even more importantly, it positions landowners in a privileged position in the Mexican nation.

As my conversation in the Restaurant Susy suggests, landowners' positioning in relation to class and race was also shot through with particular constructions of gender (and vice versa). Historically, caciques and landowners have served as the template for depictions of Mexican machismo (e.g., Paz 1985). This macho character, as Evelyn Stevens (1973:90) observed, is steeped in a "cult of virility," characterized by "exaggerated aggressiveness." He is, in Oscar Lewis's classic formulation, a man who will "never give up or say, 'Enough' . . . [who wants] to go to his death smiling" (quoted in Gutmann 1996:231).

In many ways, Chiloneros affirm this stereotype through violent bluff and bluster. One landowner carries a gun, he tells me, "because at least that way I'll take some Indians to my grave with me when they get me." At the same time, as Matthew Gutmann (1996:241) cogently argues, machismo is not an essential identity. Rather it is a category with "multiple shifting meanings," always existing in tension with other discourses and practices of masculinity. In Chilón, macho violence was often offset by another current of masculinity steeped in notions of responsibility and careful governance, closely associated with agricultural production. Thus the meanings of masculinity turned not just on violence and virility but also on caution and hard work. This intersection of macho virility and racialized paternal responsibility manifested itself clearly in Chilón's agrarian politics. Paternalism played a key role in defining landowners' relations with their indigenous workers, constructing estates as hierarchically ordered patriarchal families. In other contexts, this construction of masculinity as careful paternal guidance constituted one of the central idioms through which landowners experienced agrarian conflict. As I explain later, the tremendous psychic dislocation of land invasions arose not out of a frustrated macho impulse to fight to the death, but rather from a loss of connection to production, understood broadly as the coming together of hard work, progress, masculinity, and vocation.

So what is a landowner?

In popular and academic writing on Chiapas and in everyday speech the terms *terrateniente* (landlord), *latifundista* (owner of a large estate), and *ganadero* (cattleman) carry enormous unstated meanings. Particularly since the Zapatista uprising, these words have served — more or less accurately — as a sort of shorthand for a string of negative characteristics: oppression of indigenous peoples, land concentration, corrupt politics, violent repression, and grinding structural violence. This discourse, however, often groups landowners with other "bad guys": "In Chiapas," Thomas Benjamin (1996:223) wrote, "[landowners] and the state are the same thing." Similarly, especially in the early years of the Chiapas conflicts, analysts often lumped landowners with peasant paramilitary organizations.[5]

Much writing on Chiapas ultimately transcends its own simple shorthand. Indeed, Thomas Benjamin's classic work (1996) admirably traces complex, often conflictive relations among landowner factions and between these groups and state actors, particularly in its discussions of prerevolutionary Chiapas. Similarly, Fernández and Tarrío's *Ganadería y estructura agraria en Chiapas* (1983) provides a highly nuanced look at the relation between landowners and the state in mid–twentieth-century Chiapas despite its painfully mechanical understanding of class power. Even Antonio García de León (2002:27) has acknowledged the historical "displacement of the traditional oligarchy" in Chiapas and focused substantial attention on this process.

My goal in reflecting on the study of landed elites in Chiapas is not to create a straw man or to frame my arguments against "bad" portrayals of landed elites. Rather it is to highlight the limited extent to which landed elites have been studied at all in this heavily studied region of rural Mexico. A few lesser-known works on indigenous mobilization craft multidimensional portraits of landowners (e.g., Alejos García 1999, 1996), while an even smaller group effectively centers its attention on the history and contemporary challenges of landed production (e.g., Toledo Tello 2002, Reyes Ramos 1998b). More often, however, landowners haunt the margins of the voluminous literature on indigenous Chiapas. Or, more accurately, landowners act as foils: interesting only insofar as they shape the contours of indigenous communities and provide the historic target for indígenas' resistance.[6] When landowner agency is framed in this way, it is limited to the narrow palette of ideological and coercive control, ignoring the more complex processes of subject formation, cultural struggle, and diffusely working power found in recent works on indigenous Chiapas.

Yet, as the stories that begin this chapter suggest, landowners' identities and interests are far from monolithic. Two challenges present themselves immediately if landowners are to be conceived as full-fleshed actors, not foils. First, landed elite must be seen as a constantly shifting, culturally constructed category, not as a fixed position in relation to land, labor, capital, or the state. And second, we must carefully parse the complex ways in which landowners and the state have interacted over time, sometimes supporting one another, sometimes undermining one another, and often generating unexpected outcomes.

How can we find a useful framework for understanding this unwieldy assemblage of divergent class, race, masculinity, and numerous other positions? If responses to agrarian conflict arise from a set of interests, what leverage does social theory provide for understanding how these interests — landed interests, if you will — get formed out of such an ungainly assortment of positionings?

For decades, most studies of landed elites everywhere (not just in Chiapas) and their roles in agrarian conflict have deployed narrow readings of political economy aimed at grouping those elites according to purely economic types arrayed on predetermined paths of economic transition. In rejecting this trend, I do not reject political economy. Quite the contrary. Cultural politics and political economy are inseparable in the study of estate agriculture. As should be clear shortly, Marxian-inspired agrarian political economy — long the central (or only) site of vibrant scholarship on the nature of modern landed production — remains fundamental to my thinking on the subject.[7]

Theorizing Landed Interests: Political Economy and Cultural Politics

From their origins in nineteenth-century debates about capitalist development, the categories of landed production and landowner were addressed by political economists at oblique angles with ulterior motives. Not only was discussion of landowners typically harnessed to anti-landowner politics, but, more importantly, classical political economy deployed the category as a way of working through lines of argument only tangentially related to the real social relations of landed production.[8]

Nevertheless, classical political economy — particularly the ideas of the conservative political economist David Ricardo and his radical critic Karl Marx — has irrevocably branded the study of landed elites. Indeed, in the more than 150 years since Marx and Ricardo wrote, interest in landed production has not strayed far or advanced much from its nineteenth-century foundations.

Not surprisingly, then, when I entered Chiapas as a twenty-first-century ethnographer interested in categories of identity and difference, race, gender, class, and meaning, Ricardo's and Marx's enduring formulations weighed heavily on me. Their central analytical tool for understanding landed production — the concept of rent — seemed stodgy and ill suited to nuanced conceptions of power, at least on the surface. In plain terms, Ricardo, Marx, and most subsequent theorists have agreed that landed elites derived their wealth from political control over territory rather than from efficient production. That is, landowners used monopoly control over land to reap excess profits (called rents in the obscure language of classical political economy) without having to reinvest profits in increasing productive efficiency, simply because their historically privileged access to land and labor allowed them to produce at lower cost than other competitors.[9]

Although this monopoly position clearly gave landed elites short-term advantages, for most theorists it also sealed their fate. Without reinvestment of profits, landowners' production would stagnate and become increasingly unable to compete with more innovative capitalist agriculture (Fine 1979). Modern landed production was an unstable form that eventually would be undone by capitalist competition. Thus subsequent debates took as their primary tasks the typologizing of actually existing landed properties according to purely economic variables and the locating of these forms on objective paths of capitalist transition away from antiquated estate agriculture.[10]

Meanwhile, by the mid-1980s, scholars studying peasant production had found economism and class-centrism challenged and destabilized from all directions.[11]

On one hand, studies of peasant resistance (e.g., Scott 1985, Smith 1989) dramatically expanded earlier understandings of the limited modes and possibilities of peasant politics (e.g., Paige 1975, Wolf 1969). On the other hand, engagements with feminist theory (e.g., Hart 1991, Carney and Watts 1990, Deere 1990), subaltern studies (e.g., Guha 1982), critical race studies, and Foucauldian understandings of power (e.g., Stoler 1995b) shifted the study of peasant actors away from economism and toward a broadly construed cultural politics of economic and social change. From my perspective, there was a clear double standard: peasants received nuanced analyses tacking between political economy and cultural politics, while the interest in landed elites remained confined to the economic logic of landed production.

At the same time, confronted by the concrete realities of landowners' struggles to maintain their livelihoods and influence in the Chiapan countryside, I understood that Marxian political economy had a lot to offer — particularly once I came to understand the political economy of estate agriculture not as a definite "logic" but rather as a process of cultural-political struggle over space operating in multiple registers, including race and gender. But there was still a problem: according to key theorists, landowners, finding themselves increasingly unable to compete against more innovative capitalist agriculture, would be thrust by the economic logic of ground rents toward increasingly violent responses to peasants' challenges to their control over territory (Paige 1997, 1975; B. Moore 1966). While these works brilliantly demonstrate how challenges to the economic logic of landed production propel landowners toward violence, the case that confronted me in Chiapas suggested that understanding economic propulsion is not sufficient. Why would rentier landowners respond to challenges from the peasantry with quiescence and resignation rather than with thugs and guns? If the political economic insights into landed production were to be as useful to the study of landed elites as, say, gender or race — which I strongly felt they should be — they had to be modified to avoid the pitfalls of economism. My goal, then, was to reaffirm the importance of political economy in the study of landed elites, while reworking the limited way in which political economy is usually conceived in this type of study. To do this, I returned to Marx.

Although they are closely related, Marx's understanding of land-owners' ability to earn unusual profits without productive reinvestment differed from Ricardo's classic formulation in one fundamental way. Ricardo's economics naturalized landowners' profits (rents), presenting them as a "gift of nature" arising out of naturally occurring differences in fertility and location. Marx countered that landowners' control over territory was not a natural gift but rather a process of distributional struggle, "written in the annals of mankind in letters of blood and fire." Landowners' profits (rents) presupposed and depended on the existence of a historically specific system of landed property; a distributional struggle in the present that was itself the outcome of distributional struggles in the past (Hall 1974). Simply put, landed property, like all political economic categories in Marx's writing, is not a fixed "thing"; it is a social relation (it is also, as I discuss below, a spatial relation) whose specific forms and outcomes could be understood only through concrete analysis of particular historical-geographic conjunctures (Ollman 1976, Hall 1974).

Thus, while many theorists have taken to heart Marx's suggestion that landed production would tend to disappear in the face of capitalist competition, treating it as an iron rule of capitalist transition, Marx himself expressed less certainty. In a letter cited by David Harvey (1999:345), Marx criticized those who turned his "historical sketch of the genesis of capitalism into an historico-philosophical theory of the general path of development prescribed by fate to all nations, whatever the historical circumstances in which they find themselves . . . events strikingly analogous but taking place in different historical surroundings led to totally different results."

Ultimately, I argue that this quote neither settles the question of landed production's "final fate" nor implies the need for further wrangling over whether landed production is truly transitory. This question, around which so much ink has been spilled, has little meaning for me, for peasant movements struggling against landed production, or for the landowners who live out the daily mess and madness that slowly accretes into long-term social change. Indeed, while I trace a specific form of landed production through a historical arc of decline and transformation, I make no claims whatsoever about the long-term existence of landed production as a category. What is central to me is precisely Marx's "different historical surroundings" and "totally different results."

Stuart Hall's theory of articulation (Hall 2002, 1996; Slack 1996) arose from this nonreductive analysis of Marxist method and offers a less economistic way of understanding the logic of landed production. Articulation, for Hall, moves beyond theorizing necessary connections and determinations (e.g., Paige's attempt to theorize a necessary connection between economic pressures and landowners' violence) to focusing on the concrete ways those connections and determinations are actually made in the real world. In this light, the goal of scholarship is to reveal the complex and undetermined power relations through which subjects, ideologies, and practices articulate in particular moments and places. My specific aim is to trace the historically and geographically singular ways in which landowners in Chilón have been positioned by multiple pressures, from the exigencies of political economy to the changing meaning of neoliberal citizenship to geographical imaginaries of race fear, and have actively positioned themselves in relation to those pressures. Landowners' interests and identities are deeply and unavoidably etched by the unique pressures and logics of their form of production — but not reducible to them. Only by conceiving landed production in this way can one understand the unexpected ways in which landowners responded to the pressures of economic restructuring and peasant mobilization.

One further lesson is to be gleaned from Marx's understanding of landed production, a lesson that will help organize the diffuse forces that make up the cultural politics of estate agriculture. It is the obvious fact that Marx treats landed production as a social relation geared toward ordering space in particular ways. Estate agriculture is a struggle over space and territory.

Articulating Territorial Struggles in Chilón

This book examines struggles over territory in Chilón. In particular, it traces ongoing attempts by ladinos to defend the spatial order of landed production in the face of indigenous claims to land and autonomy. Thus, it is a book about territoriality, defined in its most basic sense as the social creation of a bounded space in an effort to exercise control over that space, its contents, and the practices of people within that space.[12] I take this definition further: territorialities (or territorial projects) are constellations of spatial practices aimed at delimiting, representing, and enforcing spatial boundaries in the service of complexly constructed interests. Henri Lefebvre's (1991) meditations on social practices and the production of space help refine this definition. First, for Lefebvre, all social practices are spatial. They both produce space and are themselves shaped by existing spatial configurations. Struggles over land in Chilón, for example, with their attendant spatial practices of invasion, mapping, lobbying, leafleting, assassination, and legal wrangling, shape the material landscape. But they are also the products of the way that landscape was configured in the past. For example, small buffer properties split off from large estates and given to loyal peasants in the 1950s (described in chapter 5) were immediate spatial outcomes of previous agrarian conflicts. At the same time, by serving as one of the physical bases for the development of indigenous territorial claims played out in 1994–1998, buffer properties also shaped the trajectories of subsequent agrarian conflict.

Second, Lefebvre cogently demonstrates that spatial practices operate in multiple registers. His dialectical scheme for understanding the politics of space has been reworked (e.g., Harvey 1990) and critiqued (e.g., Keith and Pile 1993), but its central point remains that space is produced through both material and representational practices. Indeed, material and representational practices are inseparable, recursively connected by relations of mutual constitution. Landowners' discursive racialization of space, for example, has had profound effects on Chilón's material landscape, just as more clearly physical practices such as building fences and roads have been essential components of the representation and imagining of space.

Thus the "how" of territoriality as presented here is quite broad. As Nikolas Rose (1999; cf. Watts 2003) argues, power operates, in large part, through the creation of "governable spaces": "a matter of defining boundaries, rendering that within them visible, assembling information about that which is included and devising techniques to mobilize the forces and entities thus revealed" (33). These spaces, in turn, "make new kinds of experiences possible, produce new modes of perception. . . . They are modalities in which a real and material governable world is composed, terraformed, and populated" (32). Thus the creation of governable spaces is also the production of governable subjects. At its core, however, three intertwined types of practice play pivotal roles in the construction of territory: the classification and delimitation of bounded spaces, the sedimenting of those spaces with meanings that shape subjects and naturalize the territory, and the enforcement of boundaries through surveillance and coercion.[13]

These processes of territoriality and subject formation do not unfurl automatically and unchecked: they are always contested and reworked. Struggles to bound and define territories always and everywhere encounter "a fractured landscape saturated with power, cultural meanings, and the legacies of past struggles" (D. Moore 1998:367). Efforts to forge governable spaces and subjects constantly articulate with and are transformed by other territorial projects (Watts 2003; cf. Ong 2000, D. Moore 1999, Li 1999). In this sense, territoriality rests on a constantly shifting process of hegemony formation.[14]

The techniques, goals, idioms, and channels of the struggle for hegemony are shaped by existing configurations of territory and in turn generate new boundings of space. Following Gramsci (1971), I consider hegemony not as monolithic ideological domination but rather as the fragile balancing of coercion and consent in "a continuous process of formation and superseding of unstable equilibria between the interests of the fundamental group and those of the subordinate group" (182). As William Roseberry (1994:361) contends, it is a "problematic, contested, political process of domination and struggle . . . [that] constructs . . . not a shared ideology but a common material and meaningful framework for living through, talking about, and acting upon social orders characterized by domination." Thus, in this reading with its emphasis on the way hegemony shapes subjects, consciousness, priorities, and expectations, Gramsci presages Foucault's interest in the productive, diffuse, and multidirectional workings of power (Foucault 1990:95). Subjects are never "located 'outside' fields of ideological and cultural domination," as Gastón Gordillo (2002a) succinctly argues. "The images and symbols used by subordinate groups to understand or resist their domination are shaped by the processes of domination itself."

Seen in this light, landowner territorialities — the territorialities of estate agriculture — must be seen as a constellation of diverse social-spatial practices through which different actors construct estates as bounded spaces of landed production through struggles over hegemony. The territoriality of estate agriculture is not something constructed exclusively by landowners, but rather is a set of relations among actors — contingent manifestations of the articulation of various landowner, indigenous, and state territorialities as they intersect over time, sometimes undermining, sometimes reinforcing each other, always creating new kinds of subjects, opening new opportunities for action and foreclosing others.[15]

Estate Formations

4

Children of the Magic Fruit

The Making of a Landed Elite, 1850–1920

In the late 1880s, Chiapas's governor Manuel Carrascosa mounted a massive campaign to attract international investment to the state. The 1889 Universal Exposition in Paris was to be Chiapas's cotillion, its grand entrance onto the world stage. "Only [the world's] ignorance of what we are actually worth, the resources we have, and the resources we could have in the future," Carrascosa wrote, "can . . . hold back the arms, the intelligence, and the foreign capital that will work with our own to build a prodigious progress" (1889).

As the exposition neared, Carrascosa amassed an enormous display of Chiapas's natural wealth, brought in from the far reaches of the state on steamships, mules, and the backs of indigenous porters: amber came from the department of Simojovel, quetzal feathers, wildcats, and medicinal herbs from Comitán, natural dyes from Tonolá and Palenque. He gathered samples of mineral water from six springs, ginger, cane liquor, artificial flowers, palm wine, artisan cheeses, rare table salts, and indigenous textiles from the entire state. Chiapas's indigenous population was touted as "a labor force in search of an entrepreneur" (quoted in Baumann 1985:12).

Every aspect of Mexico's broader participation in the Paris Exposition extolled the new "science" of liberal government spreading through the nation during the late nineteenth century. Mexico's national pavilion, an Aztec pyramid at the base of the just-built Eiffel Tower, was filled with exhibits on hygiene, medicine, sanitation, criminology, anthropology, statistics, and public administration (Tenorio-Trillo 1996). Systematic presentation of Mexico's vast riches to the world would, in the minds of the country's Liberal technocrats, inexorably attract foreign investment and buoy the Mexican economy.

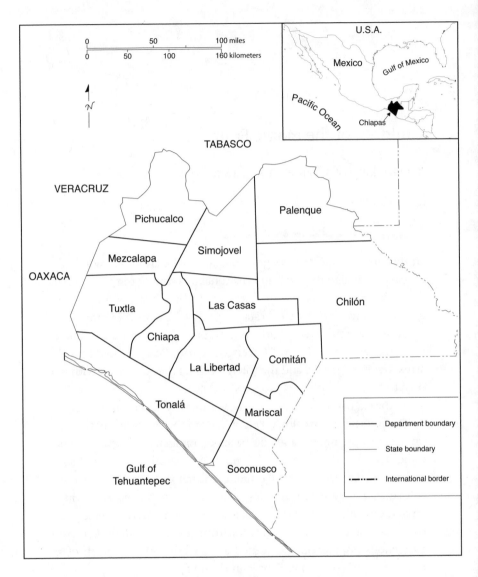

Map 2. Departments of Chiapas, 1910 (based on Benjamin 1996:36)

But amid the cornucopic display of Chiapas's potential gathered by Carrascosa for the exposition, Chilón — still sparsely populated by ladinos — was hardly represented.[1]

Less than three decades earlier, in 1861, the French traveler Désiré Charnay had noted nothing of particular interest in Chilón. The Indians were poor and most ladinos produced only corn and beans, he reported. Even sugarcane was "not found until Guaquitepec" (Charnay 1956:135). Other reports from the same period suggest that early ladino estates around Chilón did produce substantial amounts of sugarcane, but Charnay got one thing right: ladino agriculture in the region was, for the most part, a ragged affair conducted by poor farmers on marginal estates.

The countryside around Chilón had seen trickles of ladino and Spanish in- and out-migration since the seventeenth century, and marriage records show that most of the ladino surnames carried by Chiloneros today were present by 1800. Yet even as late as the 1892 census, the vast Department of Chilón reported only 8,237 ladinos, and those were mostly concentrated in or around Ocosingo, far to the east of the towns of Chilón, Sitalá, and Guaquitepec (Rabasa 1895). Cristina Cancino, a young Chilonera, complained in 1896, "There are so few ladino families in this town, it's hard to find someone of your own class to tie the knot with."[2]

While tensions between ladinos and indigenous communities clearly existed (as evidenced by a major 1712 indigenous uprising discussed in chapter 9), it would be a long stretch to call Chilón's early ladino population a landed elite. It was largely a class of poor frontier farmers. The inventory of Mariano Constantino's possessions at his death tells this story well: born in Chilón, probably in the 1830s, Constantino died in 1888. He owned more than 900 hectares, but he had lived in a thatched-roofed, mud-walled house with sparse furnishings. His other property consisted of a few religious artifacts, two horses, two mules, a few burros, five head of cattle, and a broken *trapiche* (sugar mill). After the value of his land (410 pesos), the debts of two male servants (110 pesos) were his largest asset. Like his neighbors, Constantino produced corn, beans, a little fruit, and some dairy products, primarily for local consumption. His main commercial product, sugarcane, was likely carried on the backs of indigenous porters to San Cristóbal or Comitán, where it could be distilled into cane liquor. Constantino was not alone in his rustic life. An 1842 ecclesiastic report on the payment of the 10 percent annual tithe in Chilón offers an intimate glimpse of ladino agriculture: only a handful of ladino farmers tithed that year, providing the parish with a total of less than 50 pesos' worth of corn, beans, and sugar.[3]

This was about to change. Thanks in part to the efforts of Carrascosa and a succession of Liberal governors, the number of commercial estates in Chilón soared during the last decades of the nineteenth century as a globally integrated cane-coffee complex began to define the region's economy. By the 1880s, sugarcane was so intensively cultivated that north-central Chiapas became one of the state's most important centers of sugar production. By the 1890s, coffee production had taken root, with 125,000 coffee bushes bearing fruit or about to bear fruit (Rabasa 1895). And by 1900, nearly all of the ladino families and fincas that would endure, in some form or another, through the 1990s were present in Chilón. The late nineteenth century and the early twentieth formed a critical moment when the intersection of Liberal rule and the local logics of landed production forged key enduring features of estate agriculture and landowner territoriality.

Progress, Privatization, and the Making of a Landed Elite

Some sixty years before Chiapas' trip to the Paris Exposition, Mexico resolved a long struggle over its border with Guatemala that would set the stage for the subsequent development of the state. In 1824, after vacillating for almost a decade between Guatemala and Mexico, Chiapan elites, led by the landed oligarchy of Ciudad Real (now San Cristóbal de Las Casas), engineered Mexico's annexation of Chiapas (Benjamin 1996:11). Chiapas was firmly lodged in the national body of Mexico — at least on the maps. On the ground, however, Chiapas was a remote periphery barely connected to the rest of the nation, and many landowners still opposed the annexation. The task of producing Chiapas as a governable space within the Mexican nation had barely begun.

Through the latter half of the nineteenth century successive Liberal governments worked to incorporate Chiapas into the nation, in the process binding it to the larger Liberal project of "order and progress" exemplified by rationalized public administration, the subjugation of competing centers of authority within the nation, a radically expanded role for the market, and the spread of modern communication and infrastructure. This project reached its apex under the Liberal dictator Porfirio Díaz (1876–1910). By the 1880s, Díaz, surrounded by a group of technocratic advisers called *científicos,* centralized decision making in Mexico City and extended military and bureaucratic control into the countryside. Díaz waged military campaigns to "tame" marauding indigenous groups in northern Mexico, undermined local political bosses throughout the nation, presided over an epochal period of land concentration, and attracted unprecedented levels of foreign investment, particularly in commercial agriculture. Roads and railroads served as both avatars and agents of Porfirian state formation and export promotion.[4]

In remote Chiapas "order and progress" unfurled unevenly. Roads — occasionally passable, normally thick with mud — snaked their way slowly through the state during the late nineteenth century. Rail connection between Chiapas and Mexico City remained an elusive goal. Begun in 1880, the Ferrocarril del Sureste (Southeastern Railroad), would not be successfully completed until 1935, and English investors repeatedly failed in efforts to link Chiapan agricultural producers by rail to the state's deep-water ports (Chanona 1952). Chiapas remained physically remote and incompletely incorporated in the nation. At the same time, however, a whole array of new forms of state rule were working their way slowly into the Chiapan countryside and steadily transforming the terrain of social relations. By the early twentieth century, even as diverse actors ignored or appropriated the institutions and functions of a distant central government, struggles over landowner hegemony were increasingly articulated through the idiom of government.

In order for Chiapas to truly claim a place in the Liberal utopia of order and progress dreamed of by Díaz's científicos, the state's "astonishing exuberance" (Carrascosa 1883) would have to be tamed, settled, and made productive. The late nineteenth century in Chiapas, as in much of Mexico, was a time of an unfolding Liberal territorial project grounded in land surveys, settlement, an expansion of private property, and the promotion of particular forms of capitalist accumulation. These practices, harnessed to a vision of Mexico as a modern, rational nation, profoundly shaped the Chiapan landscape.

From the 1830s on, a series of federal and state laws opened vast quantities of "unused" or "underutilized" land to privatization. Under the Ley Lerdo of 1863, for example, anyone with sufficient institutional savvy and money to pay prices as low as 75 centavos per hectare could claim up to 2,500 hectares (Toraya 1985). Until the 1880s, investors mostly took advantage of these laws to claim land held by the Catholic Church in Chiapas (de Vos 1994). Under Porfirio Díaz, however, land held collectively by indigenous communities came under increasing pressure. Thanks to Porfirian laws facilitating the privatization of indigenous communal lands, the number of estates in Chiapas more than tripled between 1837 and 1889 (Rus 2003:7). The toll on indigenous communities was palpable. By the turn of the century, independent indigenous communities with secure control over village lands had almost entirely disappeared from Chiapas (Rus 2003, Pedrero 1981). Indigenous peasants dispossessed of their land—often through egregious fraud—were reduced to near slavery on estates. By 1892, 20,000 of the 34,000 indigenous residents of the departments of Chilón and Simojovel were *baldíos*—resident workers, often heavily indebted to landowners, receiving the right to a plot of land in return for three to four days of labor per week in the landowner's fields (Rus 2003:10). It was a dramatic change, one that has been widely chronicled by historians.[5] But, while many popular and scholarly accounts of this moment in Chiapas glide smoothly from the facts of Porfirian land privatization to the existence of a stable and powerful landed elite, in Chilón things were not so simple. There, the creation of estate agriculture and a landed elite was hard work; not something that unfurled automatically, but rather a multistaged process that saw the rise and fall of several groups of landowners and enormous amounts of cultural, political, and economic struggle.

The Origins of Ladino Estate Agriculture in Chilón

In July 1848, Fr. Marciano Trejo, Sitalá's parish priest, responded to a request from his superiors to report on the state of indígena-ladino relations in the district. "In all the Towns of my charge," he wrote, "there is not a single ladino resident."[6] As we have seen, a scattering of ladino families had farmed land around the towns of Chilón and Yajalón since the eighteenth century, but the region as a whole was still dominated by indigenous subsistence production. Fr. Marciano complained that ladino cane-liquor merchants had begun to pass through the region and alluded to faint stirrings of trouble "because of something to do with land measurements," but ladino landed production had not yet taken root around Sitalá.[7]

Exactly fifty years later, the priest's successor, Fr. Manuel Zetino, would tell a completely different story: reporting to the same ecclesial office on the state of affairs in his region, the priest grumbled, "Things in [the town of Sitalá] have come to a complete standstill . . . because the majority of residents have all gone away to the fincas."[8] Whereas an agricultural census in 1851 had found no fincas in Sitalá or Guaquitepec, there were almost twenty in 1885.[9]

These two priestly letters bookend a process of rapid social and spatial change in which nonindigenous colonists poured into north-central Chiapas, dispossessing and privatizing indígenas' communal lands and expanding the landscape of ladino farms. This wave of privatization and modernization followed two separate paths into the region: one moved northward from San Cristóbal and led to the establishment of large, often absentee-owned estates producing corn, beans, cattle, and, most important, sugarcane beginning in the 1850s; the other, driven by coffee production, spread south from Yajalón, Palenque, and Tumbalá beginning in the late 1880s. While ladino elites from San Cristóbal pioneered the northward colonization and focused their efforts on production for domestic markets, the latter wave of colonization took place in the shadow of foreign-owned coffee estates and looked north toward Gulf Coast ports.[10]

By 1900, these two movements had collided and commingled in Chilón, laying the basic foundations of landed production that would endure into the twenty-first century — with one important caveat: today's landed elites are not necessarily the direct descendants of either group of late-nineteenth-century land colonizers. Many or most of the area's contemporary landed elites trace their ancestries to itinerant merchants, skilled laborers, and poor professionals who poured into north-central Chiapas during the late nineteenth and early twentieth centuries to take advantage of employment opportunities created by the expansion of cane and coffee estates. Typically these newcomers found work as trusted estate administrators and foremen or started businesses that provided estates with transportation and supplies. Eventually they saved enough money to buy portions of either declining foreign-owned estates in the north or ladino-owned sugar haciendas in the south. They married into local ladino families, and by the early twentieth century the forebears of Chilón's and Sitalá's contemporary landowners had completed an unlikely transition from city to country, merchant capital to landed production.

Northward Expansion into Chilón:
The Liquor Road to Agrarian Capitalism

How and why ladino investors from the highland town of San Cristóbal de Las Casas began to purchase land in north-central Chiapas is
still shrouded in uncertainty.[11] Nevertheless, several things are clear.
First, beginning in the 1850s, a growing number of ladinos began
purchasing large tracts of land in the region. This wave of land claims
and investment, carried out by prominent merchants and politicians as
well as by relative unknowns, involved both the seizure of indigenous
communal lands and the purchase of already existing ladino farms. In
most cases, however, San Cristobalenses seem to have purchased land
previously surveyed and claimed by land speculators. The prominent
Porfirian-era landowner and merchant Vicente Pineda, for example,
purchased some 2,200 hectares near Guaquitepec from two land speculators a few years after that property was originally surveyed, in 1849.
Less well-known San Cristóbal merchant families such as the Alcázars
and Zepedas, as well as such regional *jefes políticos* (political bosses) as
Abraham Suárez and Porfirio Navarro, also obtained large tracts of
land in this way, taking over existing land claims and cobbling together the basic topography of ladino property that would dominate
the region for more than a century. Many, if not most, of the estates
that appear in subsequent chapters of this book — San Antonio Bulujib, Junacmec, San José Sierra Nevada, Las Delicias, and Golonchán to
name a few — trace their origins to this process.

Second, sugarcane seems to have animated this wave of expansion.
Nearly all of the almost seventy estates established in the region by
around 1900 claimed sugar as their primary commercial crop (Estado
de Chiapas 1909). Although these new estates grew sugar extensively
and according to "the most primitive system," Chilón emerged as an
important center of sugar production, famous for the high quality of
its output (Rabasa 1895, Estado de Chiapas 1895). In 1900, just the
dozen or so fincas circling the town of Guaquitepec produced 400,000
kilograms of sugarcane, 4,000 kilograms of refined sugar, 15,000 kilograms of raw sugar in brick form, and 18 hectoliters of legally distilled
aguardiente.[12] The fact that sugarcane production boomed during decades of rapidly expanding coffee production is no coincidence. In
north-central Chiapas, sugarcane distilled into cane liquor and sold on
credit to indigenous laborers made coffee exports possible. Tax records
from 1903 speak to the lucrativeness of this connection: every two

weeks, five or six legal producers in Sitalá alone declared 50 to 150 liters of liquor each, and one landowner, Caridad Alcázar, paid 20 to 35 pesos in taxes *per week* to municipal officials for his aguardiente production. Extrapolated over a year, Alcázar's liquor tax payments would range between 1,000 and 1,800 pesos. This was an enormous amount of money at a time when a head of cattle sold for 15–20 pesos, a hectare of land averaged 3 pesos, and a hectare of cane yielded about 25 pesos.[13] Countless other stills operated on the margins of the law, and archival evidence of ceaseless fighting among ladinos for control of the clandestine liquor trade speaks to the high value of the business. Wenceslao López recalled, "Because [aguardiente production] was illegal and because it made lots of money, aguardiente producers had to be hidden and tough. Sitalá was hidden enough. The aguardiente producers had their own gunmen because there was so much money to be made. Just like drug traffickers today."

By the early twentieth century, the northward expansion into Chilón had slowed considerably and the region's largest landowners had begun to sell off their estates in pieces to a new wave of ladino settlers. Numerous factors contributed to the dissolution of late-nineteenth-century estates. Many of San Cristóbal's elites originally set their sights on north-central Chiapas because of its abundant supply of cheap labor (Estado de Chiapas 1895), but by the 1900s supplies of indigenous indentured labor seem to have been in short supply. In 1906, for example, Samuel Pascacio, who administered Finca La Naranja for Manuel Pineda, complained that "the growing difficulty of getting fieldworkers because of the daily forced recruitment of workers [*enganches*] for coffee groves and lumber camps in the Department of Palenque [to the north of Chilón]" was "well known to all residents in the region."[14] It is also possible that many landowners had fallen deeply into debt, a problem exacerbated by a major downturn in the coffee market at the end of the 1890s (Rus 2005). Participants in the late-nineteenth-century colonization of Chilón regularly used their land claims as collateral for large loans — often totaling thousands of pesos at 6–18 percent annual interest — and by the early twentieth century there are reports of landowners subdividing their estates in order to liquidate debts.[15]

Thus, for whatever reasons, Chilón's large Porfirian estates had begun to change hands by the end of the nineteenth century, and growing threats of land reform in the wake of the Mexican Revolution (1910–1920) served as the final blow to this wave of land claims and the formation of large estates. Wenceslao López, who purchased El Carmen Saquilá in 1940, at the tail end of this shift, is one of the last people alive who participated directly in these changes. López's father had come to north-central Chiapas to work as a mason on El Triunfo, a vast foreign-owned coffee plantation to the north of Chilón. Eventually he left the estate, married a local woman, and settled in Yajalón, where he and his wife opened a hotel. While they built the family business, adding coffee processing and the region's first ice factory, Wenceslao took to the roads. As an itinerant merchant, Wenceslao accumulated a small fortune plying the region's rugged mountain paths to buy the produce of local estates and supply them with whatever they needed. In the course of his trekking, López found El Carmen Saquilá, abandoned for more than fifteen years by its wealthy absentee owner, Manuel Penagos. Penagos had claimed the property in 1897 but never developed it, leaving it instead in the hands of Porfirio Navarro, the region's political boss. "Navarro was a very delicate man, and I showed up on the porch of his estate all muddy from my walking, so at first he didn't trust me," López recalled, laughing at his youthful audacity, "but when I told him I could put down a thousand pesos on the ranch then and there — in those days having a thousand pesos was like being a millionaire — he changed his mind."[16]

When López purchased El Carmen, it was covered with cornfields farmed by indígenas who had carved out nominal independence on the abandoned estate. "I put an immediate stop to that," he remembered, "but I told them that if they wanted to come help out on the ranch, they could have all the milpa they wanted." In return for continued access to its cornfields, this new labor force — fourteen families in all — would now work in López's fields three days a week, do estate maintenance on Saturdays, and tend their own crops the remaining two days. Like most of the new ladino landowners, López planted sugarcane. Particularly around Sitalá, which remained a center of clandestine liquor production well into the twentieth century, sugar was still a lucrative crop. At the same time, like many of his neighbors, López increasingly turned his attention to coffee.

Coffee and the Southward Expansion in Chilón

Two mid-nineteenth-century changes in the international coffee economy fueled land privatization and commercial development in Chilón: first, independence struggles hampered production in Brazil and sent world prices soaring; second, land suitable for growing coffee in Guatemala had been saturated, largely by German investors. Together, these factors, combined with the Mexican government's efforts to promote foreign investment, shifted coffee capital across the border from Guatemala to the Chiapan coast (Hernández 1979). As new plantations saturated the coast and Soconusco regions, investors looked north to the possibility of growing coffee in Chilón and Simojovel.

Two Germans, Friedrich Kortum and Karl Setzer, led the expansion of coffee into north-central Chiapas. Kortum arrived around 1894 and founded the Finca Mumumil in Tila. Karl Setzer, an employee of a German commodity trading firm, followed eight years later, establishing a series of estates outside Yajalón. Others followed—Frederico Schilling, the Morrison brothers, the Kanters, and Enrique Mahr—quickly establishing a belt of coffee estates north of Chilón and Yajalón. These estates were large; one of them, El Triunfo, owned by the German-American Coffee Company, covered 20,000 hectares and employed 3,000 workers in the contemporary municipios of Tila, Tumbalá, and Salto de Agua (Alejos 1999:283).

A century later, Carlos Setzer reflected on his grandfather Karl and the other German immigrants:

> After Germany's victory over France in 1870, Germans were looking for new places to go. . . . Basically, Germany wanted cheap tropical imports, so it sent its sons out to secure them. My grandfather first went to Guatemala and discovered that all the good land had been occupied from the highlands all the way down to Tapachula. So the Bundrum [Trading Company] sent him to Comitán, where he met other Germans who sent him on to San Cristóbal. There, making his way with no Spanish and no guide, he found other Germans who told him about Yajalón. He left with a group of shanghaied [*enganchado*] Chamulan Indians heading to work on the Kortum finca. The Kortums were the first Germans in the area, and they dealt with the lack of labor by getting groups of Indians from Oxchuc, Chamula, and Cancuc, whom they gave 5 pesos to go work at Morelia. When my grandfather got to Yajalón . . . all the production [there] was sugarcane. . . . My grandfather bought land from a guy named Romero who had gotten it from the Kelly Streeter Land Company [which had surveyed and claimed much of Chilón and Yajalón]. He was looking for a place where he could put a water wheel, and he found it. He returned to Guatemala and found his boss, who went to Mexico City to carry out the purchase.

Miguel Utrilla, a ladino whose family established a firm base in the liquor trade before taking on the mantle of landed property, explained the next step to me — the transition from foreign-owned to ladino-owned coffee estates:

> The first people to bring coffee to the region were Germans. Working with their German trading partners, part of a German commercial exodus, these men established the first plantations in the area: Bremen and Hanover. . . . The few mestizos who lived in the area — mostly small farmers — began to study the German plantations and see an opportunity for commerce. Typically the father bought the son one or two mules and set the son up transporting coffee from the plantations to Salto de Agua, where it could be moved on navigable rivers — the Tulijá and Grijalva — to the coast. These traders would take coffee to ports and return with salt, kerosene, and other necessities. At the same time, these families . . . began to pocket coffee beans — spiriting them away in their coats or saddlebags — in order to try planting this magical fruit on their own little farms. . . . The mestizos saw the foreign example of how to be progressive, how to communicate with the rest of the world, how when the boss told people to do something, they did it. They learned how to run a farm from the foreign fincas.

This quaint story paints a charming, harmless picture of the rise of ladino domination in Chilón, obscuring a whole history of displacement, enclosure, and serfdom. Nevertheless, it raises two important points: first, that the regime of domination and subordination put in place on these estates was, in some ways, a transnational hybrid, adopting practices found on European estates and plantations in Germany's African colonies;[17] and second, that commercial coffee production devolved from foreigners to ladinos during the first decades of the twentieth century. It is important, however, to add a dose of political economy to Utrilla's Promethean epic. By 1899, investors buoyed by steadily rising coffee prices had planted more than four million coffee plants in Chiapas, and almost twice that many sat in nurseries awaiting transplant (Rus 2005). This bubble was soon to burst. In the space of one year, between 1898 and 1899, the price of coffee fell from 35 pesos to 15 pesos per *quintal* (100 pounds, or about 46 kilograms), while costs of production continued to rise.[18] Amidst the devastating collapse in coffee prices, which continued through the early twentieth century, owners of large estates complained bitterly about the cost and difficulties of securing a labor force (Baumann 1985).

North-central Chiapas's large foreign-owned estates, weakened by this crisis, began to sell plots of land to ladinos as early as 1909. But it was the Mexican Revolution that struck the final blow. Although consolidation of the Revolution with its contradictory agrarian reforms and counterreforms lasted well into the second half of the twentieth century in Chilón, the region's large Porfirian estates — particularly foreign-owned ones — came under attack early. By 1915, Karl Setzer complained in a letter to the German consul, Enrique Rau, that, thanks to a new law freeing debt-bound laborers, only six of forty permanent workers remained on the Hanover estate (cited in Baumann 1985:46). The owners of El Triunfo and other foreign-owned estates began to preempt agrarian reform by partitioning their land to sell parcels to ladinos, but even these strategies eventually failed. By 1940, El Triunfo, which had once covered 20,000 hectares, had fewer than 400 hectares (Alejos 1999). By 1946, when El Triunfo's German-born administrator, Frederico Schilling, battered by low coffee prices and a decade of agrarian struggle, hanged himself from the rafters of a storeroom on the estate, the foundations of ladino landed production had been laid from Tumbalá to Guaquitepec. Abelardo Gómez, whose father had bought several parcels of El Triunfo, mused, "Now we [ladinos] had our own problems, our own struggles with workers, our own agrarian reform problems."[19]

Father Figures and Finca Indians: Making Landed Elites, Making Estate Workers

Cacique has a lot of negative connotations, but really to be a cacique is just to be an intermediary. We are the bridge between the city and the people who work in the country. . . . At least until there was television, we were the cultural bridge that integrated isolated indígenas into the national culture. — Fausto Trujillo

When Wenceslao López decided to buy El Carmen Saquilá, he had the means. Well into the twentieth century only treacherous footpaths and mule tracks connected Chilón to the outside world. As a result, the economic viability of coffee and sugar production in this remote region turned on the provision of inexpensive transportation, usually in the form of Indian porters or mule trains.[20] The men who ran these trade routes, organizing the portage of coffee and sugar to Salto de

Agua and San Cristóbal and returning laden with basic goods for sale to estate workers and owners, quickly accumulated capital to buy land. Drawing on their commercial experience and connections, men such as López knew they could market estate produce better than any of their competitors, but could they make the estates produce? How, in effect, did a group of merchants, craftsmen, and professionals remake themselves into agrarian capitalists? The answer to this question lies in the embodied, everyday practices of debt-bound servitude on estates —practices that literally made ladino father figures and loyal finca Indians as subjects.

The Cultural Politics of Debt Servitude

By the end of the nineteenth century at least half the heads of indigenous households in the department of Chilón were tied to estates as debt-bound resident workers (Rus 2003). In 1904 a census of cane- and corn-growing estates around Sitalá reported a range of "servant populations," from fifteen heads of household on the Finca Tula- quil (200 hectares) to 133 on Zapacuná (300 hectares).[21] Resident workers—called *peones acasillados* or *baldíos*—coercively "freed" of their land by nineteenth-century Liberal "reforms," exchanged their labor (along with the unpaid work of their families) for minimal wages and the right to cultivate a plot of land on the estate. Under customary practices, peons worked two or three days for the land- owner and two or three days tending their own crops each week. On the seventh day workers and their families "voluntarily" contributed unpaid labor—the *faena* or *fajina*—toward the general upkeep of the estate. Typically men repaired roads and buildings, cut firewood, or mended equipment, while women and children washed clothes, cooked, and cleaned the *casa grande*.[22]

Except for this "voluntary" work, heads of households were, thanks to Liberal labor reforms, ostensibly capitalist wage laborers, paid be- tween 50 centavos and a peso for a day's work on the estate. Access to land, however, served as the primary incentive for workers. Wages, mandated by the state, in almost all cases returned immediately to landowners' pockets as workers purchased basic goods through the estate's *tienda de raya* (company store), or through a regionally spe- cific variation of it. While tiendas de raya purportedly existed to sup- ply workers with cloth, seeds, tools, medicine, and other goods not produced on the estate, in practice they primarily trafficked in cane

An indigenous worker dries coffee beans on the patio of a ladino estate, spring 2001. *(Photo by author.)*

liquor. As Oscar Franz, former owner of the Finca Verapaz, reminisced about the 1930s and 1940s: "In those days the patrón sold a lot of aguardiente . . . on Saturdays after the day's work at five or six p.m. — [the faena] was a long day's work — the patrón would sell the workers aguardiente and they'd get drunk, and that's how their debt got bigger and bigger."

Informally recorded with notches in a wooden stick or hash marks (*rayas*) on a tattered piece of paper, workers' debts followed them through life and were inherited by their children. They were often quite substantial. Peons' debts ranged from the equivalent of a month's to more than a year's wages. In 1949, for example, a fifty-year-old worker had accumulated a 200-peso debt — enough money to purchase a hundred-hectare estate at that time.[23] Indeed, inventories taken after landowners' deaths suggest that workers' debts were some of landowners' most important assets, accounting for 10 to 30 percent of the total value of their estates.[24] In a vivid testament to the value of one worker's debt, a landowner personally tracked a runaway worker one hundred treacherous kilometers into Tabasco in order to collect 60 pesos owed him.[25]

This system of debt servitude left considerable room for abuse. Landowners exercised considerable, and unlawful, control over workers' mobility, used corporal punishment liberally, and inflated workers' debts through a variety of dubious means. Some landowners claimed seigniorial rights to intercourse with indigenous brides on their wedding night, and rape played an important part in shaping both patrón and peon as subjects (Toledo 2002, Olivera 1980). It is difficult to assess the extent of abuses on estates because debt-bound workers had few opportunities to express their complaints in writing, but rare cases that do appear in public documents offer a glimpse of everyday violence: Doroteo Maldonado was tied to a post and beaten by an estate administrator; Sebastián Hernández was dragged by a horse until dead; Antonio López was pistol-whipped by a *mayordomo* (steward) letting off steam.[26]

At the same time, the widely perceived scarcity of labor allowed considerable room for resistance. While indígenas' denunciations of abuse rarely found their way into public documents, Chiapas's archives overflow with landowners' complaints about indígenas cutting fences, burning crops, and killing animals. In 1930, to cite one of many examples, Absalón Zepeda complained that estate residents, sometimes armed with machetes and shotguns, constantly stole corn, beans, and tools from his estate.[27] Archival records also suggest that workers enjoyed some freedom to play one landowner against another. In a case from 1876, for example, workers moved en masse from one finca to another because they "couldn't stand the mistreatment they received," and by the 1940s fleeing from one estate to another had clearly become a well-defined tactic of resistance.[28] Workers who took this course did not escape debt—it was transferred to the new landowner's ledger—but presumably they gained some improvement in conditions.

Despite landowners' abuse and peons' resistance, however, debt servitude provided a coherent basis for landed production that endured from the 1880s into the 1980s. As a system of social relations on estates, Chilón's debt servitude followed a common pattern. Indeed, during the late nineteenth century, estate agriculture began to develop along remarkably similar lines around the globe, from the Nile delta to the Elbe, from the island of Sicily to the mountains of Chile (Richards 1979). Despite impressive geographic differences, these estates all shared a relatively analogous pattern of labor relations. By any name, this system turned on what Karl Marx called "labor-rents." On these estates, Marx observed, "the direct producer, using instruments of labor (plough, cattle, etc.) which actually or legally belong to him, cultivates soil actually owned by him during part of the week, and works during the remaining days upon the estate of the feudal lord without compensation from the feudal lord" (Marx 1967:790).

"Actual" or "legal" landownership by peasant producers was often only a temporary right of use, and in Chiapas, as we have seen, peons received a symbolic wage along with access to land. Nevertheless, the basic elements remain consistent: access to land was exchanged for labor, and labor for oneself and labor for the lord were separated by time and space.[29] The system worked well for Chilón's landowners, whose control over land leveraged virtually free labor bound to estates through coercion, debt, and more subtle ties of loyalty.

In their work on revolutionary-era Yucatán, the historians Allen Wells and Gilbert Joseph (1996) offer one of the more subtle studies of the cultural politics of Mexico's labor-rent estates available. Departing from previous examinations of such estates, which typically conceived of power as something monopolized by landowners and wielded over workers like a stick, Wells and Joseph highlight the much more dispersed way in which power operated on henequen estates, which functioned as spatial technologies of disciplinary power that shaped workers into subjects through layered isolation, coercion, and the provision of security. Chilón's cane-and-coffee estates shaped subjects through layered isolation, the twinned coercions of debt and alcoholism, and paternalism. My relabeling of Wells and Joseph's third category points to an important difference between us: I am interested not just in how peons were shaped as subjects but also in how social relations on the estates created landowners as subjects, particularly through the workings of paternalism.[30]

Layered Isolation

In 1898 unidentified elites from north-central Chiapas offered Governor Francisco León a 30,000-peso bribe to cancel the planned construction of a road that would have connected coffee and sugar estates in the region to distant markets and ports. Later that year, León complained to Porfirio Díaz that north-central Chiapas's geographic isolation allowed landowners and merchants to virtually enslave the indigenous population. With essentially free estate labor and cargo transport provided by indigenous porters who cost less to maintain than mules, landowners and merchants had no reason to invest in productivity.[31] León (and other governors before him) attacked this isolation with roads in the hope that physical infrastructure would channel resources to more productive parts of the state, freeing labor for coastal plantations. These efforts met severe opposition, and it took decades to effectively connect north-central Chiapas with the rest of the state. Well into the 1960s, most landowners and merchants in Chilón relied on bush aviation to move supplies and crops into and out of the region.

Physical isolation of the region was just one of the modes and scales through which the production of bounded space articulated with landowner hegemony. More than one hundred years after León complained to Porfirio Díaz about Chilón's isolation, another Díaz, a former landowner from Guaquitepec, summarized the biggest transformation of estate relations that had occurred over that century. "Before, the peons lived *inside* the finca," he told me, stressing "inside" with an encompassing gesture. "Now," he declared, throwing open his arms, "they aren't inside the finca any more. They live outside the finca, and maybe come to work if they feel like it." In the simplest of terms possible, Díaz had struck to the heart of the spatial upsetting of landowner hegemony. For more than a century, landowners in Chilón struggled against myriad obstacles to maintain a sharp boundary between inside and outside, and worked to make sure that peons were inside.

Beyond the efforts to ensure the region's isolation, this spatial project worked most immediately at the level of the individual body. "Peons," as the Finca Verapaz's former owner reminded me, "didn't have the right to leave the finca. If they left or fled, the landowner would send people after them, or other landowners would catch them and send them back." Under Liberal labor reforms, peons did, of course, have the *legal* right to leave, but this right was typically denied in the day-to-day operation of estates. Even trusted overseers could face severe punishment if they tried to leave their employers without permission. When one overseer tried to leave San José Inapilá in 1922, the patrón hogtied him, threatened to shoot him, and held his child hostage until the local judge intervened in the overseer's favor. Disenfranchised indigenous peons were not so lucky. Landowners tightly controlled traffic on roads through their properties, tracked down runaway workers, and in one case recorded in 1911 stripped a former peon of all his possessions, even though the man had left the estate legally. Landowners maintained informal jails on estates and frequently confined workers who ran away or threatened to do so. One woman who had tried to flee service in a landowner's house was raped and then forced to continue her housework naked, with her family watching.[32]

In all estate relations — indeed, as a direct result of the spatial workings of estate social relations — landowners interposed themselves as the sole or central nexus between inside and outside. This system operated through commerce, as Israel Gutiérrez explained: "The peons weren't free at all. They needed the patrón's permission to leave. Or, for example, if they had a pig they had fattened and wanted to sell it, they had to pay a tax to the patrón for permission to sell the pig to a merchant." Thus landowners interposed themselves between peons and traveling merchants like the young Wenceslao López. They also mediated between the outside world and peons through the institution of the tienda de rayas.

Landowners actively insulated peons from outside ideas as well, In 1861 Désiré Charnay (1956) noted that Chilón's indigenous population was particularly obedient to the church. Landowners skillfully mediated peons' relationship with traveling priests to ensure that this obedience extended to estate relations as well. Fr. Mardonio Morales, a Jesuit priest who helped spread liberation theology through Chilón, remembered that during his earliest visits to estates in the 1950s, landowners interceded in his interactions with workers: "The first time I went to one of the fincas, when I was very new, I went to San Juan Cabtejaj. The indígenas invited me to come say mass, but the finquero sent his horse to get me and he put me up with a very nice meal in the *casa grande*. I didn't even see the indígenas until the next day, when I said mass and did baptisms. Because I didn't speak Tzeltal yet, the owner translated for me."

Notably, as Fr. Morales made clear, this mediation operated not just by creating tangible barriers between priests and peons but also by shaping estate workers' own understandings of their (inferior) relation to the outside world: "When I told the indígenas that I was going to visit them without the finquero's knowledge, they got very worried and said, 'But we don't have any horses to bring you,' and I said, 'I've always walked, I don't need horses.' And they said, 'But we don't know what you eat,' and I said 'A few beans are fine with me,' and then finally they said, 'But where will you sleep? We don't have any beds,' and I said I'd sleep on the floor. That's when we began to start *hermitas* — that was what we called our little communities — and train catequistas." Thus it was not just the priest's breaking of the physical distance between inside and outside but also his transgression of deeply felt cognitive geographies that truly challenged landowner hegemony; it was, in Morales's words, "pure dynamite" (Human Rights Watch 1997:3).[33]

Despite these challenges, the system continued to shape docile dependent subjects well into the second half of the twentieth century. But if isolation shaped subjects, it could do so only in conjunction with two additional features of social relations on estates: the dyad of debt and alcoholism and the variegated workings of paternalism.

Debt, Liquor, and the Performance of Domination

In her study of women and drinking in highland Chiapas, Christine Eber (1995:30) quotes a landowner as saying, "Take aguardiente away from the Indian, and what will become of coffee? Coffee plantations run on aguardiente as an automobile runs on gasoline." This insight speaks powerfully to the importance of cane liquor to labor relations. Liquor sales, as Eber rightly notes, were the fundament on which debt was built and labor coerced. Yet the statement might also have read: "Take aguardiente away from the Indian, and what will become of the categories of peón and patrón?" The very existence of peones and patrones as subjects rested historically on the not-so-subtle workings of intoxication. Even today, long after formal systems of debt bondage have been extirpated, they continue to define the indigenous and ladino identities.

Alcoholism among indígenas was a constant presence weaving its way through my fieldwork—not the poverty-riddled livers and devil possessions that Eber evokes so clearly, not the embodied cultural meanings of alcoholism in indigenous communities, but "indigenous alcoholism" as an abiding part of the construction and performance of ladinoness. Whether it was by trying to draw me into the pitiless ridiculing of an indigenous worker who had come to beg money for "one more drink" or by lecturing me on the difficulties of finding "good workers," instructing me in the nuances of indígena alcoholism was one of the central ways in which ladinos taught me how to be ladino. Never during my entire time in Chilón did I, in the company of a ladino, pass an obviously drunk indígena—whether sprawled on the roadside or staggering along the street—without having my attention pointedly directed to the spectacle by the ladino. Only rarely, however, did I see ladino landowners refuse workers' requests for an advance to buy the next drink.

The ritual went like this: a landowner pulls up to Restaurant Susy in his blue Dodge Ram. He's come for lunch and given three workers a ride into town. Two—a young Guatemalan couple—hurry off together to buy supplies. The third, an older local worker—grizzled, drunk, and singing to himself—hangs around. The inevitable comes quickly. The man adopts a servile tone, "*Patróóón* . . ." His words go on in Tzeltal, their meaning obvious. Laughing, the landowner translates for me, for everyone listening: "He's asking for money. We all know what that's for. I shouldn't give it. He'll just drink it up like the last bit." In Tzeltal, paternal and stern: "*Mayuk* [No can do]."

The worker, in Tzeltal, pleading: "Ayy, patrón, please . . ."

This is a staged production, with a script as old as coffee in Chilón. The outcome is preordained. Once the landowner has lectured enough and the peon groveled sufficiently, once the roles of domination and subordination have been appropriately reinforced, 20 pesos—more than a day's wage—change hands and the man scuttles off.[34]

Ladinos may perceive alcoholism as destroying indigenous communities and as a main cause of indigenous poverty, but they do not trace its origins and sources to ladinos. Most ladinos categorically refuse to draw connections between the historic co-evolution of ladino prosperity and indigenous alcoholism, but the connections could not be more clear. Landowners eager to secure a reliable workforce for their labor-intensive coffee groves had many ways to create new debt-bound workers and encourage existing workers deeper into hock. Landowners held workers financially responsible for damage to property under their care, added the debts of deceased parents to those of their children, and converted seasonal workers into permanent ones by charging high prices for food.[35] Liquor, however, was quicker.

As coffee production spread through the region, estates combined sugar and coffee production into a seamless cane-coffee complex in which aguardiente distilled from the first crop lubricated the production of the second. Carlos Cañas—old enough to remember the 1930s and 1940s—was brutally honest, pointing to Saturday afternoons, after the fajina had been completed, as a critical moment in the production of debt servitude: "The owner would invite workers to a drink on Saturday, supposedly to thank them for the week's work, but really it was to get them going." Every subsequent bottle was duly added to the workers' debts.

If fights and disorderly conduct erupted among indigenous drinkers, all the better, especially if they were seasonal workers not yet tied to the estate by debt. For landowners eager to augment their debt-bound labor force, delinquency was more a boon than a bother; crimes committed under the influence of alcohol served as a convenient source of workers' original debts. Numerous cases stretching over more than fifty years follow a remarkably similar pattern: An indigenous freeholder, all sense obliterated by cane liquor, stumbles into an argument with a neighbor. Machetes flash, and one of the men wakes from his stupor in the municipal jail. Authorities impose an impossibly high fine and hold him until a local landowner pays the penalty. "Freed" in this way, the man and his family are now legally bound to work for their benefactor until the debt is fully discharged; in other words, most likely for the rest of their lives.[36]

When an indígena had committed no offense, a landowner could invent one. In a telling case in 1896, investigations by a district court in Ocosingo found that Juvencio Gallegos, owner of Chilón's Finca Chapapuil, colluded with municipal authorities to forge a document in which two indigenous freeholders "confessed" to killing Gallegos's horse. In the end, the court in Ocosingo ruled that it had no reason to hold or charge the two peasants, but fined them 50 pesos each anyway. Several weeks later a second landowner, José Lara, paid their fine and welcomed them as workers on his estate.[37]

Tiendas de raya also played a central role in the cycle of ever-deepening liquor-induced debt. While some estates in the region were large enough to pay workers with scrip redeemable only at their own tiendas de raya,[38] most made special arrangements with a merchant from a nearby town. Miguel Utrilla, whose family operated a cantina, a general store, the region's most important legal still, and at least two large estates, explained how this system worked:

> Tiendas de raya were found only on the foreign-owned fincas. . . . Mestizo ranchers weren't big enough to have tiendas de raya. . . . The mestizo landowner had no money to pay wages and the peasants always needed money to buy basic necessities — they'd come to the patrón asking for money for medicines and other things. Before the fiestas in July and December the indígenas would want to have cloth to make new clothes. So my grandfather would make an arrangement with a merchant in Yajalón to get cloth, medicines, whatever for the indigenous workers in return for the promise of coffee after the harvest. The

indígenas would get their supplies in return for promising to work for the patrón, the landowner would get an assured workforce, and the merchant would get an assured market and source of coffee.

While Utrilla's description emphasizes benign staples — cloth and medicine — his family's fortune was founded on liquor, and whether a tienda de raya entered the picture or not, liquor accounted for a major part of a landowner's sales to peasants. As Fr. Morales observed, landowners were "always buyers and sellers [*compraventistas*], buying peasants' labor and selling them liquor."

If the heady effects of liquor on landowner-indígena financial interactions are fairly obvious, alcohol's more subtle influence on other aspects of social relations is no less important. It not only provided a means to coerce labor through the legal strictures of debt but also shaped governable subjects — subjects whose character, will, and aspirations were harnessed to the success of the estate. It hardly needs saying that rampant alcoholism, made possible by ladino liquor merchants' steady supplies of aguardiente, produced a secure workforce. If anything, liquor has at times proved all too effective at shaping subjects, creating docile workers who were difficult to get to work. Furthermore, while addiction forced laborers to turn to landowners for money, this practice could drain scarce cash from landowners' wallets into debts unlikely to be repaid — a phenomenon landowners decry today, and did as long ago as 1914 (Gremio de Agricultores 1914).

Organizations arrayed against landowners quickly realized the ability of liquor to produce submissiveness. According to Fr. Morales, political consciousness could not be raised in indigenous communities without first breaking the bonds of alcohol. Today, not surprisingly, communities organized around Catholic liberation theology or the EZLN prohibit militants from drinking alcohol.

The disciplinary relations of indigenous alcoholism produced subjects who lacked autonomy, who were physically addicted and mentally subordinated — ultimately dependent on their patrones. Thus, even when alcohol failed to produce docile subjects, instead generating the garrulous and unwieldy drunks prone to injury and machete duels who populate Chilón's court records, it served to reinforce the landowners' sense of superiority, providing yet another opportunity for landowners to ritually reinforce their domination. Extrapolating from contemporary relations, one can fill in the paternal displays that must have surrounded countless occasions in the past, documented in archival records, when landowners calmed fights among workers and bailed drunken peons out of jail. As Jorge Martínez explained with pride, "The relation between [landowners] and the workers was good. It was a relation of patriarchy. I use that word instead of *cacique* because that has a bad connotation. . . . The patriarch was judge, lawyer, and protector. Whatever kind of problems the indígenas had, they'd bring them to the patrón for resolution; family problems, especially problems arising from alcohol, which was a major cause of their poverty." In sum, alcohol consumption shaped, and was shaped by, the social relations formed under paternalism, but those relations are never simple.

Paternalism

More than any economic logic, landowners use cultural discourses of paternalism to explain the workings of labor relations on their estates. For landowners and many indigenous workers, the estate is a clearly constructed family, with well-established roles assigned to each of its members. Landowners pose themselves as parents and act accordingly. They take extremely seriously their paternal responsibility to fairly balance discipline and forgiveness, affection and force. In this way, landowners successfully recast the benefits of debt bondage as burdens. In 1914, highland landowners responding to the Revolution's prohibition of debt bondage, wrote, "The master enslaves himself to his servant because their contract obliges him to give [the servant] a house . . . land . . . forests from which to extract his natural products . . . clothing . . . and health care for his family" (Gremio de Agricultores 1914:7).

These words echo in the present, even though most workers now live on ejido land rather than on an estate.[39] Paternalism, or the notion that estate social relations conform to an implied contract of reciprocal responsibilities, still stands as a central justification of the relations between landowners and indígenas. It is not an entirely cynical notion, either. Paternalism did and at times still does provide workers with various forms of security (c.f. Wells and Joseph 1996). Although landowners usually profited from their "benevolence," pay advances and emergency loans formed a critical safety net for workers, and these safeguards extended into other realms as well. Numerous court cases indicate that estate workers frequently sought refuge in the casa grande during violent incidents, appealing to landowners for protection against abusive administrators or rival indigenous groups. At least in documented cases, landowners usually complied, and their actions reinforced their place at the head of the estate family. But "security" is never simple. What is absolutely central is *not* whether landowners provided security out of altruism (as they sometimes claim) or more self-serving motives (as many outsiders argue). Rather, I hope to illuminate the multiple effects of paternalism in shaping subjects— something completely missed in debates about intention.

In July 1998 Gustavo Utrilla received me in his living room attended by a daughter who served strong coffee as we spoke. As a young man Utrilla had studied at Mexico's prestigious Polytechnic University, then returned to Yajalón in 1976 to take over the family's estate. He was articulate and fiercely passionate about his work, his family, and his relations with the indígenas. Despite all the problems that have strained ladino-indígena relations since 1994, he told me, he still maintains close ties with his workers and former workers. Even those who now live on independent ejidos still invite him to drink *pozol* (a corn gruel) with them. Like his father before him, he was the godfather of many of his workers' children, and just the previous week had sponsored one of their school graduation parties.

As I prepared to ask him to elaborate on this point, the doorbell rang. Standing in the patio was a Tzeltal man and his weary-looking son. Utrilla received them from his doorstep, speaking Tzeltal and gesturing at the son. The tone was grim. Soon Utrilla retreated into the house and returned with 150 pesos for the man. This was a substantial sum, more than a week's wages, and the man broke into a relieved smile, jostling his son to thank Don Gustavo. After the two left, Utrilla explained: The man was a seasonal worker who farmed his own ejido plot. The son was sick—some undefined stomach ailment not helped by the government doctor—and the money was a loan to pay for a private doctor. The man secured the loan by promising Utrilla some of his corn crop—expected in January, some six months away. Not a word of the agreement reached paper, but Utrilla was confident he would be repaid.

This story can be read in many registers. Utrilla would probably benefit—maybe even handsomely—by reselling the man's corn. As an out-of-town representative of a multinational coffee company told me, local landowners who also try their luck as *coyotes* (commercial go-betweens) can outcompete corporate buyers by drawing on strong networks of paternalism, *compadrazgo* (fictive kinship), and reciprocity in indigenous communities. On another level, Utrilla has done his best to make sure that this worker will continue to leave his own fields during peak harvest time to pick Utrilla's coffee. This loyalty can extend even further: many landowners I spoke with hoped their workers' loyalty would protect their properties from invasion, and numerous cases dating back to the nineteenth century suggest that trusted estate workers served as hired guns charged with enforcing discipline on estates. All landowners regularly counted on loyal workers to pass on warnings and rumors about upcoming violence. On yet another level, Utrilla, acting instrumentally or not, provides a safety net for his workers, as the gratitude on this man's face clearly attested. Finally, at the deepest level of all, regardless of whatever interpretation of the event the two men hid in the depths of their consciousness, at least some part of their respective identities was shaped by this ritual enactment and reinforcement of the father-child, patrón-peon dyad.

Operating at all these levels and more, paternalism has played a central role in shaping estate social relations for more than a century. The most basic component of this system has always been land. By consolidating monopoly control over land in Chilón, landowners effectively seized the very substance of security: indígenas' subsistence could be secured only by maintaining good relations with their patrones. In the most wildly disingenuous way possible (given that the land had just been stripped from the indígenas' control), landowners presented access to land as a paternal gift to "apathetic . . . [and] drunk . . . Indians" (Gremio de Agricultores 1914:19) as well as an economic exchange.

At the same time, landowners provided wage advances, medicine, cloth, and alcohol for workers with paternal aplomb, blurring the distinctions between gift and loan, generosity and usury. Often landowners' ties to workers — particularly the strong bonds of compadrazgo — passed from generation to generation, just like peons' debts (Olivera 1980). Roberto Trujillo, for example, continues to provide occasional monetary support to one of his father's godchildren, now in his seventies. But paternalism can also have unintended effects. As Joseph and Wells (1996) remind us, a landowner's gift can easily be experienced in a radically different way. Joseph and Wells document cases in which indigenous workers who were "generously" provided Western medical care by estate managers in Yucatán experienced this treatment as sadistic torture.

One of the most evocative descriptions of the unstable nature of paternalism comes, as so many of the more subtle portrayals of social relations on estates do, from fiction. In *War and Peace,* Leo Tolstoy, with his unrivaled eye for the nuances of landowner-peasant relations, describes the Russian peasantry as "baffling." With Napoleon's army bearing down on the Bogucharovo estate, the owner's daughter Princess Mary learns of the hunger and ruin war has wrought on her serfs. Torn by sorrow, she impulsively orders her steward to distribute all the estate's stockpiled grain to the peasants before it can fall into French hands. Upon hearing the order, the serfs assemble angrily outside Princess Mary's house. Confused, she thinks they have misunderstood her command, and restates the offer: the serfs will take her grain and can even follow her to her Moscow estate, where she will provide them with housing and more food. The peasants respond with dead silence. Slowly they begin to chant: "Oh yes, an artful tale! Follow her into slavery! Pull down your houses and go into bondage! . . . I'll give you grain indeed! She says" (Tolstoy 1996:649).

Princess Mary's magnanimous gesture has completely failed; the peasants perceive it as a ploy to mire them in debt. Princess Mary leaves for Moscow convinced that she has seen yet another manifestation of peasants' witlessness. Both groups believe that they intuitively understand the other. Both groups have completely misunderstood the other. My research turned up many Princess Mary moments, as we shall see in chapters 8 and 9 — moments when landowners discovered that the peasants they thought they knew so well were in fact entirely incomprehensible. Yet in the process of acting out these mutual mis-recognitions, landowners and peasants also made themselves as subjects — father figures and finca Indians.

Liberal Rule and Estate Mediations

> For a while now, the government of this state has felt the need to put an
> end to the servitude of indebted peons. The humanity and the political
> economy, civilization and the character of our institutions demand it.
> — Governor Francisco León to President Porfirio Díaz, May 25, 1896

Despite landowners' nostalgic evocations of frontier independence, the development of landed production in Chilón during the late nineteenth century was a direct result of state practices. Government encouragement and underwriting of land enclosures and commercial coffee ventures made landed production possible in Chilón. The specific forms it took, however, were not always what government officials intended. As we will see, practices that the state hoped would enable it to tame and subordinate the landowners ironically buttressed their dominant position in the countryside.

Throughout the nineteenth century, state officials in Chiapas struggled to rationalize and control their most troubling offspring: entrenched conservative landowners in central and north-central Chiapas, whose very existence depended on Liberal land laws but whose actions (particularly their control over debt-bound workers) were seen as threatening to the progressive development of Chiapan agriculture. Considerable research on this period has quite ably focused on high-level wranglings between and among elites, and has spoken broadly of victories won and losses sustained by competing camps.[40] A microlevel approach, however, reveals that the extension of liberal government — through censuses, resource studies, taxation, and an expanding legal system — subordinated Chilón's landowners to a particular form of state rule even as it provided them with opportunities to buttress their position as the sole nexus between countryside and nation.

In broad strokes, during the last decades of the nineteenth century Chilón's landowners found themselves tangled in a statewide dispute that pitted Liberal lowland and coastal agro-export elites against conservative highland landed elites in debates over whether Chiapas's indigenous population should remain debt-bound in highland haciendas or be freed to work as wage laborers on lowland coffee plantations. Coffee planters in the lowland Soconusco region had millions of coffee plants reaching maturity after years of waiting, but no one to harvest the crop. Only one thing stood between the Liberal agro-export elites and progress: highland landowners' backward system of debt-bound servitude. "The time has come," Governor Francisco León wrote to President Díaz in 1898, "to put an end to the incredibly sad condition of the indebted peon, because this is the obstacle impeding progressive development of agriculture and the birth of the industries that [progressive agriculture] creates."[41] While León and other critics invoked "humanity" and "civilization" to condemn "this monstrous social disease," planters complained that debt servitude drained capital from more productive investments and prevented labor from seeking its most efficient occupation (Baumann 1985).

Through the 1890s, Chiapas's state legislature passed a series of laws aimed at limiting highland control over labor. Afraid that too sudden a repeal of debt servitude would precipitate a major crisis in the state, legislators instead attacked some of the system's worst abuses: torture and forced labor were prohibited, and after a major statewide debate at the Agrarian Congress of 1896, a new law required landowners to record workers' debts at the office of the Jefe Político and limited pay advances to two months' wages (Baumann 1985:24). Nevertheless, even these palliative measures met strong resistance from highland landowners and were almost impossible to enforce. Ultimately, despite the formative impacts of Liberal labor reforms, Chilón emerged from these struggles with a modified but still formidable system of debt-bound servitude that in some places would last well into the 1980s. It is important to note, however, that while Chilón's landowners resisted and co-opted liberal rule, they did not remain independent of state projects. Rather, in important ways they became the state, simultaneously shaping and being shaped by the workings of state rule.

Chilón's landowners, like landowners throughout Chiapas, dominated local and state government, filling the seats of municipal presidencies, congress, courts, and most public bureaus. To say that this translates into a state apparatus subordinate to landowner interests, however, implies a relatively simplistic and monolithic understanding of both class and state. Landowners' interests are not unified and predictable, but rather are shaped by struggles over hegemony — often struggles that take place within the conceptual framework of the state itself. More importantly, the workings of state power transcend the interests of groups of political functionaries, operating instead (often in unintended ways) in multiple arenas and shaped by diverse agendas. State actors — even landowner-state actors — sometimes acted in ways that undermined landowners' defense of the spaces of landed production.

Here, however, I want to take seriously for a moment the often repeated notion that in Chiapas the state and landowners were "the same thing" (see Benjamin 1996). I do not mean to suggest that the state's and the landowners' interests meshed perfectly; rather I ask: What does it mean when certain actors are put in the position of, quite literally, embodying the state in a remote corner of the nation — of being the agent through which state practices unfold? Records of resource studies, taxation schemes, attempts to impose order on the clandestine liquor trade, and censuses of all kinds — of estate workers, of buildings, of voters, and of agricultural crops — stacked in staggeringly high dusty piles in the municipal archives of Chilón and Sitalá attest to the state's efforts to know and make legible this far corner of the nation. Porfirian officials wanted counts of aguardiente stills, corn harvests, houses, useful trees, and estate workers. They demanded reports on phytosanitary conditions in coffee groves and "the height in meters of every tree."[42] But mostly they wanted lists of men: of voters, taxpayers, workers, and potential soldiers. Numerous documents speak of ongoing attempts to count, track, and tax resident estate workers. In an age when freeing labor for coastal plantations was a central goal of government intervention, efforts to know and control the population of estate workers constituted a direct threat to Chilón's landowners. At the same time, Porfirian officials tried to challenge landowners' mediator position by extending the reaches of its legal system into Chilón and onto estates. An 1849 law, for example, snaked the tendrils of criminal justice into the realm of landowner authority, regulating which peasant offenses landowners could punish directly (by "confinement, chains, or yokes") and which infractions they were required to refer to "the competent authority" (de la Peña 1951:356).

Both the extension of rational calculability and legal accountability can be seen as attacks on landowners' hegemony. Not surprisingly, landowners resisted with gusto. Indeed, a major reason that archives in Chilón and Sitalá swell with census, taxation, and similar records is the sheer truculence of landowners in the face of these new requirements. In 1901, for example, a landowner drove two tax collectors off his estate at gunpoint. When higher officials issued charges against the landowner, a friendly doctor helped him evade arrest by certifying him temporarily insane. In 1888 an official based in Ocosingo complained to the mayor of Sitalá that landowners were exhibiting "extreme listlessness in the collection of [workers'] taxes."[43]

The landowners' resistance is hardly surprising—another case of backwoods small-arms fire in the struggle between states and localisms. What makes it interesting and what makes these nineteenth-century feuds echo down through the next hundred years is that the state's efforts to make the countryside legible and manageable were not disembodied and abstract; landowners themselves were called to serve as direct agents of state rule. When that landowner drove the tax collectors from his land, he was attacking two neighboring landowners who also served as government officials. The grid of liberal government did not deploy itself over the countryside. People placed it there, and the people who placed it there were precisely the people the state sought to make into tractable subjects.

During this period, municipal presidents, acting as a sort of administrative assistant selected by landowners from among their own ranks, received new policies from the state government. Then, through an endless stream of "circulars" addressed to the owners of major estates, municipal presidents passed the new policies directly to landowners for enforcement. Thus landed elites essentially became the state, called upon to carry out state functions: building schools, repairing roads and bridges, taking censuses, and reporting on the condition of local agricultural production. Within the bounds of the estates, landowners were asked to register births and deaths of peons, organize workers to pay a new head tax by providing free labor on public works, and organize voters to go to the polls. Perhaps most important, landowners exercised de facto judicial power on their estates, playing the roles of police officer and judge in disputes among workers.

In the end, the collision of state and landowner territorialities produced two kinds of "governable space." Landowners, as agents of state rule, advanced state territorial projects, helping, in effect, to subordinate themselves and their indigenous workers to the rationales of a liberal government. Yet at the same time, these practices — particularly the delegation of law enforcement and taxation functions to landowners — strengthened landowners' ability to police the boundaries of their estates. Control over the municipal governments and the populations of their estates would serve as the primary channels through which landowners defended their estates against a new set of state and indigenous territorial projects that emerged after the Mexican Revolution.

Killing Pedro Chulín

Landowners, Revolution, and Reform, 1920–1962

From 1916 to 1920, young ladinos in Chilón joined with landowners across Chiapas to wage a successful guerrilla campaign against the encroaching forces of the Mexican Revolution. Fighting Venustiano Carranza's Constitutionalist army to a stalemate, Chiapan landowners secured seats of power in every state government that would follow. After the national triumph of the revolutionary forces, however, landowners quickly began to shape the discourses of revolution into a language of domination. Only eight years after their counterrevolutionary victory, former fighters from Chilón quoted Karl Marx in their announcement of a new regional political party: "The emancipation of the workers is the work of the workers themselves," the landowners declared, but their party would support "the legal mobilization" of rural laborers in the hopes of creating "effective revolutionary proposals."[1] For many commentators who pose Chiapan landowners as titans of domination, these words alone would confirm the ineffectiveness of revolution in Chiapas, the emptiness of its promises to poor peasants hoping to free themselves from exploitation by landowners. As novelist Carlos Fuentes wrote shortly after the 1994 EZLN uprising, "In Chiapas, the revolution did not triumph . . . not only have oligarchic practices not returned land to the peasants, they have stripped it away piece by piece." Chiapas was "a colonial reserve" operated by and for landlords.[2]

I propose a different reading of the Revolution and its effects on the relation between landowner, peasants, and the state in Chilón. Even in landowner-dominated Chilón, postrevolutionary state rule was territorialized in radically different ways than it had been under previous administrations. In the violent decades that followed the overthrow of

Porfirio Díaz, groups struggled to define postrevolutionary rule at all levels of Mexican society, from Chilón's back roads to the Presidential Palace in Mexico City. In this context, landowners did not defend autonomous domains of despotism — "colonial reserves" — amidst quickly thickening postrevolutionary rule. Rather, the contours of landed production were shaped and reshaped by the complex interactions of landowners, the state, and indigenous peasants as they struggled to define the forms and meanings of postrevolutionary rule. Landowners quickly and effectively reworked the logics and practices of postrevolutionary rule to further their privileged control over land and labor. Nevertheless, by appropriating the Revolution in this way, landowners also subjected themselves to the legitimating discourses of agrarian reform and social justice, and increasingly found themselves forced to shore up their crumbling authority with substantial concessions to a peasantry also empowered by state practices.

The Struggle for San Antonio Bulujib

Carlos Bertoni, generally described as a short, corpulent Italian, was the son of Corsican pirates who escaped the French navy by fleeing into the wilds of Chiapas. "In Mexico," Bertoni's grandson and namesake informed me, "the family did what it had always done — it smuggled illegal alcohol," using the 2,000-hectare San Antonio Bulujib estate as a base of operations in the hills around Guaquitepec and Sitalá. Even Bertoni's claim to San Antonio was shrouded in controversy and rumors of brigandage. During the Mexican Revolution, in one of the twisted intrigues that make Chiapan property rights so hard to decipher, San Antonio's ersatz owner, the Porfirian political chief Abraham Suárez, placed the estate in the care of Límbano Penagos, who in turn named Carlos Bertoni as its legal administrator. In 1918, however, Suárez initiated a court case arguing that Bertoni had "rendered not one accounting of his administration" and was "using the estate as if he were the perfectly titled owner."[3] Suárez's claims quickly prevailed at various levels of the justice system, but as late as 1920 Bertoni greeted visiting court officials at gunpoint, tore up their documents, and drove them off the estate.[4] The case's final resolution remains unclear, but by 1934 Bertoni effectively controlled San Antonio and had built it into a center of coffee, cattle, and illicit cane liquor production worth nearly three times as much as any other estate in the area.[5]

Beginning in the early 1940s, however, San Antonio came under increasing attack from within and without as the estate's resident workers and neighboring indigenous communities mobilized land reform claims against the property. For two decades Bertoni fought back against the agrarian committees of Sitalá and Guaquitepec with a broad array of maneuvers ranging from clever manipulation of land law to ambush and assassination. By 1962 the Bertonis had lost nearly a third of San Antonio to land reform, leaving Carlos's daughters and sons to sustain the decades-old defense of San Antonio into the 1980s, when they sold most of the 1,300 remaining hectares during a wave of invasions.

Today a third-generation Bertoni carries his grandfather's name, but unlike his grandfather, Carlos Bertoni Unda stands tall and fiercely lean. With domineering charisma and jet-black eyes that flash between avuncular and crazed, Carlos could easily pass as a Corsican pirate king, but instead he cultivates the *ranchero* image of Emiliano Zapata, whose portraits fill his office. Unlike his grandfather, Carlos presides not over a lucrative and shady estate but over one of the busiest offices in the somewhat shabby quarters of Chiapas's state congress. Carlos Bertoni Unda has come a long way from his early years as the owner's son on San Antonio, through the ranks of peasant organizations and into a seat in congress as leader of the left-opposition Partido de la Revolución Democrática (PRD, or Party of the Democratic Revolution) in Chiapas.

Our conversation stretches over parts of two days, continually interrupted by journalists, politicians, and an endless stream of peasant constituents soliciting financial aid, development projects, and dispute resolution. Through these hot Tuxtla Gutiérrez afternoons Bertoni shows his street-smart brand of leadership, delivering fatherly advice and promises of patronage with an alligator smile. Once he presented me to impressed ejido leaders as a potential foreign investor. Always he steered our discussions far from San Antonio and his family history toward more pressing concerns: international trade agreements, the specter of U.S. imperialism, and an upcoming conference he organized to resolve peasant-landowner disputes remaining after the implementation of the 1996 Agrarian Accords. The family stories Bertoni didn't tell me — pieced together from fragmentary archival records and scattered interviews — sketch a picture of the ways landowners stalled, stymied, and crushed nascent peasant mobilization in Chilón for more than three decades.

In the late 1920s, inspired by the rise of reform-minded politicians in Chiapas's landowner-dominated government, some 240 families of indigenous estate workers united to form the agrarian committees of Guaquitepec and Sitalá.[6] The two groups launched separate petitions for the restitution of more than 1,300 hectares they claimed ladinos had stolen from them during nineteenth-century enclosures. Together the petitions demanded expropriation of land from at least nine estates, including San Antonio Bulujib (see Map 3). The peasants of Guaquitepec would have to wait two decades for a positive presidential response to their claims, while the agrarian community of Sitalá received a provisional land grant after only a few months. But for both groups, the state's rulings in their favor were only the beginning of their struggles. For Carlos Bertoni, the Revolution had finally reached home, and the rest of his life would be spent defending San Antonio.

As holder of strategic government posts, including leadership of the liquor excise police, Bertoni had significant contacts and resources to mobilize against the Sitalá and Guaquitepec agrarian committees. When Sitalá received provisional possession of 600 hectares in 1933 — almost 300 of which were to be taken from San Antonio — Bertoni allied himself with other affected landowners to delay implementation of the decree into the 1950s. Together the landowners bribed a series of officials in the Secretaría de la Reforma Agraria (SRA, or Secretariat of Agrarian Reform) to fraudulently survey the land grant, threatened to drive off peasants legally occupying their estates "with a hail of bullets [a balazos]," and concealed the names of the true owners of the affected estates.[7]

Bertoni proved particularly adept at turning the confusion surrounding agrarian property rights in Chiapas into a protective smoke screen. Reports published by the SRA still named Límbano Penagos as San Antonio's owner well into the 1960s, while still others listed Bertoni's five children (who "purchased" San Antonio from their father in small parcels days after peasants from Sitalá lodged their land reform claim). While the agrarian committee of Sitalá contested the legality of San Antonio's subdivisions, pointing out that the sales took place after they had filed their petition, Bertoni effectively stalled expropriation by responding that the subdivisions took effect after the claim was filed but before it was officially published.[8]

In 1946 federal officials rejected Guaquitepec's demand for restitution of land lost during the nineteenth century, but declared that since the peasants had demonstrated a legitimate need for land, they should

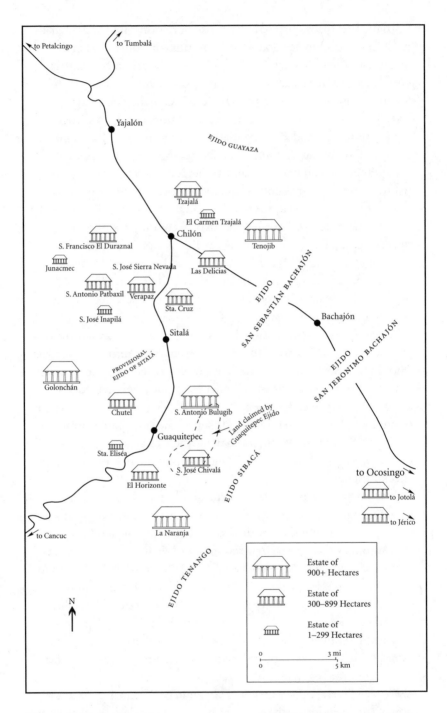

Map 3. Chilón's estates, c. 1950–1960 (approximate locations)

be allocated 3,016 hectares — at least 300 of which would come from San Antonio.[9] With this decree, 170 heads of households should have received provisional possession of a significant piece of San Antonio, but Bertoni refused them access, treating them as land invaders. From 1946 to 1953 a series of struggles ensued in which peasants occupied San Antonio and Bertoni resisted. He used connections in the Forestry Department to accuse peasants of environmental crimes (setting forest fires), drew on support from the municipal governments of Chilón and Sitalá to press trumped-up charges against peasant leaders, and obtained multiple stays of execution from judges in Ocosingo and Tuxtla Gutiérrez.

After a presidential resolution supported Guaquitepec's claim, final possession was granted to peasants in 1953. This settled nothing. Bertoni continued to fight, pointing out that the final act of possession was riddled with technical errors, while peasants complained that, with the help of corrupt Agrarian Reform technicians, Bertoni avoided ceding hectares of valuable coffee plants promised in the original endowment.[10] Within weeks of the "final" resolution of the case, Bertoni filed for a *certificado de inafectabilidad agraria* (or certificate of exemption from expropriation), swearing that his properties "had absolutely no agrarian problems." At that the peasants of Guaquitepec forcibly occupied San Antonio's coffee groves.[11]

In the fall of 1960, Carlos Bertoni, his daughter Alfa, and her husband, Alberto Gutiérrez, orchestrated the arrest of four peasant leaders from Cantajal (an indigenous settlement within the bounds of San Antonio) who had championed Guaquitepec's claims since the 1940s. Pedro, Alonso, and Sebastián Chulín along with Pedro González resisted arrest, "taking up their shotguns . . . and machetes," but were eventually captured and charged with damaging Carlos Bertoni's property and with "threats and injuries against Alberto Gutiérrez and Alfa Bertoni de Gutiérrez."[12] The peasant leaders eventually won their freedom, but they met a worse fate two years later.

On February 4, 1962, Alberto Gutiérrez, accompanied by his brother and a squad of (presumable loyal peasant) supporters, ambushed Pedro and Alonso Chulín on a narrow path across the fields of San Antonio. Pedro died instantly from bullet wounds in the head and chest, but Alonso escaped with a bullet in his side. For three days, from February 4 through February 7, Pedro's body lay untouched in the field while the local judge found pretexts for inaction. Under pressure from the municipal president in Chilón, the local judge, Luciano Díaz

Peasant-produced coffee beans drying on the road between Sitalá and Guaquitepec. San Antonio's now abandoned *casa grande* sits in the background, surrounded by an indigenous settlement. *(Photo by author.)*

Cancino, finally did investigate the attack: in a meeting with Alberto Gutiérrez and Alfa Bertoni, he drew up another round of charges against surviving peasant leaders for threats against the Bertoni family.

Sometime between the fatal ambush and the end of March, the town of Cantajal burned to the ground and its residents took refuge on a neighboring estate. Government officials blamed the fire on "indigenous malefactors,"[13] but it seems likely that Bertoni, or judicial police pursuing indigenous leaders at that time, razed the town. The fire proved convenient for the Bertonis, allowing them to demand an administrative ruling that Cantajal did not exist: "It is in the interests of this estate to make known that the . . . town, which woefully or with intent to confuse the authorities was named 'CANTAJAL,' has always been recognized by this estate as SAN ANTONIO, since CANTAJAL does not appear and has never appeared in the records of any Office."[14]

Thus Cantajal could not be considered a legal subject with its residents entitled to lodge agrarian reform claims. The administrative disappearance of settlements was a common tactic used by landowners to deflect land claims because agrarian reform bureaucrats depended on local municipal governments for rulings on the existence of population centers. In this case, Guaquitepec's municipal representative reported that the town had formed around the time of Alberto Pineda's counterrevolution with "the common agreement of patrón and peons," but then corrected himself a week later, "at the behest of our good friend Carlos Bertoni," saying that Cantajal had "ceased to exist."[15] A year later, even San Antonio had "no buildings whatsoever and for that reason no town exists."[16] With that, the peasants' claim fizzled and their hopes for expanding their communal lands faded until land invaders seized the remaining pieces of San Antonio in 1994, almost thirty-two years to the day after the killing of Pedro Chulín.

Citizen Peasants and Revolutionary Rulers

Citizen Peasants of the finca SANTA CRUZ in this municipio, property of Sr. Enrique Flores . . . request the intervention of this authority in a dispute. . . . They declare that they have lived for more than forty years on finca land . . . and that Sr. Flores makes them work for one peso a day, giving them daily tasks that can be completed only in two days and that Sr. Flores is trying to . . . evict them from the finca. . . . These peasants see all this as unjust, and for that reason they have asked this authority to write out this act so that it can be presented to the Governor of the State in the capital of the State and so that he will give them justice and make the land where they live into an [ejido] and by so doing remedy all the injustices that they suffer under Sr. Enrique Flores. — Act presented by the municipal president of Sitalá, October 2, 1954

The "Citizen Peasants" of Santa Cruz, like their neighbors at San Antonio, fought a difficult battle. Like the agrarian committees of Sitalá and Guaquitepec, they endured decades of delays, small victories, limited concessions, and almost overwhelming obstacles in their struggle for land. Like their neighbors on San Antonio, the peons of Santa Cruz would not win complete control over their land until the 1980s. Indeed, these struggles seem to confirm conventional understandings of landowners' violent defense of territory. Nevertheless, the mere fact that workers on these estates sustained an organized struggle for land over several decades speaks to remarkable changes in the nature of politics in the Chiapan countryside.

Through the middle decades of the twentieth century, processes of postrevolutionary state formation — attempts to create governable spaces by subsuming the countryside in corporatist relations centered on the ruling Revolutionary Institutional Party (Partido Revolucionario Institucional, or PRI) — gave rise to new indigenous identities and territorial claims. These state efforts to reorder networks of political mediation by incorporating Chilón's estate workers into class (peasant) and ethnic (*indigenista*) organizations ultimately undermined landowners' position as the sole nexus between peasant and state. The creation of a novel spatial form — the ejido — lay at the heart of this process by providing a physical, institutional, and social base for the elaboration of new indigenous territorialities.

Jan Rus (1994), in his superb account of the consolidation of the postrevolutionary state in highland Chiapas, describes the making of "institutionalized revolutionary communities" (IRCs) in which young bilingual indigenous leaders tied to the federal government infiltrated the structures of traditional community political, religious, and economic leadership. Cultivated during the apex of radical social policy under President Lázaro Cárdenas by Erasto Urbina, the ladino director of the Chiapas office of the federal Department of Indígena Protection, the new indigenous leaders emerged as the central mediators between the state and indigenous communities in highland Chiapas. Urbina had brilliantly "not only penetrated the Indians' internal community governments, but enlisted them in the task of subordinating the state's landowners and planters to the national government and party" (277). Yet, outside of the highlands, little is known about how the state's expanded postrevolutionary presence in the countryside articulated with existing forms of power.

In the landowner-dominated periphery of Chilón, as in the central highlands, new mediators emerged to integrate indigenous communities into national politics. Often these new mediators clashed with ladinos and provided indigenous communities with alternative channels for patronage and appeal. Yet Chilón's landowners, unlike those in the highlands, maintained considerable ability to co-opt and obstruct the new mediators. Thus, if the story of postrevolutionary state formation in the highlands can be told as the story of the rise of the institutional revolutionary community, in peripheral Chilón it is the story of ongoing tension between the institutional revolutionary community and estates.

Displacing Landowners, Unbounding Estates

In 1939, a letter distributed by the municipal president of Sitalá instructed landowners to organize "all the peasants who live on your finca" to greet "but not bother" the governor on a visit to their town.[17] This marshaling of peasants through their patrón recalls the prerevolutionary system of landowner-centered mediations, but the contours of rural politics were shifting.

In the late 1920s a handful of indigenous communities in Chilón had launched campaigns to restore lost territory through Mexico's embryonic Agrarian Reform bureaucracy. Then in 1934 a campaign tour by the presidential candidate Lázaro Cárdenas triggered a wave of land reform petitions across northern Chiapas. After taking office as president, Cárdenas deepened federal influence in the Chiapan countryside, creating a series of new institutional actors charged with supporting indígenas' struggles, arming peasants against landowners, and granting more than 400,000 hectares to petitioners throughout the state. These reforms made new forms of peasant territoriality possible, but because the bureaucratic requirements for land claims were so extensive and arcane, they also subordinated peasants to a new legion of state specialists and political mediators, a "sort of priests who served as intermediaries between the remote state and the ordinary person" (Arturo Warman quoted in Ibarra 1989:191).

Chilón lagged behind much of the rest of the state in land reform and peasant organizing. Nevertheless, the emergence of new mediators — bilingual teachers, indigenous political bosses, agrarian committees, and federal officials — in the decades following the Revolution had long-lasting consequences for the way landowners, peasants, and the state interacted in Chilón. Writing in 1927 to denounce the poor treatment, harassment, and forced labor of indigenous peasants in Sitalá, Celedonio Constantino, representative of the military sector of Ocosingo, would go so far as to proclaim, "Those days are gone forever."[18] Those days were not gone forever — not by a long shot — but some things had changed. Through the 1930s and 1940s, new institutions and actors, including the Department of Social Action and Indigenous Affairs, federal labor inspectors, federal rural teachers, and special prosecutors for indigenous affairs, began to intervene in landowner-peasant relations, receiving peasants' complaints, pressuring land-owners and local governments to resolve disputes, and offering alternative channels for aid.

In 1938 Erasto Urbina even extended his hand into remote Sitalá, angrily addressing the "municipal president of Sitalá": "I respectfully entreat you to arrange all kinds of protection for the members of the ejido of [Sitalá] . . . because we have knowledge that Sr. Ramiro Ramos[19] . . . has fenced a piece of land that belongs to them. . . . I beg you to take care that indigenous workers are not exploited now that the Mexican social movement and the revolution have made Laws benefiting these groups that had been totally abandoned to their own fate, but now have Sr. General Cárdenas and Sr. Efraín A. Gutiérrez eager to give them all kinds of protection."[20] As a dependency of Chilón from 1922 to 1944, Sitalá did not, in fact, have a municipal president in 1938, and Urbina's error illustrates the region's remoteness from central state influence. Nevertheless, after the 1930s, peasants in Chilón did have unprecedented access to higher authorities. They sent delegations to San Cristóbal and Tuxtla Gutiérrez, penned appeals to Mexico City, and consulted with new allies in the government. In response, the new state actors conducted a paper war, defending organized peasants against distant oppressors and sometimes clashing with state actors more closely tied to landowners. Most of the cases involved peasants' attempts to seize territory under the agrarian reform legislation and landowners' violent responses to these efforts. But the new state actors also intervened in the tightly formed bonds linking patrones and peasants. In one case, the director of indígena affairs, having spoken with a peon who journeyed to San Cristóbal to denounce a beating dished out by his patrón, wrote to Sitalá berating the landowner and ordering the municipal president to "make Sr. Bonifaz appear in your office . . . and warn him that if he relapses or mistreats any other person of the indigenous class, he will be turned over to the appropriate authorities for punishment."[21]

Even more threatening than bureaucrats in distant offices who composed antilandowner diatribes, federal bilingual teachers who streamed into the countryside beginning in the late 1920s directly mobilized indigenous peasants, teaching agrarian law along with literacy and hygiene.[22] These teachers caused landowners considerable consternation. In 1935, peasants in the nearby municipio of Sabanilla wrote to Lázaro Cárdenas relating the penury of life as estate workers and declaring: "Today, now that we have a federal teacher who has explained to us about the wages we should receive and the hours we should work, we sent our complaints to the Governor and . . . they sent a Delegate to see these injustices."[23]

In Chilón, federal and state officials tried to force landowners to accept responsibility for the rural education campaign. They urged owners and administrators of estates to fulfill their patriotic duty by sponsoring the construction of a schoolhouse for the federal teacher program, conducting censuses of school-aged children on their estates, and financially supporting the new teachers.[24] Landowners resisted. As early as 1927, federal teachers in Sitalá came under attack despite frequent interventions on their behalf by the governor's office.[25] In the years that followed, landowners and local authorities expelled teachers from the region several times, while indigenous communities fought to keep them in place (Maurer 1983).

At the same time, *indigenista* policies, which developed in conjunction with land reform in the late 1940s and 1950s and sought to westernize Mexico's indigenous population and incorporate it in the economic life of the nation, were also implicated in the construction of new forms of political domination in Chiapas (Romano 2002, Fabregas Puig 1988, INI 1988, Favre 1985). During this period, the state cultivated new forms of indigenous identity that turned on a more direct relationship between state and peasants. In 1940, for example, the Department of Indigenous Affairs called on the region's indigenous communities to send delegates to a congress at which workshops would discuss production cooperatives, municipal electoral processes, agrarian reform law, and how to negotiate a collective labor contract.[26] New government agencies charged with prosecuting legal complaints in indigenous communities displaced landowners and the landowner-dominated municipal judge's office as the sole dispensers of justice in the region. The first evidence of this change preserved in the archives is a handwritten note from an assistant prosecutor in the Department of Indigenous Affairs informing ladino officials throughout the region that "as of this date" his office "would handle all indigenous legal problems" in the region.[27] Similarly, the new agencies began to provide peasants with alternative sources of much-needed material support, including seeds, credit, housing, and other resources previously accessible only through landowners. In short, the "benevolent" state increasingly replaced the fatherly landowner. As Daniel Nugent and Ana Alonso (1994:227) argue, the processes of postrevolutionary state formation—particularly those related to land reform—construed peasants as "children" of "the state as paterfamilias."[28]

Ejidos and the Making of Indigenous Territoriality

The most important change that occurred during this period was the creation of an independent indigenous land base and political identity outside the estates. One simple document written of 1940 graphically illustrates the change. Written by the municipal president of Chilón to the municipal agent of Sitalá, the letter concerns arrangements for an upcoming census. Unlike the scores of census-related documents in local archives going back to 1882, this letter distinguishes between ejido and nonejido populations. Whereas in the past the state had summoned estate owners to survey the region's indigenous population, now indigenous leaders, organized in agrarian committees, carried out their own counts.[29]

By 1950, agrarian committees had formed in dozens of Chilón's indigenous communities and estates and exercised legal control over some 25,000 hectares, with thousands more pending. By 1962, when Pedro Chulín was killed, the land covered had expanded to almost 70,000 hectares.[30] In this context, indigenous authorities increasingly provided a counterbalance, however weak, to ladino local government. Archival records show a new arena of conflict emerging alongside the struggle for land: competition between indigenous authorities and ladino local governments. Increasingly, new indigenous leadership organized around agrarian committees and ejido governing bodies campaigned against abuses of their ladino counterparts. Indigenous authorities in Bachajón, for example, challenged ladinos' ability to levy taxes on ejido members and their coffee production. In several occasions, this competition forced the ethnic integration of low-level municipal government, as "higher authorities" called on local ladinos to appoint officials "more identified with the peasants."[31]

The most unsettling evidence of change in the countryside, however, is the explosion of accounts of inter- and intracommunity indigenous disputes during the 1940s and 1950s. Violent confrontations within indigenous communities were nothing new in the region. Archival evidence from the late nineteenth century suggests that violent crime—usually individual disputes associated with drunkenness and accusations of witchcraft—had long been a part of daily life in indigenous communities and on estates. By the 1940s and 1950s, however, these accounts began to reflect the emergence of indigenous land claims as a locus of political struggle. In the rather typical year of 1950, for example, authorities in Chilón heard cases related to one fatal shooting of an indigenous man by a ladino and one ladino-indígena land dispute. Meanwhile, fifteen land disputes between indígenas, three homicides of indígenas by indígenas, and thirteen nonfatal machete and firearm attacks in indigenous communities passed through the courts. While many of these crimes followed the time-worn pattern of witchcraft accusations and drunken brawls, disputes over ejido land and authority grew more and more prevalent, reflecting the elevated stakes a modicum of indigenous autonomy brought to internecine struggles. A gruesome murder reported in the large ejido San Sebastián de Bachajón, for example, clearly articulated with attempts by one peasant faction to intimidate rivals within the ejido.[32] At the same time, members of smaller ejidos increasingly quarreled with outside rivals.[33]

As in the highland IRCs, indigenous caciques like the Chulíns led these struggles. José Lazos exemplified this new breed. By the 1940s, Lazos's name appeared frequently in complaints about disputes between indigenous communities. In one case Lazos was accused of burning crops and invading land claimed by rival groups, and in another of farming land that belonged to an ejido of which he was not a member.[34] The latter case in particular nicely illustrates both Lazos's tactics and the deep divisions that accompanied the rise of indigenous caciques. In April 1942 the municipal judge of Sitalá wrote an injunction in support of Lazos:

> José Lazos [in the company of several others] was getting ready to burn a plot designated as part of the planned land grant to the Ejido of this town. Around three in the afternoon, Juan Ramírez, Auxiliary Agent of the Prosecutor for Indigenous Affairs; Lorenzo Núñez, president of the Ejido Commission of this Town; and Juan Ruiz. Ramírez asked them, "Who authorized you to work this plot? Don't you know you can't work this land because you're not in the ejido?" . . . Lazos answered that he had special permission, and then [his companion] answered that the congressman who had come through these parts told them they could work the land. Ramírez answered: "The Congressman can go *fuck* himself, he has no reason to get involved in these land questions" . . . and that he had some . . . Forestry Agents who were going to the municipal palace that afternoon [to stop Lazos from burn-

ing his fields] . . . and Lazos, to show they couldn't stop him from burning his fields, answered that they could do as they pleased and he would find a way to defend himself.[35]

In this tense world of competing government and indigenous factions, the new caciques championed community demands for land and a role in political decision making, but also began to accumulate land and wealth within the ejidos. By the late 1970s a peasant told Pedro Ovalle Muñoz (1984:68), "There is monopolization of land among us also. Sometimes someone's father dies and the children are still small, and [caciques] try to invade the parcel, and since we have no documents to protect it, the other guy takes over and starts to put up fences or make a milpa, plant coffee, or make a pasture. . . . There are people who have 100 [or] 200 [hectares] they've taken over like that without working it, without making it productive."

Those Days, Gone Forever? Landowners and Revolution

As never before, after 1930 peasants circumvented the tyranny of local ladino authorities by appealing to the higher-ups.[36] In this way, Chilón's peasants won important concessions and found themselves integrated into complex structures of authoritarian corporatist political representation. How much these shifts — visible in the paper world of memos, reports, and circulars — changed the daily workings of ladino domination is more of a mystery.

Strong evidence indicates that much remained the same in Chilón. While radical peasant unions proliferated in the other regions of Chiapas, large organized groups made few inroads into Chilón. There peasant organizing remained isolated and episodic. In an area long cleaved along stark ethnic lines, indigenous communities had won remarkable concessions, but serious inequalities remained.

By 1962, presidential resolutions had decreed the creation of twelve ejidos covering almost 70,000 hectares in Chilón and Sitalá. Seven of the twelve ejido petitions had reached the final stage of legalization: definitive possession of land. Five claimants had received only partial possession, while at least four other groups awaited responses to their petitions and three requests for expansion of preexisting ejidos worked their way through the land reform bureaucracy.[37] Nevertheless, ladino landowners still controlled more than 15,000 hectares of the region's most productive land, dominated every aspect of local politics, and monopolized all levels of commerce. In 1962, all twenty merchants registered in Chilón and Bachajón were ladino, and indigenous leaders were not to take high-level posts in municipal government until 1994. Hundreds of indigenous peasants still lived on estates, and when the agrarian committee of Cantajal, facing arrest for land invasion while the murderers of Pedro Chulín went free, asked, "Are the laws different for Indians, or do they apply to everyone?" the answer was clear.[38] Despite challenges from ejido authorities, a handful of ladino landowner-merchants continued to dominate local government. In 1954, a letter to the governor from representatives of the ejido council of Guaquitepec protested:

> Gustavo Vera Cruz . . . holds the offices of Municipal Secretary, Municipal Treasurer, and Municipal Judge, and has filled these posts for years because all the Presidents who hold office are his cousins, for example: Don Rafael Martínez Vera, who was President, is his COUSIN and COMPADRE; Benjamin Trujillo, who was [municipal] PRESIDENT, is his COUSIN and COMPADRE; Don Ramiro Vera Cruz, who was PRESIDENT, is his BROTHER. Now the PRESIDENT Don Humberto Martínez Vera is his COUSIN and COMPADRE. Of course, these presidents let him do whatever he wants [and] any issue must be taken to Sr. Gustavo Vera Cruz and negotiated with money.[39]

Ladinos also co-opted the new patterns of mediation and indigenous leadership. In 1946, for example, Isidro Jiménez, multiterm municipal president and owner of the fincas Las Delicias and Shishontonil, led a faction of indigenous supporters in an attempt to seize control of the Bachajón ejido council. Another landowner audaciously petitioned for membership in the ejido that had just taken over part of his estate.[40]

Landowners even broke ranks from the shared defense of property to organize groups of agrarian reform claimants. When Cantajal burned, for example, its residents fled to the estate of Manuel Díaz Cancino, cousin of Luciano Díaz Cancino, the judge who shielded Pedro Chulín's assailants. As recently as 1948, the agrarian committee of Guaquitepec had lodged numerous complaints against Manuel Díaz Cancino for encroachment on community land, but by the 1960s he had mysteriously joined with the Chulíns and two federal teachers in denouncing landowners' treatment of the Guaquitepec community. Manuel Díaz Cancino may have been "a real nut case," as Roberto

Trujillo remembered, or even "a real lord of the manor, a guy who treated his people like slaves," as a relative recalled, but he also understood the benefits of using the postrevolutionary institutions to advance his interests. Díaz Cancino was able to use his position to steer land reformers' attention away from his property and toward San Antonio Bulujib.[41]

In sum, landowners managed to appropriate and rework important elements of postrevolutionary rule to their own benefit. Yet they in no way remained untouched or unchanged. Indeed, landowners had to rework themselves as they reworked the Revolution.

Defense in a Time of Reform:
A Landowners' Survival Primer

By 1962 the Bertoni family had lost nearly a third of San Antonio to land reform but still had more than 1,300 hectares in various parcels. The story of how the Bertonis buffered themselves from peasants' claims provides an overview, in capsule form, of the diverse tactics landowners used against their challengers: violence, creative twisting of Mexican property law, and tapping of allies in municipal, state, and federal governments.

Violence

Archival accounts are replete with cases in which peasant groups decried landowners for threatening them with evictions, police actions, or other sorts of repression. When the indigenous residents of Golonchán tried to form an agrarian committee, for example, the estate's owner Gustavo Flores crashed the meeting and sent more than half the assembly fleeing into the night with his violent shouting.[42] Other tactics used to dissuade peasant organizing included the burning of settlements, as in the case of Cantajal, and frequent assaults on community subsistence by cattle deliberately loosed on peasant cornfields. When bluster and other indirect methods failed to discourage peasant land claimants, landowners mustered loyal peasant followers to attack them or enlisted local authorities to evict them, whether or not the "invaders" had a legal right to occupy the land. Violence was by no means a one-way street; peasants threatened and intimidated landowners too, but landowners backed their thuggery with the ever-present specter of state support. Indeed, landowners' ability to parry

Prominent ladinos in Chilón, c. 1940. *(From the private collection of Alí Reyes.)*

land invaders has always rested on a foundation of state support. Before the 1970s at least, this support came primarily in the form of *impunity* — the ability to carry out violent evictions, occasional assassinations, and ongoing campaigns of harassment without fear of legal reprisal. Only occasionally did the police and other authorities directly carry out repression for landowners, and while the drama of violence earns it a prominent place in popular conceptions of landowners' defense against land reform, most of their efforts took more quotidian forms.[43]

Ambiguous Tenure and Tactical Partitioning

Landowners consistently resisted the rationalization of property rights either deliberately or through neglect. Land changed hands informally, often within families or between close friends, with delays as long as two decades in the official recording of title transfer. This practice allowed landowners to avoid substantial land-transfer taxes, but also fouled agrarian reform claims by generating a paper trail of confusing and contradictory reports. In a similar vein, landowners legally subdivided land among children, spouses, other relatives, and, less frequently, loyal peasants. On one level, this practice innocently reflects the natural progression of family succession, but, as in the case of San Antonio, it frequently reflected intentional efforts to circumvent landholding limits. While many heirs farmed and administered their subdivided properties as separate units, more frequently the divisions existed only on paper. As one classified ad in a local newspaper plainly stated: "Pedro Martínez sells his beautiful cattle estate . . . with a total of 640 hectares in three divisions appropriately protected with certificates of exemption from land reform."[44]

As land reform claims intensified in the 1950s and 1960s, many landowners formalized the usufruct enjoyed by loyal peasant workers by giving them legal title to their plots in return for promises of labor. This practice ensured access to a stable labor force at a time when the expansion of ejidos drew workers away from estates, but it also buffered large properties from land reform. No record exists of Bertoni's creation of buffer properties in the struggle over Sitalá's land reform petition, but we do have evidence that his neighbor José Monterrosa settled indigenous laborers from Bachajón on the margins of his property. In subsequent conflicts, the agrarian committee of Sitalá complained that these peasants "defended Monterrosa's land as if it were their own."[45]

Finally, when landowners were forced to concede land to agrarian reformers, they naturally attempted to hold on to their most productive fields. Some of the most virulent resistance to land reform erupted when government surveyors included valuable coffee groves in land allocated to peasants. Workers on the Jotolá estate, who had simultaneously invaded and petitioned for redistribution of a large tract of that estate's uncultivated land in the 1940s, must have been pleasantly surprised when, in 1961, they were granted a substantial portion of Jotolá's best coffee plants. In response to the landowners' protests, a subsequent survey in 1963 reported that "the planned [redistribution] does not concur with the reality on the ground," and this mistake delayed further action until 1975.[46] Thus most of the newly formed ejidos inherited the least developed and least productive land in the region, while estates retained control of their best lands.

Landowners in Chilón also ably exploited loopholes in the law to have their properties declared "small properties," not subject to expropriation. These practices reflect some of landowners' most cynical abuses of the spirit, if not the letter, of the land reform law. Bribery and intimidation sometimes induced government surveyors to falsely report the sizes of estates, but more legal means usually sufficed. When government surveyors assessed an estate's exposure to land reform, they calculated its "theoretical equivalent in irrigated farmland" — a national yardstick used to compare distinct types and qualities of land. By adjusting this value, landowners and their allies in officialdom could bring even large estates under legal limits. San Juan Cabtejaj, for example, a nearly 400-hectare estate with ten buildings for debt-bound workers, large banana and citrus orchards, and 100 head of cattle alongside its coffee groves, received an exemption certificate with an irrigated equivalent of only 62 hectares. Similarly, one 294-hectare estate qualified as small property despite the fact that its five motorized coffee dryers and other coffee-processing equipment made it one of the most valuable estates in the region and suggested far greater production than the 40 hectares of coffee officially reported. Thus, whether through subterfuge, false reporting, or legal technicalities, by the middle of the century most estates in Chilón fell under the legal limit for landholding.[47]

As we will see in due course, landowners' efforts to paint themselves as small property owners were more than just means to duck legal landholding limits; they were part of a discursive attempt to find a place for themselves in the postrevolutionary nation. In the wake of the Revolution, vast estates of the Porfirian era came to symbolize evil and injustice. "Small property" represented Mexico's future in new visions of the nation, and framers of the 1917 Constitution enshrined it as the most privileged and desired category of land tenure (Ibarra 1989:110). Not surprisingly, landowners' self-definitions adapted to this climate. Today, as in the early postrevolutionary period, landowners universally reject the imposition of such labels as *finquero* and *terrateniente*, with their strong connotations of injustice and iniquity. Their self-identification as *pequeños propietarios* (small property owners) or *rancheros* (country folks) reflects Chiloneros' deep-seated belief that they epitomize the yeoman farmer ideal of the Mexican Revolution.

Allies in the State

When disputes arose over the physical existence of a settlement of land reform petitioners, state-level authorities deputized the municipal president to determine whether or not the community existed. As with Cantajal–San Antonio, in case after case the municipal president informed distant authorities that no town could be found. In 1957, for example, state-level officials, responding to a suggestion by a corrupt local SRA technician, asked Isidro Jiménez, the municipal president of Chilón, for a ruling on the existence of the town of Shishontonil. The group had solicited redistribution of the estate of the same name, and, not surprisingly, Jiménez, who was also the owner of Shishontonil, wrote back quickly informing the SRA that he "found no town with that name and no group of peasants soliciting land with that name."[48]

As in the case of Pedro Chulín's death, ties of kinship and compadrazgo bound landowners to municipal authorities and secured their immunity to prosecution. In case after case, landowners were found innocent or simply not charged with the murder of peasants — but impunity also extended to more quotidian abuses.[49] As one former municipal president told me, "The ranchers split up power in the municipio among themselves and put the one they wanted in the post of president . . . . That way if someone was injured on their ranch, they'd never have any legal problems. They just took care of it." During this period, state and federal officials complained frequently about local handling of legal disputes between landowners and peasants. In 1945, for example, the regional court in Ocosingo returned an indictment of Alonso Chulín to the judge who had issued it in Sitalá, suggesting that he "take more care next time . . . because it seems to have absolutely no validity, since neither the plaintiffs nor the witnesses were examined under oath. . . . At the same time, I hope you also submit the records I've requested pertaining to injuries suffered by Juan Alonso Chulín of Guaquitepec that we have reason to believe were turned in to you. . . . Next time, to avoid being held responsible for any problems, please be sure to follow . . . the Penal Code Procedures."[50] Nevertheless, as evidence of subsequent cover-ups confirmed, the regional court had little influence over Sitalá's landowner-dominated municipal government.

Indigenous petitioners often refused help from officials in the state government and called for support from presumably more sympathetic federal agents, but such attempts to circumvent local authority did not always work. Landowners also filled the ranks of federal institutions, including the SRA and indígena protection agencies. In the late 1930s, at the height of state support for radical agrarian policy, for example, Humberto Martínez Martínez, owner of the 136-hectare San Antonio Patbaxil in Chilón and sole heir of a Porfirian political boss, served as federal labor inspector in northern Chiapas. Not surprisingly, records indicate that Martínez enthusiastically defended landowners in at least one labor dispute brought before him by estate workers. Other officials could be wooed with bribes—as the San Antonio case illustrates—or simply through social networks. In those days, as one peasant group noted, landowners and SRA agents often spent long nights together sharing cane liquor.[51]

Landowners' networks also extended into higher echelons of the state government. For example, one of the Bertonis' neighbors told me, "One day, during a period of land reform, the governor was over at our house. He was here to inaugurate some public work, and when he got my father alone he told him he was going to have to lose one of his farms to land reform in order to settle agrarian conflict, but he could choose which farm it would be. My father got him to agree that if he gave up [one] without any problems, the government would never touch [the other]." Agrarian pressure did finally dissolve both of that landowner's properties, along with the Bertonis' holdings and most ladino-controlled land in the area, but not until new waves of land invasions swept through the region in the late 1970s and 1994.

We have seen that the relationships between landowners, peasants, and the state followed two contradictory trajectories: landowners' skillful appropriation of the Revolution on one hand and the proliferation of new indigenous identities and forms of territorial struggle on the other. Landowners successfully defended their privileged positions but increasingly found themselves working to navigate a tricky system of politicized property rights and multichanneled political mediations. To say that landowners have become fluent in the language of the Revolution does not reduce the Revolution to an upper-class artifice. Intertwined notions of the Revolution, the nation, and revolutionary institutional forms of rule have colonized the lives of all Mexicans. Everyone has learned to speak the language of the Revolution, to bend it to serve his or her aspirations, and in turn to be bent by it.

Today the men who waged Alberto Pineda's counterrevolution are the sepia-toned heroes of Chiloneros' family albums. "The *Pinedistas* were young guys from around here and the landowners liked them because they didn't touch their farms like the *Carrancistas* [followers of the revolutionary leader Venustiano Carranza]," Carlos Setzer informed me. On another occasion, Carlos Cañas spread out photos of his father, Rubén Cañas, a Pinedista officer, and explained that most of the landowners I met had fathers, grandfathers, and uncles who fought against the "Carrancista invaders." Contemporary landowners enshrine the cruel tactics of Carranza's invading army in memory and compare them to current indigenous mobilizations. For Chiloneros, *carrancear* still means "to sack" or "pillage."[52]

At the same time, larger-than-life visions of other heroes of the insurgency—Francisco Villa, Francisco Madero, even Emiliano Zapata—constitute such a fundamental aspect of national education and civic ritual in Mexico that few landowners escape an uneasy admiration of both the sanitized pantheon of a distant revolution and the protagonists of a local counterrevolution. Landowners generally approve of the Revolution even as they condemn its more radical manifestations and pine for a return to the "order and progress" of Porfirio Díaz's dictatorship. One Chilonero cattleman even named his children and farms after significant places and events in Pancho Villa's life. Once a year he makes a 1,400-mile pilgrimage to the birthplace of the "Centaur of the North."[53] Such is the power of the Revolution.

In Mexico, whose constitution provides that property vests ultimately in the nation and is administered by "the state" in accordance with "the dictates of public interest, including regulation of social well-being . . . equal distribution of public wealth . . . [and] balanced development for the nation," access to land hinges on participation in politics, or, more exactly, engaging with and being incorporated in the discourses and practices of postrevolutionary rule.

In 1962, the year Pedro Chulín died in one of San Antonio's fields, thirty men from Chilón's most important landowning families came together to form an association that would tightly knit Chiloneros into the fabric of postrevolutionary state rule. The founding of Chilón's cattlemen's association (AGL) reflected changes sweeping across southern Mexico: cattle ranching, once an ancillary and poorly developed aspect of tropical agriculture, had taken on vast proportions. Within a few years, spurred by state subsidies, pasture would cover more than half the surface of Chiapas. In Chilón the AGL's founding members initially reported owning more than 2,500 head, a number that would double over the next twenty years.[54] Perhaps even more important, as a corporatist sectoral organization created under state auspices and intimately tied to the PRI, the AGL linked ranchers in Chilón to regional and national lobbying efforts that won substantial concessions and allowed Chiloneros to participate in an unprecedented wave of cattle-based prosperity.

The AGL's founding also responded to another trend. Along with provisions for technical, marketing, and financial assistance, new legislation promoting cattle raising authorized Chiapas's local and regional cattlemen's associations to form special rural police forces and otherwise protect the security of land tenure (Fernández and Tarrío 1983). Nineteen-sixty-two was a violent year, with the death of Pedro Chulín, numerous attacks against land claimants on other estates (particularly Jotolá and Jérico), and increasing conflict within and among newly formed ejidos. As the number of land invasions soared in Chilón through the late 1960s, the AGL stood as landowners' paladin—the central coordinating body for the legal, political, and coercive defense of property. By working through the AGL, landowners could effectively articulate the importance of their production to the nation and defend the spaces of estate agriculture in the postrevolutionary context. At the same time, something fundamental had changed about the relations between landowners, the state, and indígenas. Where once landowners stood as the sole nexus between countryside and nation, now both landowners and their indigenous neighbors related to the state and each other through channels of corporatist mediation.

Change loomed on the horizon, and some landowners understood this. Jorge Martínez, who grew up in the 1950s and 1960s, reminisced, "Our father always told us that our time was limited. There was always a sense that it was only a matter of time before the indígenas would take the land away from us, through agrarian reform." This premonition meant that, even during a period of remarkable agricultural prosperity brought about by the expansion of cattle ranching, children's real futures lay off the land. The Martínezes, like many other prominent families, channeled the riches of cattle into education. Thus in the 1960s young ladinos began to trace their grandparents' footsteps backward, out of the countryside and into nearby cities. Some went farther. Like Jorge Martínez, several of Roberto Trujillo's older siblings attended secondary schools and universities in Mexico City, following trajectories that led toward executive offices in PEMEX, Mexico's national oil company, and in various multinational firms. This exodus did not lead to the abandonment of rural roots or agriculture, as teleological modernization narratives might suggest. Instead, professional salaries subsidized family estates. Roberto Trujillo's brother Fausto observed, "When ranchers talk they always say that 'the ranch paid for this education,' but the truth is that it was usually the other way around. People would study and work to subsidize the ranch."

In the difficult decades of the 1970s and 1980s, the professional careers of estate owners' sons and daughters carried estates through agricultural crises. They could do little to defend landed production against political change, however. Even in boom times, two processes had been set in motion that would shatter ladinos' virtually unchallenged control over land and politics. By the mid-1990s, professional careers and urban life were more than ways to diversify a family's economic base. They represented the only attractive escape from political turmoil and agrarian conflict and, as we shall see in chapter 9, played an important role in shaping landowners' calculations of the risks of violent response to land invasions.

In sum, during the decades that followed the Mexican Revolution, landowners maintained considerable ability to defend themselves against emerging forms of indigenous territoriality produced by postrevolutionary state rule. Landowners twisted the institutions, legal frameworks, and ideologies of the Revolution into new forms of domination, but in doing so, found the spaces of landed production changed forever. Attacking peasant leaders, subdividing estates, creating peasant-owned "buffer properties," corrupting agrarian reform officials, and lacing the paternal language of estate social relations with Revolutionary fervor, landowners mounted a tactical defense of landed territory. But, increasingly, these practices had long-lasting unintended consequences. Violence and corruption forestalled conflict, but inflamed tensions and contradictions in the countryside. The creation of buffer properties reconfigured the estates in ways that solidified indigenous usufruct land claims and helped consolidate indigenous territoriality. As Oscar Franz reflected, "We thought that giving the indigenous their own land would make them want to defend our properties—and it did—but it also gave them a sense of what it's like to be an owner, and made them want to own more." Most importantly, while landowners continued to dominate local government, shifting patterns of political mediation during this period that displaced landowners as the sole nexus between peasant and nation, undermined the material and discursive bounding of estates' "insides" and "outsides." By the late 1970s and 1980s, with economic crisis deepening in the Chiapan countryside, all of these contradictions exploded into large-scale agrarian conflict.

The Dead at Golonchán

Cattle, Crisis, and Conflict, 1962–1994

What was the catastrophe at Golonchán like? At five in the afternoon landowners in state police uniforms came with the army, and . . . they all came carrying guns. They were dragging along a cannon, and when the shooting began, a bullet that looked like an ear of corn hit the house and exploded beside us into metal shards. We fled to the edge of the forest, crawling on our bellies because there were a lot of bullets. Lots of people died. Twelve of us died, eighteen wounded, and the wounded are loaded up with debt now because of the cost of medicine. . . . This is the tragedy that happened on June 15 at five in the afternoon.
— Anonymous witness, 1980

On June 15, 1980, landowners dressed in police uniforms, along with federal soldiers under the command of General Absalón Castellanos Domínguez, descended on a meeting of indigenous land invaders affiliated with the Partido Socialista de los Trabajadores (PST, or Socialist Workers' Party) occupying part of the Golonchán estate. When the shooting stopped more than two hours later, at least a dozen peasants lay dead.[1] Countless more were injured, and hundreds of people had fled Golonchán for nearby estates occupied by members of the PST. Many other refugees disappeared into distant settlements in Chiapas's eastern rain forests.

The dead at Golonchán have a way of cropping up in unexpected places. Don Roberto remembers meeting one of the dead deep in the Lacandón forest while traveling for his work in the Ministry of Health. Another dead man purportedly farms a small plot outside nearby Ocosingo. Amidst this confusion, the very real dead at Golonchán also live on in indígenas' and landowners' memories of agrarian struggle. For landowners, particularly those not directly involved in the events of June 1980, "Golonchán" symbolizes a moment when "the government acted quickly and with a heavy hand" to protect property rights. Not surprisingly, after 1994 many landowners consciously deploy "Golonchán" as a foil for understanding the government's response to more recent land invasions. For example, Alfredo Pinto, whose San José Sierra Nevada estate was invaded in both 1980 and 1994, denied that he had faced any agrarian difficulties before the Zapatista uprising. When I challenged him with my knowledge of the invasion of his property and of the invaders' eviction by the army in 1980, he replied, "Those weren't *real* invasions. Not like in 1994 — complete invasions that forced us out, with death threats and all that. They were just little invasions and the government intervened quickly to restore the properties. It resolved the problem."

The occupation of Golonchán by PST members formed part of a massive wave of land invasions that spread across the state, and indeed the entire nation, during the late 1970s and early 1980s. Beginning in the late 1960s, peasant organizations, often critical of the state, flourished in Chiapas, and violent conflicts erupted between opposition peasant groups, peasants and landowners, PRI-aligned peasants and state forces. By 1980, peasants representing various political leanings, but primarily aligned with the PST, had seized almost seventy of the largest estates in north-central Chiapas.[2] The massacre of PST members at Golonchán was but one event in a massive wave of repression by landowners and government forces that followed close on the heels of this escalation of land conflicts. Indeed, when land invasion was made a federal crime in 1977, a coordinated military campaign was launched against land invaders, peasant leaders were increasingly harassed, and landowners evicted peasants with impunity. The years from 1976 through 1983 came to be called the period of "bloody populism."[3] Not surprisingly, after the Zapatista uprising of 1994, journalists and activists dredged up the dead at Golonchán as emblematic evidence of landowners' ongoing domination of Chiapas by force.

At Golonchán landowners won a tremendous victory, striking a decisive blow against peasant mobilization. Or did they? For landowners affected by the other PST invasions, memories of that period are not so clear-cut. A conversation with one landowner, who as a young man helped lead landowners' opposition to the PST and may have participated in the events of June 15, 1980, provided a glimpse of this ambiguity. After he described landowners' organized efforts to lobby state officials for the eviction of invaders from Golonchán and the subsequent response by the army, I interrupted the story to comment:

Bobrow-Strain: So you got what you wanted in the end.

Anonymous landowner: No, we didn't. Once the agrarian movement ended, the government told us to participate in its plan to purchase the invaded properties and turn them over to peasants.

Bobrow-Strain: Why would the government evict the invaders if it was just going to turn the land over to peasants in the end?

Anonymous landowner: Because they wanted to get rid of the invaders from the opposition party [the PST]! Then they gave the land to peasants who were still loyal to the government. There were so many that the government proposed to buy other ranches. They bought Golonchán. They bought Picoté, San Antonio Bulujib, San Juan Cabtejaj, which is now called San Juan de la Montaña, and Verapaz. That was the end of cattle ranching in Sitalá!

In the end, government repression of land invaders from militant opposition groups coincided with landowners' demands for evictions — a fact that has allowed many observers to gloss the events at Golonchán as an unalloyed triumph of landowner hegemony. Nevertheless, as this landowner's words suggest, careful examination of this moment in the formation and re-formation of estate agriculture in Chilón tells a far more complex and ambiguous story.

The public file on Golonchán at the National Agrarian Registry in Tuxtla Gutiérrez stands almost eight inches high. It has been meticulously cleaned of references to the events of June 15, 1980, but not of stories, ambiguities, and contradictions. Without challenging the fact of collusion between landowners and state actors in the heavy-handed repression of land invaders, I dredge up the dead at Golonchán once again to tell a different story — a story not of clear-cut class conspiracy between landowners and the state but rather of an unstable moment in the relationship between landowners and the state. The massacre at Golonchán and subsequent evictions throughout Chilón and Sitalá illustrate a further movement in the shifting terrain of political mediations described in chapter 5; shifts in which a growing body of competing peasant organizations gradually displaced landowners as the mediators between state and countryside. These shifts both arose from and gave rise to new articulations of landowner, state, and indigenous territoriality.

In order to understand these changes, we must follow the unfolding of a state project aimed at reorganizing the spaces of agricultural production in southern Mexico. The state's efforts to supply the country's growing urban industrial workforce with beef by promoting cattle production in southern Mexico resonated powerfully with Chiloneros' defense of territory, providing new political and economic underpinnings for landed production. But the transition to cattle ranching also had devastating consequences for peasants' livelihood. By the 1970s, the combination of cattle ranching and organizing by new political actors—priests preaching liberation theology and adherents of the opposition PST—radicalized indigenous territorial struggles. This process culminated in the invasion of Golonchán and scores of other estates in the late 1970s and early 1980s.

Cattle and Conflict

In the spring of 1949, Francisco Cancino, the owner of Sitalá's Zapucaná estate, complained that stray cattle had trampled several of his cane and corn fields.[4] The animals' owner, Enrique Flores, was one of the region's pioneering cattlemen. He and his brother Gustavo (owner of Golonchán) owned more than a third of the cattle in Sitalá and Guaquitepec, and if those animals caused conflicts among landowners, they would eventually cause even greater troubles between landowners and their indigenous workers.[5]

The 1950s and 1960s saw cattle spread rapidly across the landscape of north-central Chiapas. It was a time of land enclosures, with landowners clearing trees, crops, and workers to make room for pasture. Barbed-wire fences snaked around once open estates and Chilón's Local Cattlemen's Association emerged as one of the region's preeminent social, political, and economic institutions. Massive new government subsidies aimed at promoting livestock production throughout the nation fueled a profound change in the countryside that came to be called the *ganaderización* (literally, "cattle-ization") of Mexico. In Chilón the expansion of livestock production also came as a direct response to more locally specific shifts in the political economy of estate agriculture: first, competition from large sugar producers outside Chiapas and government crackdowns on clandestine cane liquor production caused the collapse of small-scale sugarcane farming and left cane-growing landowners eager to find new sources of income. Second, growing labor-scarcity—the result of land reform programs that offered indigenous workers their first chance to leave the estates and farm their own plots of land — encouraged landowners to switch from labor-intensive coffee production to almost laborless cattle ranching.[6] The shift toward closed pastures and cattle ranching provided a powerful boost to landowners' incomes but displaced peasants, destabilized basic food provisioning, and set the stage for massive social protest.

The Ganaderización of Mexico

Before 1950, despite the central place of cowboys and cattle ranches in Mexico's popular culture, Mexicans in general ate relatively little beef (Martín 1960, Sanderson 1986, Robles 1988). As the country industrialized after World War II, dissonance between a romantic cowboy culture and a peasant corn diet exerted an increasingly powerful pull on agricultural policy, with production of beef for domestic consumption taking on a new urgency. President Ruiz Cortines (1952–1958) rushed to implement an emergency plan for promoting the livestock sector based on "ample and well-timed credits for all cattlemen . . . ; control and eradication of disease; expansion of artificial insemination programs . . . ; [and] energetic repression of cattle rustling" (quoted in Robles 1988:78). Over the next three decades cattle would emerge as a principal source of accumulation for national development and a pivotal ingredient in efforts to consolidate the government's post-revolutionary legitimacy.

From 1950 to 1960 investment in livestock nearly quadrupled and, thanks in large part to massive injections of heavily subsidized credit, the livestock sector grew at a phenomenal rate (Chauvet 1999, Robles 1988:80). By 1970 almost 70 percent of all agricultural land in the nation was dedicated to livestock (Chauvet 1999:52, Sanderson 1986). Importantly, it was medium to large private property owners, not the ejido sector, that reaped the benefits of this remarkable expansion. Indeed, between 1950 and 1970, the lucrative endeavor of livestock production became the almost exclusive domain of private property owners such as Chilón's coffee planters (Rutsch 1984:24). In 1960, only 595 of Chilón's almost 4,000 cattle were to be found on ejidos (Secretaría de Industria y Comercio 1960).[7] With ranchers' claims to large tracts of land legitimated by the exigencies of national development, the livestock sector increased production without a significant investment in labor, remaining an overwhelmingly extensive endeavor (Chauvet 1999, Robles 1988, Rutsch 1984).

Once confined to the bleak northern deserts where a hundred hectares supported one scraggly steer, cattle found a new home in the lush southern tropics. Pasture metastasized across the tropical "cattle frontier," particularly in the states of Chiapas, Veracruz, and Yucatán. Between 1940 and 1960, ranchers in these states increased the total herd by 3 million head (Villafuerte et al. 1997:20). In contrast to the export-oriented tropical ranching found in many other Latin American countries, cattle ranching proliferated across southern Mexico to supply *domestic* markets. In this sense, while ranchers in northern Mexico continued to export cattle and beef to the United States (Sanderson 1986), tropical ranching truly existed to underwrite Mexico's urban industrial growth. Ranching in the tropics was also explicitly linked to the need to dominate, populate, and conquer territory. As one policy maker wrote in 1955, "We live in a time that will pass into history as the liberation of colonial nations; this liberation depends in large part on the conquest of the tropics and their integration into the economy and civilization of . . . the world" (quoted in Villafuerte et al. 1997:14). Champions of this grand conquest boasted that "the tropics have cattle as a vocation" (quoted in Fernández and Tarrío 1983), but it was sweeping state support that enabled southern ranchers to follow this "vocation."

Backed by initiatives of the World Bank, the U.S. Agency for International Development (USAID), and the Inter-American Development Bank (IADB) to promote tropical ranching, the state poured funds into the south as never before. In Chiapas, four consecutive governors sponsored programs designed to stimulate cattle production and convert the sector "into one of the state's firm bases of economic sustenance" (Governor Aranda Osario, quoted in Fernández and Tarrío 1983:49). Through the 1950s and 1960s, cattle ranchers received tax breaks of up to 70 percent on profits, roads built to transport cattle to markets, a wide range of technical assistance, and virtually free credit, fencing material, and veterinary medicines (Fernández and Tarrío 1983:50; Villafuerte et al. 1997). The number of cattle in Chiapas grew 260 percent between 1950 and 1970, and throughout that period private ranchers consistently controlled more than 70 percent of Chiapas's livestock. Even more importantly, the number of cattle classified as purebred (*fino*) — animals owned almost exclusively by private ranchers — increased more than 2,000 percent (see Table 1).

Cattle promised to transform the backward colonial structure of Chiapas into modern agribusiness, and boosters of the state's "magnificent livestock future" (de la Peña 1951:491) zeroed in on Chilón as an unexploited reserve ripe for cattle. Despite the "vast possibilities for

Table 1 Number of cattle throughout the state and on private property, Chiapas, 1950–1970

Year	All Chiapas		Private property*	
	Total	Fino grade	Total	Fino grade
1950	480,308	11,278	351,771	6,811
1960	682,512	57,982	525,086	49,954
1970	1,249,326	148,185	890,094	140,191

* Larger than 5 hectares.
Source: Calculated from Villafuerte et al. 1997:196.

livestock in this rich district" (de la Peña 1951:513), Chilón, held back by rampant disease, ticks, vampire bats, and lack of market infrastructure, lagged far behind other parts of Chiapas. With roads into the region impassable much of the year, stud bulls had to be flown in and out of the region aboard propeller-driven cargo planes, and production was so extensive that landowners referred to it as cattle "hunting" rather than "husbandry." Through concerted state effort to combat threats to livestock health and open up roads into the region, however, this was about to change.

For Chiloneros, incentives to go into cattle ranching couldn't have come at a better time. In the mid-1950s both the coffee and sugarcane markets experienced major contractions, the former crippled by cyclical overproduction in international markets and the latter done in permanently by changes closer to home.[8] Thus, by the time cattle production began to take off in the 1950s and 1960s, Alejandro Díaz explained, "people who had grown sugarcane weren't able to make a profit anymore so they were looking for other ways to make a living and they turned to . . . cattle. With cattle there was more circulation [of money] than ever before. . . . Cattle raised the economy up. . . . People were also happy because when they had depended on coffee or sugarcane, they always had to wait for the harvest in order to have money. With cattle they could get money whenever they needed it. If they had an expense, they could sell cattle. . . . Cattle was more constant." Thus, coupled with lucrative state supports, the year-round liquidity of livestock proved a boon to producers, long constrained by the seasonal cycles of coffee. "Cattle brought tremendous wealth to the region," Enrique Díaz Pérez remembered. "Cattle are living capital, and they made the municipio rich."

"Ganado fue ganado" (cattle was profit), as they liked to say,[9] but cattle ranching also provided a much-needed solution to another problem. As more and more estate laborers formed or joined ejidos in the postrevolutionary period, securing an inexpensive and reliable labor force became increasingly difficult. Miguel Utrilla remembered this period: "In the 1950s, the common people began to see that coffee was a good thing and wanted to have their own coffee plants. They want to have their own place to plant coffee, which they see as gold. Once people have their own land and coffee plants, it gets harder and harder to hire labor. You'd go to someone you'd hired for years to harvest coffee and he'd say [mimicking a self-effacing voice], 'No-o-o, patró-ó-ón. Why don't you ask my son? Why don't you ask my brother?'"

Delio Ballinas, who lost two properties to invasion in the early 1980s, lived through the same process. "[Organizers] came and started telling the indígenas that if they'd lived on the property for ten years, they had a right to it." Peons who did not form or join an ejido in Chilón, Ballinas continued, "abandoned our ranches and went to the jungle, where the government gave them land, and we were stuck without a workforce." Ballinas recruited temporary workers from as far away as San Cristóbal, but he never could get enough.[10] Yet the alternative — coercing resident workers to remain on the estate — was losing its appeal. As land reform petitions by resident workers proliferated in the 1950s and 1960s, workers living on estate grounds posed a constant threat.[11]

Landowners turned to a number of solutions. Most fractioned off portions of their estates to give loyal workers small properties that they could pay for in labor. This widespread practice established a secure workforce with fewer legal claims on landowners' estates and, ideally, a debt of gratitude to the landowner.[12] Cattle production, with its phenomenally low labor requirements, provided another method of reducing reliance on resident workers. Perhaps even more importantly, landowners quickly realized that the state's increasing support for cattle production carried with it an array of new laws, institutions, and political mechanisms that allowed landowners to remake the territoriality of estate agriculture.

In 1965 the Unión Ganadera Regional de Chiapas (UGRCH, or Regional Cattlemen's Association of Chiapas), based in Tuxtla Gutiérrez, posted a memo to its member associations celebrating its phenomenal success in lobbying the Secretariat of Industry and Commerce to establish a higher guaranteed price for dressed beef carcasses "than had even been promised."[13] But, judging from the correspondence in the AGL archive, Chiloneros were less concerned about economic guarantees than about legal and political guarantees. Letter after letter complained of actual and threatened land invasions, trumped-up agrarian reform claims, and the disruption of production by peasants' sabotage. Landowners' cries did not fall on deaf ears.

A zealous patron of cattle production, Governor José Castillo Tielemans (1964–1970) clearly expressed the dual requirements of an expanding industry. The livestock sector, he argued, required both economic stimuli and all "the legal guarantees . . . necessary to develop its activities without threats or uncertainties" (quoted in Fernández and Tarrío 1983:51). Or, as a later governor put it more forcefully, "I reiterate the firm determination of the executive chief of the state not to permit any invasion that would disrupt the peace of the people of the countryside . . . [so that] the cattlemen of the state may feel secure and continue producing benefits for the whole Chiapan family" (Governor González Blanco, quoted in Fernández and Tarrío 1983:55).

The governor's words have a revealingly ironic double meaning: the exact term he uses to indicate the state's population as a whole — "the Chiapas family" — is also commonly used to describe the state's wealthiest landed elites. Whether or not he intended this double meaning, it reflects precisely what the institutions and legal frameworks of *ganaderización* achieved: guaranteed ongoing political benefits for landowners because of their perceived ability to produce for the larger social body. These benefits took two forms: the provision of extensive legal protections for pasture and the creation of new institutions to enforce and defend these protections.

In 1937, in an effort to "conserve and increase the wealth of [Mexico's] livestock sector," the radical land reformer President Lázaro Cárdenas decreed an addendum to the federal agrarian code that would have long-lasting and decidedly conservative consequences in Chiapas. The addendum granted cattle ranchers exemption from the land reform law and dramatically raised the legal limit of "small property" to whatever area of land was required to sustain 500 head of cattle. Under Cárdenas, this exemption was temporary — limited to twenty-five years — and applied only if the agricultural needs of all peasant communities within a radius of seven kilometers had already been met (Reyes 1998b:159–160). Nevertheless, by the end of the 1940s Lázaro Cárdenas's temporary concession had become permanent. To ensure the eligible landowners' immunity, federal bureaucracies offered them *certificados de inafectabilidad* specifying that their property was exempt from land reform. Beginning with the administration of President Miguel Alemán (1946–1952), the "businessman president" (Krauze 1997) and architect of Mexico's agrarian counterreform, tens of thousands of hectares of land received exemption certificates in Chiapas. Although actual cattle ranching lagged behind in Chilón, Chiloneros were quick to take advantage of this trend. Every major estate in the area petitioned for exemption, and more than half of the applications were filed between 1952 and 1955.

While exemption certificates were key signs of state support for landowners, applying for one could be quite onerous, as Enrique Pinto, owner of the 136-hectare San Antonio Patbaxil estate, complained to the Departmento de Asuntos Agrarios y Colonización (DAAC, or Department of Agrarian and Colonization Affairs) three years into his petition process: "I can't work my lands with any enthusiasm because of constant threats from peasant groups who want to apply for land reform in this region, something that has harmed me greatly. At the same time, I can't apply for loans at the Bank because I don't have an exemption certificate, so please, I beg you again to update me on the progress of my case, since on my last visit to Mexico City I visited [your] offices and was told verbally that it was about to be resolved — that was a year ago."[14]

Eight years later, Pinto did receive final confirmation of exemption from land reform, after being rejected and having to go through the whole process again. While the rationale behind both the rejection and subsequent granting of exemption are less than clear, the fact that San Antonio Patbaxil operated as one estate in tandem with the adjacent San José Sierra Nevada property, also owned by the Pinto family, may suggest a reason for the delays. In another case, federal authorities repeatedly sent back an application made by Esperanza Zepeda for clarification, once even noting that the local SRA technicians who surveyed her land had failed to notice the existence of an entire town of indigenous land reform claimants located within the estate's boundaries. Another letter asked how it was possible for Zepeda to deny that Santa Cruz lay within the radius of seven kilometers from any land reform community, when she also listed the ejido of Bachajón as her immediate neighbor to the east.[15] Despite these complications, the federal government did eventually grant Zepeda a certificate of full exemption in 1972. As the case suggests, while exemption was far less automatic than it was often portrayed, most Chiloneros received relatively quick and positive responses to their petitions, whether or not they really satisfied the lenient requirements of the agrarian code.[16]

Given the politicized nature of property rights in Mexico, exemption from land reform would have little impact on producers without effective means of enforcing it under PRI rule. Accordingly, beginning in the late 1930s, a series of hierarchically organized corporatist cattlemen's associations emerged as the institutional guardians of property in Chiapas. At the top of this pyramid, authorized by a 1936 federal law, the UGRCH served as the coordinating body for the local associations that began to crop up throughout the state by the mid-1940s. Then as now, the UGRCH acted as a clearinghouse for livestock subsidies and extension programs, a sponsor of cattle fairs and competitions, and a general booster of cattle production in the state, but its primary function was to provide a channel through which landowners could exert pressure on the state to resolve land reform claims in their favor (Reyes 1998b). To this end, it sponsored preemptive lobbying efforts against peasants' claims and helped landowners negotiate the warren of land reform bureaucracy. Throughout the 1960s, it circulated regular broadsides to its members with such titles as "How to Report a Land Invasion."

If the UGRCH coordinated high-level lobbying for the state's cattlemen, local associations formed the front line of landowners' defenses. In Chilón, the AGL (founded in 1962) backed individual landowners in their disputes with peasants, providing a counterweight to the emerging activism of corporatist peasant organizations such as the Confederación Nacional Campesina (CNC, or National Peasant Confederation).[17] In numerous cases, the AGL affirmed landowners' complaints in letters of support directed to various state agencies. In 1965, for example, the AGL, wielding its weighty affiliation with the Confederación Nacional de Ganaderos (CNG, or National Cattlemen's Confederation), wrote to the DAAC to "set the record straight" about underhanded dealings and false assertions made by peasant invaders of the San José Mequeja estate. Often, however, the AGL played a more immediate role in resolving land conflicts, as the ill-fated owner of the Jérico estate revealed in a 1965 letter to the AGL: "The last time I spoke with Lic. de Cosas, he told me that whether or not the invaders get evicted, *all depends on our association,* because they are the ones who can intervene with the municipal president and lock up that bunch of punks [*vivales*] who take advantage of those stupid indígenas."[18]

The AGL's ability to intervene directly in agrarian conflicts of course reflected both the general impunity enjoyed by landowners and the close connections between them and local officials, but it also speaks to specific policies designed to buttress the livestock sector. For most live-stock boosters, the one factor that prevented Chiapas from achieving its true potential as a cattle-raising state was rustling. "Droughts, pests, floods, with all the damage they bring, don't do as much harm . . . as cattle rustling," wrote one observer (Chanona 1952:104), and the venerable Moisés de la Peña (1951:483) concurred. At the core of the rustling problem, he argued, was a fundamental "lack of authority" in the state. The 1940 law that authorized cattlemen's associations in Chiapas attempted to address that lack of authority with a series of provisions that encouraged landowners to form police forces to combat the plague of rustlers. According to this law, members of local cattlemen's associations could form a mounted defense brigade and the state government would supply them with arms (de la Peña 1951). Not surprisingly, while archival evidence in Chilón and Sitalá point to ladino landowners as the culprits in most disputes over cattle, the antirustling police quickly found work defending estates against peasant invasions. By 1963, less than a year after the death of Pedro Chulín, the UGRCH could easily appeal to its members to "support the Police in their Police Day celebrations . . . because they have done such a special job lately of combating cattle theft *and all the recent problems.*"[19] Thus, at the same time as the 1940 law facilitated the creation of organized landowner defense brigades (often called "white guards" by their opponents), its strong rhetoric in support of development and against rustling promoted broader tolerance of repression in the name of economic progress.

In sum, by the 1960s and 1970s, cattle production offered land-owners a lucrative market, low labor requirements, and privileged claims to a wide variety of state supports. Cattle allowed landowners to rework and defend the spaces of estate agriculture while dramatically reducing their reliance on resident workers — but this strategy would ultimately backfire violently.

The Contradictions of Cattle

The ganaderización of Chilón offered many landowners unprecedented new prosperity and stability. To most peasants, however, it brought hunger and unemployment. Throughout Mexico during the

1970s, pasture and feed crops displaced basic grains (Rubio 1990, Sanderson 1986). As Chilón's landowners converted to pasture both their own cornfields and the milpas once farmed by resident workers, food supplies dropped precipitously. By 1980, the municipal president of Chilón was writing frequent complaints about the region's "great scarcity of corn and beans" due to the expansion of pasture.[20]

Five days before the Golonchán massacre, Rodolfo Domínguez sent a delegation of *ejidatarios* and resident estate workers loyal to the PRI to urge the municipal president to support them in their efforts to secure desperately needed corn and beans through the Instituto Nacional Indigenista (INI).[21] That these peasants turned to the INI for food reflects a monumental change in traditional estate social relations. For decades before, the landowner provided workers with emergency food supplies in lean times. But with the increasing importance of ranching, as Alejandro Díaz revealed, "it was no longer convenient to have [resident peons] on our estates." Beginning in 1959, court records in Chilón testify to landowners' increasing preoccupation with finding ways to get rid of workers with the right to use land that might otherwise serve as pasture. A man who had bought part of Patbaxil, for example, refused to accept the property "along with all its servants," as customary, complaining bitterly about two families who would not leave the land.[22]

Using a popular rule of thumb, landowners report that whereas one hectare of coffee requires 200 people (i.e., person-days of labor), one cowboy can manage 200 hectares of cattle. By 1978, land devoted to agricultural crops had dwindled to only 12 percent of the state, and cattle occupied more than 40 percent of the entire surface of Chiapas. Yet ranching still employed only a third as many people as the shrunken farm sector (Fernández and Tarrío 1983:138). In sum, the expansion of cattle ranching generated simultaneous declines in basic food supplies and local employment. Mercedes Olivera, an anthropologist and activist who spent time in the region during this transition, paints a graphic picture of its consequences: "We literally saw lines of peasants [who had been expelled from estates] walking on the roads. They'd come up to us to say they were looking for a new patrón and ask if we knew where they could find a new patrón to work for." As economic crisis deepened into the 1980s (Rus 1995), peasants' feelings of abandonment quickly turned to anger and mobilization. Olivera reports that she and other students organized landless peasants to claim the plots they lost in the transition to cattle ranching, sometimes watching with horror as the peasants' "feelings of sorrow turned into hatred and violence."

Priests, Parties, and the
Transformation of Indigenous Territoriality

Beginning in the 1970s and spurred on by the brutal effects of ganaderización on indígenas' livelihoods, radical new mediators drove an irreversible wedge into the relationship between landowners, indigenous peasants, and the state. Nascent peasant movements in north-central Chiapas in the 1970s formed part of a larger national response by landless and land-poor peasants to the effects of prolonged agricultural crisis, the contradictions of ganaderización, the lethargic response of the country's land reform bureaucracies, the crumbling legitimacy of the government-aligned CNC, and fallout from the repression of democratic popular movements in 1968. Encouraged by political reforms and the populist agenda of President Luis Echeverría (1970–1976), large-scale mobilizations spread throughout the Mexican countryside (and persisted despite repression under Echeverría's conservative successor).

Writing on Chiapas's agrarian struggles in this period has focused considerable attention on conflicts in Simojovel and Venustiano Carranza (Harvey 1998, Toledo 1996). In both cases, the displacement of thousands of peasants by the construction of hydroelectric dams intensified the contradictions discussed above, and the dramatic clashes that resulted frequently made national news. Little has been written, however, on the outbreak of agrarian struggle in Chilón, where two emerging forces channeled dislocated peasants toward political consciousness and organized resistance: (1) the growing politicization of community organizing efforts carried out by the Jesuit mission at Bachajón and (2) the appearance of a militant opposition political party, the PST, committed to aggressive pursuit of peasant land claims.[23]

Displacing *el Patrón:* Liberation Theology and
the Challenge to Landed Production

The Jesuit mission at Bachajón, founded in 1958 with the goals of "living with the indígenas, learning their language, preaching the Gospel, catechizing . . . and seeking [the indígenas'] social and material development" (quoted in Díaz Olivares n.d.:129), spent its first decade pursuing relatively traditional missionary work. Initially this mild approach won the mission substantial support from many landed elites, but by 1971, responding to winds of change blowing across Latin America, the mission's agenda began to change.

Encouraged by the new openness in the Catholic Church in the wake of the Second Vatican Council (1962–1965) and propelled by the contradictions of expanding poverty and deepening authoritarian rule, many Latin American Catholics began to conceive of a new kind of church. Challenging decades of conservative theology, priests and lay thinkers such as Gustavo Gutiérrez and Juan Segundo connected theology with radical social, political, and economic analysis to imagine religious praxis based on material engagement with the world. In meetings held in Brazil, in Switzerland, and, most importantly, in Medellín, Colombia, a new "theology of liberation" was hammered out and took on an inchoate institutional form. Bishops, theologians, and lay leaders argued that the church must shed its historical complicity with oppression and unwaveringly side with Latin America's poor.

Chiapas's bishop, Samuel Ruiz, was an early adherent of liberation theology and active participant in both the Second Vatican Council and the Medellín Conference of Latin American Bishops (1968). Under his influence, the Catholic Church in Chiapas began to shift its focus away from traditional missionary evangelization and *castellanización* (imposition of the Spanish language and ladino customs) to a more radical project steeped in the construction of critical political consciousness and new forms of indigenous identity.

Liberation theology took root rapidly in Tzeltal Chiapas, first in Ocosingo and then in Bachajón. Work began with the training of hundreds of indigenous lay catechists. These Tzeltal men and women walked through the mountains from community to community preaching the Gospel and linking their religious teaching to agrarian politics. "After 1971," Fr. Morales told me, "we began intensive work on agrarian issues. We translated the Agrarian Law into Tzeltal and held workshops on agrarian struggle—all under the banner of nonviolence and no invasions. People were becoming conscious of their reality."

In 1974, Tzeltal catechists from Bachajón and Ocosingo played a formative role in organizing a congress that drew indígenas from throughout the state to San Cristóbal de Las Casas to discuss land, commerce, education, and health. Conceived by Chiapas's governor, Manuel Velasco Suárez, as a simple quincentennial celebration of the birth of Chiapas's first bishop, Bartolomé de Las Casas, the congress took a more critical tack when Velasco Suárez delegated responsibility for convening the meeting to Samuel Ruiz (CENCOS 1974). Under Ruiz's direction the congress became, in Fr. Morales's words, "a process, not an event," an opportunity to bring indigenous communities together for a year of meetings in which they discussed their concerns, outlined political and economic demands, and formulated plans. In short, the preparations for the congress raised the consciousness of an entire generation of indigenous lay leaders gathered from Tzeltal, Tzotzil, Ch'ol, and Tojolabal communities.

At the meeting itself, Tzeltals from Bachajón, Chilón, Sitalá, and Yajalón denounced corrupt SRA officials, PRI-backed indigenous political bosses, ladino merchants, and landowners. They attacked the general exploitation of resident estate workers and denounced landowners' abuses and the state's failures, including eighteen years of repressed agrarian struggle on Enrique Flores's Santa Cruz estate. In the end, all the participants vowed to aggressively organize agrarian struggles and economic collectives (CENCOS 1974).

As it grew more imbued with the radical spirit of liberation theology, the Bachajón mission began to target ladinos' place at the nexus between peasants and the larger polity. Cooperative ventures, including a coffee-purchasing collective, not only sought to improve indigenous communities' "social and material development," they also explicitly challenged ladino commercial monopolies (Díaz Olivares n.d.). The Jesuits made an early decision "never to work directly with the finqueros," and Fr. Morales told me why: "The finquero was the intermediary between the priest and the people, but the finqueros dominated the people through religion. We broke that scheme by focusing on the people. We did more than hold ceremonies; we reinterpreted the word of God in light of reality. That was pure dynamite" (Human Rights Watch 1997:3).

That *was* pure dynamite. In many landowners' minds, the church that once had stood as their trusted friend and ally now only sowed division and hatred. Miguel Utrilla, who as a young man had been one of the Jesuits' strongest landowner allies, still feels betrayed by these changes. The Jesuits no longer allow indígenas to name ladinos as godparents, he complained: "Basically, the clergy are sowing ethnic difference by treating mestizos and indígenas differently; by separating them. I remember once one of my workers—he was Tzeltal but also spoke Spanish—had to go to the priests' marriage talks before he could get married. It was more convenient for him to attend the talks that were given in Spanish, but the priests insisted—*they insisted*—that Tzeltals could only attend the sessions in Tzeltal."

What was worse, to landowners' minds, was that the construction of these ethnic differences turned on painting ladinos as villains. Delio Ballinas presented a harsher but more widespread view of the priests' role in this process: "Before the priests, workers were very loyal. Yes, very loyal. But the priests began to sow hatred among them. Teach them to attack us. The priests came to Pantelhó thirty-five years ago and started teaching the indígenas to demand raises, to demand schools. Telling them that if they lived on the property for ten years, they had a right to it."

Throughout the 1970s, church organizing came under fire from landowners, merchants, PRI-aligned peasants, and state officials. In 1975, for example, a letter from the mayor of Chilón to the state legislature denounced indigenous catequistas as vagrants and troublemakers, and in 1976 the mayor of Sitalá complained to government officials about Jesuit organizing on the Golonchán estate.[24] It was the increasing presence of the PST, however, that ultimately pushed the situation on Golonchán toward violence.

Learning to Land Invade: The PST in Chilón

Independent peasant movements appeared across Chiapas during the 1970s. In Chilón, it was the newly formed Socialist Workers' Party that took up the banner of agrarian struggle. At the national level, the PST emerged out of democratization movements that arose in 1968, and was made possible by electoral reforms under Luis Echeverría's populist presidency, which facilitated the formation of new political parties (Alonso 1984). Beginning in 1973, PST militants pressured Echeverría to expand and deepen land redistribution programs, and by the late 1970s, the party's influence had spread to Veracruz, Puebla, Jalisco, San Luis Potosí, and Chiapas. In 1977, in response to the repression of peasant mobilization by Echeverría's conservative successor, José López Portillo, the PST launched a national campaign of land invasions. At its height in 1980, more than 25,000 PST militants occupied over 150,000 hectares across the country (Alonso 1984).

The PST entered Chilón and surrounding communities in 1976. Although the PST and the Jesuits would split decisively after the Go-lonchán massacre, the party worked closely with church activists at first, focusing its attention on communities where catequistas had established a base of critical peasant consciousness. A Tzeltal from Petal-cingo remembered the arrival of the PST: "In 1976 a party came . . . the PST, then from there we started to see, we had already started to realize that we hadn't been defending ourselves . . . realize how it is that they [ladinos] rob us, how they exploit us, how they mistreat us, but we didn't have strength, we didn't know how to start, how to . . . liberate ourselves from that ladino . . . when that brother [the PST activist] came, he started to help us free ourselves" (quoted in Sanchez 1999:93).

Liberation from ladinos meant struggle for land, and the PST threw itself into the fray, training peasants in agrarian law and preaching the gospel of land invasion. In Chilón, another Tzeltal remembered, the indígenas "had been pushing papers, petitioning for land reform, and no one paid us any attention. The PST comes and says, 'Now you're going to get land,' well, now that we had the PST, we started to invade the land" (quoted in Ovalle Muñoz 1984:69).

As PST-led land invasions spread, landowners scrambled to defend themselves. In cable after cable, landowners called for help: "Urgent plea for military intervention at this location to guarantee inhabitants' peace, reason[:] Unrest in Tacuba Nueva P.S.T. agitators Jesuit priests gathering people from other municipios threaten to take over this town between 10 and 15 April."[25] They mounted delegations to plead their case in Mexico City, and sometimes they took matters into their own hands. Some of the most vociferous denunciations of the PST, however, came from within indigenous communities.

In 1983, for example, leaders of the Paxbarril ejido (themselves the beneficiaries of land reform) lobbied intensively to block the PST's efforts to pursue claims against surrounding estates. This indígena-led protest against the PST speaks to important shifts in the terrain of political mediation. Eager to challenge the PRI's authority by mounting opposition candidates in ejido and municipal elections, the PST threatened the indigenous political bosses closely aligned with the ruling party. In one neatly handwritten note to the municipal president of Chilón, members of a tiny indigenous community aligned with the PRI expressed shock that "Socialist groups from outside our town want to take over [local government]."[26] The PST, according to its opponents, was undermining authority in schools, receiving arms from the Jesuits, threatening to kill PRI supporters, and seizing land in ejidos.[27] In a letter to Governor Juan Sabines, members of the San Sebastián Bachajón ejido denounced the PST for alleged abuses and appealed to the governor to intervene in a running battle over leadership in the community of Alan Sacjún: "The woman called Casilda Silvano Guzmán, a leader of the PST, told every man and woman of us that she would throw us in jail and she mistreats us all. Genaro Domínguez [another PST-affiliated leader] came to Sacjún to train the people in question in the use of arms, so they would know how to use them and then later start killing anyone they want. . . . What's more, they have chopped down a tree [and barred] the road to Alan Sacjún to keep out enemies and the army. . . . Genaro Domínguez and Casilda Silvano said that the governor is worthless and that Genaro Domínguez is better than the government."[28]

Amid this party rivalry and class conflict, land invasions multiplied across the countryside. One after another, peasants occupied some of the region's largest and most valuable estates: Golonchán, Verapaz, Junacmec, Duraznal, El Desengaño, Picoté, and Jotolá. Enrique Flores, the man who was accused of allowing his cattle to trample another ladino landowner's fields, saw *his* fences cut and land occupied by indigenous land invaders. After decades of conflict, San Antonio Bulujib succumbed to invasion. By 1980, peasants had seized sixty-eight properties in Chilón, Yajalón, Sitalá, Tila, and Tumbalá, with the fiercest conflicts erupting in Sitalá and Chilón (Pontigo and Hernández 1981).

Tensions mounted. Ladinos called for protection against hostile peasants — particularly from the PST, who were believed to be planning not only the invasion of farmland but the complete takeover of the towns of Chilón and Yajalón. In March 1980, in apparent fulfillment of ladinos' worst fears, more than a thousand militant indígenas poured into Yajalón against the express will of municipal authorities (Alonso 1984). Ultimately, however, it would be a clash between two indigenous groups that brought this conflict to a violent head.

The Golonchán Massacre

In the spring of 1980, some 800 members of the PST streamed into Sitalá from across north-central Chiapas to occupy a portion of the Golonchán estate. It was clear to the PST that Golonchán, the property of a wealthy absentee landowner covering more than 1,000 hectares of mostly unexploited hills, was a perfect candidate for expropriation. The PST, however, was not the first group to have this thought. Almost twenty years earlier, dozens of families of Golonchán's resident workers had filed their own claim to the property.

Things had not gone well for those original claimants. With few resources and little outside support, they faced a volatile landowner who frequently threatened them and who arranged for Abel Trujillo, a reportedly corrupt land reform official, to carry out "a favorable survey of the property."[29] Trujillo's groundwork ensured that the claim would not succeed. More than forty heads of households qualified to receive land had filed the original petition, but Trujillo's census found only five people eligible for land on the entire estate — too few to permit the case to proceed.[30] In the spring of 1963, land reform officials rejected the claim for lack of the requisite number of qualified persons. That summer, thirty-four heads of households from Golonchán appealed to President López Mateos, explaining their response to the verdict: "Faced with the negative ruling on the Law of Uncultivated Lands . . . we felt obliged to occupy a small piece of Golonchán."[31]

Over the next ten years, Golonchán's workers illegally occupied the estate. Several attempts were made to resolve the standoff, including a proposal to move the invaders to land in neighboring Pantelhó. The workers stood their ground and eventually received a "correction" of Trujillo's census confirming the existence of fifty-nine qualified persons.[32] It is difficult, however, to determine exactly what happened at Golonchán in the 1960s and 1970s. Factions appear to have formed among the land claimants; evidence indicates that some of the invaders worked with the Jesuit mission; and at least one feud resulted in a violent invasion of one faction's land by another group.[33] One thing is certain, however: when PST militants arrived at Golonchán in 1980, the estate was not a blank slate; it was occupied territory already tangled in a morass of disputes.

On May 31, 1980, conflicts between PST militants and the estate's original claimants erupted in violence when PST members forcefully occupied the estate. Seizing the opportunity to discredit the PST, Yajalón's municipal president, a PRI supporter, bypassed his counterpart in Sitalá by sending out a national press release: forty-five peasants had been killed in a clash between the PST and the CNC. Later, as this blatant attempt to paint the PST as violent aggressors unraveled, the official number of dead was reduced to five and then to only one.

Regardless of the number of casualties, at the end of the day the PST had routed Golonchán's original claimants from their homes and now occupied the estate.[34]

Word of the "massacre" spread rapidly. Fr. Mardonio Morales heard the news on a nightly Spanish-language program broadcast over short-wave Radio Moscow. With an appointment to see Governor Juan Sabines already scheduled for the next day in Tuxtla Gutiérrez, Fr. Morales rushed to the state capital. On arrival he discovered that his routine appointment had been changed to lunch at the governor's home, where he was joined by a top land reform official. In the course of this meeting, and at a second meeting in Bachajón, a resolution was battered out. The governor agreed to purchase Golonchán and re-distribute it to ninety original claimants while offering employment in government construction projects to the PST invaders.

Torn between wanting to resolve the conflict at Golonchán and not wanting to be associated with the government, Fr. Morales finally decided to accompany Sabines on an inspection trip to Golonchán by helicopter. In the rough, thatched-roofed settlement at Golonchán, PST militants greeted Sabines's proposal with defiance; they would leave the estate, they said, only in their coffins. Sabines compromised, promising to provide the PST with grants of land deep in the state's eastern rain forests. This offer apparently satisfied the PST, who cele-brated the successful resolution of their demands. Less than two weeks later, however, the governor's proposal would, in Fr. Morales's words, prove to be nothing more than a "bloody joke."

On June 15, 700 to 1,000 members of the PST met at Golonchán to celebrate their victory. As afternoon fell, the celebrants noticed that a detachment of soldiers had moved into position surrounding the com-munity. It's not clear how the shooting started, but when it stopped, more than two hours later, both the town of Golonchán and Sabines's promise to resolve the standoff "by peaceful means" lay in ruins. At least twelve members of the PST died.

Landowners' Pyrrhic Victory

Eyewitness reports in the press denounced landowners for their in-volvement in the massacre, suggesting that landowners paid the army to carry out the assault (*Proceso*, June 30, 1980, 12–15). One land-owner placed at the scene by eyewitnesses confirmed landowners' in-volvement but denied that they actually took part in the massacre:

"First we gave the [Public Security troops] horses so they could go in [to Golonchán]. When they got there shots were fired and the [troops] fled. . . . So then we communicated with the general, who sent about 150 of the army in. Again there was a gun battle and many were killed, four *federales* and lots and lots of the invaders. . . . That made Sitalá world famous, the government's harsh intervention. . . . I didn't go with the army to Golonchán, but afterward a soldier I was friendly with told me what had happened. . . . There were a lot more people killed than what the official report said."

Regardless of the level of landowners' involvement, the violent eviction of invaders at Golonchán unleashed a fury of anti-invasion operations throughout Chilón and Sitalá. In the wake of Golonchán, troops razed houses and routed invaders on San José Sierra Nevada, Jotolá, Duraznal, and other estates in the region (Ovalle Muñoz 1984). But this stepped-up repression of land invaders represented a Pyrrhic victory for landowners. While the invaders of some estates were evicted and the landowners regained control over their properties, Juan Sabines quickly moved to pacify conflicts and buttress support for the PRI by redistributing estates to friendly peasants. In case after case, state officials evicted peasants from opposition parties, only to turn the land over to other peasants more closely aligned with the PRI.

Ernesto Monterrosa was one of the beneficiaries of this redistribution. A former peon on San José Sierra Nevada, Monterrosa became a PRI-affiliated peasant leader in the 1970s. In the late 1970s, he remembered, "The ranchers put me in jail in Yajalón because there were lots of invasions and they thought I was an invasion leader. . . . I was there three days until the [SRA official] came and said that I was not with the PST, that I was CNC." Affiliation with the PRI meant more than release from jail for Monterrosa. It meant land. After the eviction of peasants from Verapaz, a 400-hectare estate owned by Oscar Franz, Sabines ordered Franz to "voluntarily" sell the land to Monterrosa's group under the Programa de Rehabilitación Agraria (PRA, or Rural Restitution Program). This program, championed by General Absalón Castellanos Domínguez, who succeeded Sabines as governor, administered grants to buy land from private owners to well-established land occupiers whose claims had not been resolved by the SRA. Monterrosa explained: "The government bought it for us because we respected law and order. The PST didn't respect the law and they didn't win any ranches. . . . The landowners sold because they were afraid. There was a lot of fear."

Oscar Franz, like all landowners who sold, had complex reasons for going along with the purchase. Franz carried a substantial mortgage on Verapaz—a burden that was relieved by the sale—but Franz also agreed with Monterrosa: fear figured heavily in his decision to accept Sabines's low offer. The year-long occupation of Verapaz had significantly disrupted the estate's operations and Franz "knew that the agrarian situation was just going to get worse, so why not sell now before things got even worse?" The anthropologist Henri Favre, famed for his study of the Tzeltals of Bachajón, summarized the situation cogently:

> In 1980 the government of Chiapas made it known officially to the white population of Pantelhó, Sitalá, and the rest of Chilón that it could guarantee neither their personal safety nor the safety of their property. It offered the astonished ladinos a dramatic dilemma: stay in the region and confront the risks and dangers of retaliation by the indígenas on their own . . . or give up their land to the government, which would buy it at an average price of 7,000 pesos per hectare, an infamous, even laughable price because it included cattle, crops, and infrastructure. In all, sixty-three properties, of which the largest was 310 hectares and the smallest 4 hectares, totaling 7,153 hectares, were purchased by the state and then redistributed among a thousand indigenous families through the mediation of the National Peasant Confederation." (Favre 1985:194)

While Governor Sabines expressed strong support for the institution of private property and pledged to step up protection against invasions, his actions spoke more clearly. Private property could and would be used to ease tensions in the countryside. Landowners' participation in the land purchases was not, of course, entirely voluntary, but few resisted. Substantial disagreement still exists over whether the sums paid by Sabines were as laughable as Favre suggests or windfalls that left landowners laughing all the way to the bank.[35]

Nevertheless, by the 1980s, landowners' economic situation had become increasingly precarious, as they were pinched between the state's general recession (Rus 1995), declining state support for production, and indigenous workers' growing militancy. From this vantage, it seems likely that many landowners greeted the PRA as a much-needed way to escape the stagnant world of agriculture with money in the bank, regardless of the level of compensation. In this sense, the PRA could be interpreted simply as a timely bailout orchestrated by landowners' friends in the government. Yet this explanation is belied by the fact that numerous landowners, such as Delio Ballinas, immediately used their PRA payments to purchase new land in areas less subject to political conflict, once again throwing themselves into the unsteady world of estate agriculture. Only one thing is clear: despite the evictions that followed the killings at Golonchán, many landowners had, in Oscar Franz's words, "no other option, sell or stay invaded," regardless of their economic interests or desires.

Understanding Golonchán: Parties, Mediation, and
Landowners' Place in the New Political Terrain

Days after the massacre, a group of refugees from Golonchán streamed into Yajalón. They had come to renounce their membership in the PST and beg for PRI credentials. After the army attack, merchants in Sitalá had stopped selling food to members of the PST, and PRI membership cards were increasingly seen as peasants' only safeguard against repression (*Uno Más Uno*, July 2, 1980, 4). An official from the municipal president's office — the same office that had so effectively blamed the PST for forty-five deaths on May 30 — addressed the throng with lordly condescension: "As you can see, these Indians were fooled. The PST promised that if they voted for them they'd get land, pickup trucks, and clothes. Because they're lazy, they eventually signed up for the plan. . . . [The PST] incited them to invade fincas, and now, after the deaths at Golonchán, they realized how they'd been fooled. They burned their PST flags, and now the party welcomes them" (quoted in *Uno Más Uno*, July 2, 1980, p. 4). One by one, in an almost religious act of contrition, the refugees passed before the official to turn over their PST membership documents and press their fingerprints into shiny new PRI cards.

The PST remained an important opposition force in the region through the 1980s, but in many ways the massacre at Golonchán and the subsequent repression of other land invaders it had inspired broke the party's back. After Golonchán, the Jesuit mission at Bachajón also broke with the PST, frustrated and disappointed by the party's inflammatory tactics. In perhaps the strangest twist in this story, by the late 1980s it became clear that the PST was not, in fact, the "independent" opposition force it claimed to be. From the start the PST had been an offshoot of the PRI, secretly funded by the ruling party and housed in offices paid for by the state government (Aubry 1986:2). José López

Arévalo, a landowner's son who became a leftist journalist and ran for Congress on the ticket of the Partido de la Revolución Democrática (PRD, or Party of the Democratic Revolution), told me, "Later we found out that the PST was an arm of the PRI, but . . . at the time it seemed like a real party of the left. Now we know the PRI founded it to create an outlet for agrarian conflict through invasions without getting directly involved in them itself."

In a very real sense, then, the PST represents a critical split within the PRI along class and racial lines: on one hand, through the turmoil of the late 1970s and early 1980s the traditional PRI machine remained solidly behind its ladino landowners and merchants; on the other hand, the PST, as a left-leaning PRI proxy, defied wealthy ladinos by fomenting class and racial conflict. The PRI had begun to see cultivating, controlling, and mollifying *indigenous* mediators rather than traditional ladino authorities as the only way to resolve the region's agrarian conflict — even if at times it meant backing away from the party's historical support for ladino landowners. This shift marked, in José López Arévalo's words, "the beginning of an indigenous reconquest of the region, a re-indigenization of the region."

Over the next ten years, federal and state officials institutionalized Sabines's program of pacification through land purchases in the form of the PRA. Under this program the government purchased more than 80,000 hectares for 9,253 claimants (Benjamin 1996:248, Reyes 1992:117). Like Sabines's redistribution efforts, the PRA functioned primarily as a way to buttress the indigenous CNC against its proliferating rivals, even allowing the CNC to invade properties that had previously been occupied by opposition groups. As a result of these invasions of invasions, most of the land distributed through the PRA ended up in the hands of CNC members, generating even more resentment among opposition groups in the countryside.

At the same time, Castellanos Domínguez complemented the PRA with stepped-up support for private property owners. During his regime, landowners throughout Chiapas received more exemption certificates than they had under all previous governors (Reyes 1992). Nevertheless, as events after 1994 (when agrarian officials blatantly ignored landowners' exemption certificates) would confirm, pledges of state support for private property were a degraded currency in the new political climate. Landowners would remain faithful to the PRI until well after 1994, but state officials exhibited less and less need to reciprocate their loyalty. Although the association between ladino landowners and PRI rule remained close, their efforts had proved ineffective — perhaps even counterproductive — at containing the swelling ranks of indigenous opposition in the Chiapas countryside. Landowners' interests might have to be sacrificed, or at least circumvented, to keep the PRI in power. In coming times of crisis, direct mediation with indigenous groups — sometimes to the detriment of landowners' interests — would serve as the true currency of rural politics.

Contours of Quiescence

The Invasions of 1994–1998

Estate Agriculture Unglued

———————◆◆◆———————

Still relatively insulated from conflicts raging to the east of Chilón between Zapatista insurgents and the Mexican army, members of the AGL closed their January 1994 assembly on an ordinary note. "As a last point . . . there will be a raffle in April and members should pay for all tickets issued to them by February 16."[1] Before the sweepstakes deadline, however, nearly all of the men and women present at the meeting lost their land, and they would never recover it. On Carnival Friday and through the second week of February, thousands of indigenous peasants seized forty properties covering more than 2,000 hectares in Chilón. More invasions followed through the spring and summer. By December 1999, membership in the AGL had dropped from eighty-one to fewer than forty, as state-brokered purchases distributed 7,312 hectares — 66 percent of private properties larger than 5 hectares in the municipio — to indigenous land claimants.[2] It was an odd ending to a decade that began with President Carlos Salinas's promise to liberalize Mexico's land reform laws — a promise, it was widely assumed, that would only lead to increased land concentration, the end of redistribution, and better times for landed elites.

Carlos Salinas was not the first Mexican president to pronounce the definitive death of land reform or the first to learn that, in the land of Emiliano Zapata and Lázaro Cárdenas, his postmortem was premature. In 1991, convinced that Mexico's stagnant countryside required a strong dose of market therapy, Salinas championed changes to Article 27 of the nation's constitution. The constitutional reforms called a halt to future land redistributions and allowed farmers to obtain titles to plots of land that had previously been held collectively as part of the country's "social sector" (ejidos and *comunidades agrarias*

A landowner confronts an indigenous land invader, July 1998. The land invaders had just begun cutting down the landowner's sorghum to construct houses. *(Photo by author.)*

established under the 1917 Constitution's land reform provisions).[3] While the changes did not dissolve the social sector outright, they established a series of steps through which farmers could voluntarily agree to fully privatize their holdings. For many in the countryside the message was clear: Carlos Salinas had effectively ended the federal government's sixty-year-old commitment to land reform in favor of land markets. On paper and in public rhetoric, with only small concessions to the state's long history of paternalistic support for farmers, Salinas had placed the future of rural Mexico in the hands of the market.[4]

Not more than three years later, however, land reform was back on the table. In Chiapas, land redistribution reasserted itself first as a central demand of the EZLN and then as an uncontrollable series of land seizures that seared the countryside, fueled by the political chaos left in the wake of the Zapatista uprising. While the Zapatistas are widely and rightfully famous for their unique vision of cyber-revolution, indigenous autonomy, and the struggle for human dignity in a context of neoliberal globalization, this wave of land seizures and the redistributions they won may well represent the most palpable material effect of the uprising in Chiapas.

Unlike previous waves of land seizures in Chiapas, these invasions were neither limited to poor-quality land nor undone through repression. Instead, mass land invasions forced redistribution that touched every corner of the state and included some of Chiapas's most valuable agricultural land. Yet this was more than just a physical reworking of the Chiapan countryside. The invasions in Chilón cannot be understood simply as a "land rush" (Paige 1975) in which land-poor peasants took advantage of political instability to seize a much-needed productive resource. Land represented much more than a scarce factor of production. In Chilón the events of 1994–1998 reflected a powerful resurgence of indigenous territorial projects that reshaped the spaces and social relations of landed production.

Even in Chiapas: The Difference a Revolution Makes

The acclaimed political analyst Enrique Krauze (1997:780) declared that Chiapas "was a place that Agrarian Reform ignored"; but frequently it was not the neglect of Chiapas by agrarian reform bureaucrats but rather their ministrations (well intentioned and otherwise) that caused conflict in the Chiapan countryside. Land reform *had* come to Chiapas. It had come as a practice of state rule that sought to incorporate peasants into paternalistic relations of domination. It had come as a deeply felt way of thinking about the tactics and goals of rural struggle and the relation between state and countryside. Most important, however, land reform had come as an uneven, fitful, but ultimately extensive assault on landed oligarchy.

In the early decades of the twentieth century, U.S., German, and Mexican elites owned vast estates in Chiapas producing coffee, rubber, and other crops for international markets. The 1930 agricultural census, carried out in the wake of the Mexican Revolution, found twenty-two estates larger than 10,000 hectares and 4 percent of landowners controlling 67 percent of the arable land in the state (Secretaría de Economía 1930, table 42). Since then, peasant mobilization and state-sponsored land reform have steadily and effectively broken down large landholdings. The average size of private landholdings dropped precipitously in the decades after the Mexican Revolution, from more than 200 hectares in 1930 to less than 50 in 1990, while the amount of land held by the state's social sector soared. As the effects of the most recent wave of land struggles begin to be noted, the social sector

Table 2 Hectares cultivated in private and social sectors, Chiapas, 1930 and 2000

Sector	1930		2000	
	Number	Percent	Number	Percent
Private	4,011,298	97%	2,443,694	33%
Social	104,509	3	4,244,363	57
Both sectors	4,115,807	100%	6,688,057*	90%†

* Increase of land under cultivation between 1930 and 2000 was due to expansion into the Lacandón rain forest.

† The remaining 10% is in urban and national park areas not counted in 1930.

Source: *Censo Agrícola Ganadero*, 1930, and Secretaría de Reforma Agraria tables.

controls 4.2 million hectares (57 percent of the surface area of the state) while private landowners control 2.4 million hectares (33 percent of the state) (see Table 2).

Although much of the redistributed land took the form of thousands of previously unexploited hectares opened for colonization in the Lacandón rain forest (Leyva and Ascencio 1996), sustained attack by mobilized peasants forced the state to abandon its protection of ladino landowners and landed production more than once in recent history. It is only against this backdrop of change that the 1994–1998 invasions can be understood: one dramatic stage in a slow process of agrarian mobilization and the reclamation of the countryside by peasants.

In addition to its impact on land tenure in Chiapas, the Revolution established an uneasy system of authoritarian political representation that remained committed to defending the interests of ladino landowners, but also rested in large part on the construction of peasant organizations under indigenous leaders identified with the ruling party (e.g., Rus 1994). For peasants and landowners alike, property rights hinged on participation in politics, or, more exactly, achieving and maintaining membership in a hegemonic bloc built from unstable compromises, consent, coercion, and concessions. In a nation in which property vests ultimately in the nation and is administered by the state, struggle over land tenure is also negotiation over the nature and forms of state rule. As Jorge Ibarra Mendivil (1989:18) noted, property rights are so politicized in Mexico that the ways in which they are worked out and contested not only construct particular rural subjects but also play an important role in constituting the state as an entity. Ultimately these struggles produced a fragmented and inconsistent state made up of diverse actors and institutions engaged in constantly renewed but not always unified attempts to forge balance and manage conflicts by "bargaining with the key forces in civil society" (Fox 1993:2).

The unpredictable and contradictory results of these state practices only served to generate more grounds for conflict. For example, state actors might grant a plot of land to Group A in order to quell conflict and satisfy that group's demands, while conveniently ignoring the fact that the same plot of land had already been granted to Group B years previously under similar circumstances. Long delays — decades or more — in the regularization of land grants encouraged this kind of machination. Even more commonly, one bureau of the sRA, interested in protecting landowners, might overlook peasants' claims on a property in order to satisfy a landowner's demand for a certificate of exemption from land reform. Meanwhile, another bureau, in an effort to quiet peasants' demands, might overlook a legally issued exemption certificate and authorize redistribution of a property.[5]

Not surprisingly, rural actors responded to these contradictory rulings by intensifying direct pressure. As one landowner lamented, "When two groups come together with their claims and they're both right, the only thing left . . . is to tear each other to pieces."[6] Thus the state's attempts to quell hostilities often had the opposite effects, inflaming grievances and producing rural subjects defined in large part through the violent theater of agrarian conflict. Over time this process shaped the way other struggles played out in Chiapas, as the institutions and practices of land reform — particularly the rituals of land invasion — became vehicles for a broad range of ambitions and grievances.

Times, Spaces, and Meanings of Invasion

After its debut strikes against several urban centers, the EZLN uprising left its deepest mark on three municipios in Chiapas's eastern lowland rain forests — Altamirano, Las Margaritas, and Ocosingo, which would later earn official designation as the "conflict zone." There some 65,000 hectares of private property fell directly under the control of

Table 3 Number of land invasions, Chiapas, 1994–2000

Year	Invasions
1994	960
1995	153
1996	97
1997	54
1998	16
1999	0
2000	0

Source: "Predios Invadidos 1994–2000," unpublished chart provided by Secretaría Estatal de Desarrollo Agrícola, Tuxtla Gutiérrez.

EZLN forces.[7] Outside of the conflict zone, January saw only scattered invasions. By February, however, it was clear that the new agrarian mobilizations would not be confined to any one region. On February 2 and 5, peasants seized the first of what was to total forty-five properties in Suchiate and Tapachula, home to Chiapas's most valuable agricultural land. In the weeks that followed, peasants took over properties in 70 of Chiapas's 111 municipios, affecting every corner of the state, including its richest zones of coffee, cattle, cane, and corn production (see Table 3).

Few invasions gained as much notoriety as the seizure of more than 900 hectares of the Finca Liquidámbar and its subdivisions in Angel Albino Corzo. Widely published photographs of members of the radical Unión Campesina Popular Francisco Villa (UCPFV) posing next to the estate owner's Jacuzzi and his Andy Warhol prints captured the vast gap between wealthy landowners and poor peasants, perceived as the principal catalyst of invasions. Liquidámbar, a patchwork of almost a dozen legal sections covering at least 1,910 hectares, was one of the most productive and renowned coffee plantations in Chiapas. Its larger-than-life foreign owner was cut from the fabric of rough caciques who rule the Frailesca region "by noose and club." Between 1994 and 1997 members of the UCPFV battled Liquidámbar's owner and state police, suffering multiple evictions, reinvasions, deaths in shootouts, disappearances, and assassinations. Bowing to external pressures and the UCPFV's incredible persistence, in August 1998 the state government turned over 225 hectares of Liquidámbar despite the UCPFV's strong ties to the EZLN and Ejército Popular Revolucionario

(People's Revolutionary Army). In the end, Liquidámbar remained largely intact and able to resume full operations after reportedly losing several million dollars because of the disruptions. Nevertheless, the case demonstrated the ability of peasant groups to leverage redistribution against impossible odds.[8]

The Liquidámbar case was not typical. From 1994 to 1998, opposition groups such as the UCPFV all over the state fought hard to win concessions and bore the brunt of repression and evictions, but most invaded properties were not the playgrounds of wealthy art enthusiasts and most invasion struggles were not so costly. Often the gap between landowner and peasant was much smaller, and in some cases was virtually imperceptible. Nor did the size and value of properties seem to predict whether the invaders would be evicted: smaller properties were evicted slightly more frequently than larger ones.[9] In broad terms, evictions were most common around the large productive estates of the Sierra and Frailesca regions (see Map 4), but the ten municipios with the most valuable agricultural land in the state had an average eviction rate exactly equal to the statewide average (25 percent).[10] Some 48 percent of invaded properties around the state were "voluntarily vacated" for various reasons. A few cases of reported "voluntary" abandonment undoubtedly conceal covert evictions by landowners. More commonly, peasant groups agreed to abandon contested land in return for privileged consideration in subsequent purchase negotiations. In Chilón, for example, nearly every voluntarily vacated property was eventually turned over to a peasant group, although not necessarily to the original invaders. Peasants also vacated properties in order to invade others, while still maintaining de facto control over the vacated property and pressuring for its sale. In other cases, as we shall see, peasants abandoned invaded properties because they farmed elsewhere and had carried out the invasions for symbolic or political purposes.

The Agrarian Accords

In Chiapas, state-brokered purchases of private property by peasant claimants emerged in the early 1980s as a way to resolve land disputes while bypassing the hopelessly backlogged land reform bureaucracy. In the 1990s, with the convergence of the supposed "end of Mexico's agrarian reform" (DeWalt et al. 1994; cf. Kay 1999:283), unprece-

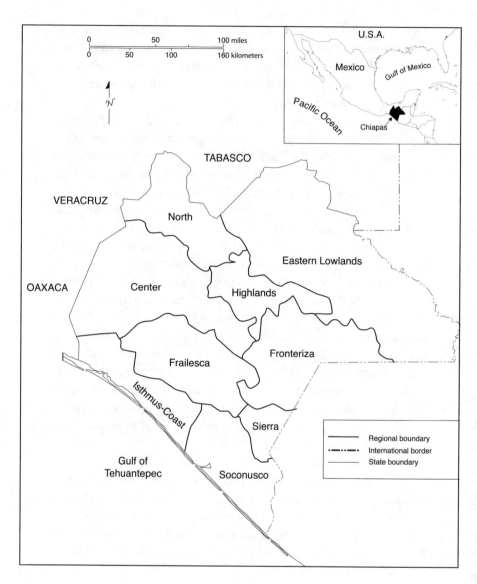

Map 4. Regions of Chiapas (official designations)

dented peasant mobilization, and high-level policy makers' desperate need to reestablish calm in Chiapas after the Zapatista uprising, state-brokered land purchases took on phenomenal new importance. In April 1994, a few scant months after the invasions began, state officials and members of the Consejo Estatal de Organizaciones Indígenas y Campesínas (CEOIC, or State Council of Indigenous and Peasant Organizations) — the most important umbrella organization of Chiapan peasant groups — established a framework for negotiations that would "facilitate and channel demands for land and reconcile invaders and property owners" (quoted in Villafuerte et al. 1999:139). A newly formed commission made up of affected landowners, peasant groups, the SRA, and the attorney general's office immediately committed themselves to subsidize the purchase of some 39,000 hectares. Peasant organizations promised to refrain from new actions and state officials pledged to evict all properties invaded after that agreement. Nevertheless, invasions continued (albeit at a slower rate), police forces carried out scattered evictions, landowners refused to sell their properties, and the purchase program stagnated in the chaos surrounding Chiapas's gubernatorial elections (Villafuerte et al. 1999:140; *La Jornada* [Mexico City], July 6, 1994).

A new impulse was clearly needed, and in the last months of 1994 state officials unveiled the first of several *fideicomisos* (trusts) that would manage the transfer of properties to peasant ownership through no-interest thirty-year loans. In an effort to further concretize plans for resolving the state's agrarian crisis, two federal agencies, the SRA and the agrarian prosecutor's office, joined the Secretariat of Agricultural Development in forming the Interinstitutional Agrarian Commission (Mesa Interinstitucional Agraria), which accepted peasant organizations' petitions centered on three themes: the backlog of land claims, the need to resolve disputes within the social sector, and land acquisition. Over the next two years the commission reviewed more than 2,000 petitions, almost half requesting acquisition of new land (Reyes 1998a:26). In March 1996, after protracted negotiations, the commission, sixty official peasant organizations, and almost a hundred independent groups signed a set of accords (Acuerdos Agrarios) at the National Palace in Mexico City. These landmark accords consolidated all previous programs and committed the government to providing loans for the purchase of up to 5 hectares per land claimant (Becerra 1998) (see Table 4).

Table 4 Agrarian Accords: Number of hectares and recipient families at various stages of implementation, 2000

	Hectares	Families
Committed	249,259	60,942
Authorized	244,201	58,441
Paid	229,112	n/a
Final transfer	195,962	n/a

Note: n/a = not available.
Source: Secretaría de Reforma Agraria, "Acuerdos Agrarios: Programa Fideicomiso (General)," 2000.

Like the invasions, the accords affected large and small properties in regions of fabulous wealth and tremendous poverty. Most land purchased fell in the medium- to low-value range (SIC 1998). Strikingly, however, the accords also targeted more valuable land. For example, statewide, about 10 percent of the money authorized by the accords went toward the purchase of more than 13,000 hectares in the Soconusco, Chiapas's rich coffee heartland. In all, some 2.3 percent of the land authorized for sales fell within Chiapas's ten municipios with the highest agricultural value per hectare (containing 7.3 percent of the state's private property). While this figure seems proportionately low, those ten municipios supplied almost seven times more land to peasants under the accords than the ten municipios with the least valuable land.

In an attempt to distance the accords from Chiapas's long history of corrupt state-led reforms, peasant groups were given subsidized loans and authorized "to find and select land to occupy according to their tastes; land that would really satisfy their needs." In the words of the federal government's special representative to Chiapas, "Never again would a government functionary choose and buy the land and then assign it to a peasant group" (Becerra 1998). All that was required was agreement between peasants and landowners, able buyers and willing sellers. In this sense, the commission sought to privatize the resolution of agrarian conflicts; to satisfy peasants' demands by creating a fluid land market. As president Ernesto Zedillo (1998) stressed, "Peasants purchase the land, not the government." On the surface, then, the accords seemed to represent a new generation of "market-led" reforms (e.g., Deininger 2003). In reality, the line between "old" state-led reforms and "new" market-led reforms was quite blurry (Bobrow-Strain 2004): massive peasant mobilization had, for all intents and purposes, forced traditional interventionist agrarian reform and state-led land redistribution back onto the political table. Despite the reform's market-based framework, peasants "purchased" land through the accords only on paper. As a land reform official, whose identity must be concealed for obvious reasons, casually remarked in 2001, "No one [in this office] expects the peasants to ever pay back the loans. They'll just melt away eventually or get converted into 'development assistance.'"

The accords also sought to depoliticize redistribution by disassociating land purchases from the act of invasion. "The accords," President Zedillo declared, "are founded on . . . devotion to the law . . . good-faith dialogue that looks for reconciliation rather than confrontation" (Zedillo 1998). As a result, the accords facilitated the purchase of twice as much land than had been invaded during the previous years. Nevertheless, without invasions, redistribution might have faded away altogether, as intended by changes to Article 27 of the Constitution. Illegal occupations compelled the state to assuage peasants' demand for land, but they also created a supply of land to meet that demand. With a median size of 50 hectares and a distribution strongly skewed toward smaller properties (see Table 5), few of the invaded properties could ever have been appropriated through the legal agrarian reform process with its higher limits on landownership. Invasions transformed these properties into the legitimate objects of redistribution proceedings.

Pandemic invasions combined with a lack of state support for evictions also generated a climate of fear and insecurity in the countryside that increased landowners' willingness to cooperate with government buyout plans. The volatility of property rights revealed by the invasions and perceptions of escalating danger in the countryside shook landowners' confidence in landownership. All over Chiapas, landowners echoed one Palenque rancher's sentiment: "No one is going to invest in land with all the invasions. If they see your land nicely planted and taken care of, they'll decide to take it." And they agreed with Roberto Trujillo in Chilón: "What good is it to get an eviction if you're always afraid of getting killed on the road on the way to the ranch?" Alfredo Pinto's fears covered the long term: "As long as the coun-

Table 5 Number of land invasions, Chiapas, 1994–1998, by size of property invaded

Size of property invaded (hectares)	Number of invasions
1–9	10
10–24	142
25–49	150
50–99	214
100–199	244
200–299	210
300–399	71
400–499	18
500–599	10
600–699	0
700–799	3
800–899	4
900–999	3
1,000–1,199	0
1,200–1,299	1
1,300 +	1

Source: Calculated from CESMECA 1998.

tryside isn't safe, I hope none of my children become ranchers . . . except maybe in another state."

The mobilizations tapped into a long history of upper-class fears of ethnic violence. Ladinos pepper explanations for their quiescence with representations of indigenous savagery, horde imagery reflecting ladinos' enclave status, and awareness that, given the large scale of the peasant mobilizations, the state was not likely to protect landowners if they chose to resist. Fear and insecurity affected the decisions of far more than those landowners dispossessed by invasions: an unknowable number of de facto invasions in which peasants did not occupy properties but used violence and intimidation to prevent landowners and their laborers from working the land never appeared in official statistics. Other landowners sold because they considered visits to their uninvaded properties too dangerous. Even in Palenque, where landowners effectively repressed numerous invasions, a prominent landowner reflected: "There were no attacks — physically — but mentally we had been attacked. Now people are afraid to go to their ranches . . . something that has taken a toll on production." In the end, with land-hungry peasants, anxious landowners, and state actors desperately hoping to quell conflict coming together, the final account of sales authorized under the accords totaled more than double the land originally invaded. Nevertheless, the Agrarian Accords frequently inflamed the very conflicts they were intended to calm.

The Agrarian Accords and the Institutionalization of Conflict

On August 3, 2000, thirty heavily armed peasants disguised as police attacked ninety-two families occupying the 193-hectare Finca Nuevo Paraíso in Yajalón. Later that week, police under the command of the federal special prosecutor for crimes committed by probable armed civilian groups swept through Nuevo Paraíso to find the original invaders routed, their houses burned, and their cornfields strewn with spent shells. On the surface, this appeared to be an archetypal case of landowner-sponsored eviction, but further investigation revealed a more complex story. The men who carried out the eviction were peasants affiliated with the infamous pro-government paramilitary group Paz y Justicia, but they were also — technically speaking — the legitimate owners of Nuevo Paraíso.[11]

In 1995 the Yajalón landowner and merchant Rodolfo Domínguez, under pressure from banks to pay outstanding debts, sold Nuevo Paraíso through a government *fideicomiso* program to residents of two nearby Tzeltal communities, Emiliano Zapata and Pinabetal. These peasants were, depending on one's source, militants either of the left-opposition PRD (as registered in government documents and suggested by Domínguez's son) or of the ruling PRI (according to Domínguez himself). Before the sale could be finalized, however, members of a staunchly pro-EZLN community occupied the finca and renamed it Tierra y Libertad (Land and Liberty). Complicating matters more, the second group of claimants, according to a Yajalón municipal official who helped mediate the dispute, was made up of "former workers on the finca . . . who had been left out of the original purchase." When asked whether this group had previously sought land on Nuevo Paraíso, the former owner's son replied, "More or less," and abruptly changed the subject.

Sometime after 1997, residents of Emiliano Zapata and Pinabetal — Nuevo Paraíso's erstwhile new owners — either converted from the PRD to the PRI or radicalized their PRI status, merging with the Unión de Comunidades Indígenas, Agropecuarias y Forestales (UCIAF, or

Union of Indigenous, Agricultural, and Forestry Communities) and Paz y Justicia and setting the stage for the eviction and reinvasion of October 2000. Critically, one of the key reasons offered for the attack on Nuevo Paraíso was not land hunger but rather the Tierra y Libertad group's support for opposition candidates in the 2000 elections. In other words, the invasion was intended to send a political message. Nevertheless, despite the aggressors' strong connection to the PRI, the federal prosecutor's office took surprising actions against UCIAF, Paz y Justicia, and the residents of Emiliano Zapata and Pinabetal. It issued warrants for the arrest of the fifty-four original beneficiaries of the government-brokered purchase and arrested eleven leaders of the October 3 eviction, charging them with "carrying firearms reserved for military use, terrorism, unlawful association, riot, organized crime, assault, [and] property damage" (*Chiapas al Día*, Nov. 8, 2000; *Excelsior*, Nov. 23, 2000). Among those jailed was Samuel Sánchez Sánchez, a PRI representative in the state legislature and highly visible paramilitary leader (PGR 2000). The charges against the paramilitary members stuck, and the episode represents a watershed moment in the government's limited crackdown on a group that had once been one of its key covert allies in the Chiapas conflict. More important for our concerns, the case nicely illustrates the central contradictions of the Agrarian Accords.

State officials conceived the accords as a decisive remedy for Chiapas's turmoil, a reagent of the ever-elusive *finiquito agrario* — the final agrarian solution (Villafuerte et al. 1999). By taking monumental steps toward ending land hunger in Chiapas, President Zedillo concluded, the accords would leave "no more reasons for clashes between different types of property" (Zedillo 1998). But despite the transfer of more than a half-million hectares, land conflicts raged on. Nuevo Paraíso was not alone. All over Chiapas invaders, reinvaders, rival peasant groups, landowners, and former landowners continued to attack one another. According to Mario Ruiz Ferro, then the governor, the accords "resolved almost completely the problem of land invasions, which in other years has been the principal cause of conflict and violence" (quoted in Reyes 1998:28). But what is most striking about the accords is that they treated only one facet of the multiple logics of land invasion, failing fundamentally to address — and sometimes inflaming — the many other factors that sparked invasion. Although the accords treated land solely as a factor of production, land invasions in Chilón arose from a variety of territorial projects. They formed part of ongoing struggles for hegemony in which the function of land as a factor of production played only a part.

Other Meanings and Materialities of Invasion

In 1976 members of the San Sebastián de Bachajón ejido sought restitution of lands allegedly stolen from the indigenous community of Bachajón by ladinos in the nineteenth century. After almost a decade of obstacles and delays, in 1983 ejidatarios wielding 200-year-old documents from the Archive of Central America in Guatemala, which they claimed proved their "primordial title" to the land in question, pressed bureaucrats in Mexico City and Xalapa for a decision. In 1990 that decision came: the documents were genuine but insufficient to prove dispossession.[12]

Ignoring the negative ruling and focusing instead on the institutional validation of their documents, the ejidatarios pressed their case further. When the Zapatista uprising created a political vacuum that facilitated the seizure of the disputed lands, ejidatarios organized under the auspices of CNPI seized more than 2,000 hectares of ladino-owned private property in early February 1994. "These [actions]," they argued, "should not be understood as theft [*despojo*] [because] we are acting according to our rights and respecting the agrarian authorities' ruling."[13]

Through the spring and summer, a diverse collection of groups from the pro-government Municipal Solidarity Committee to the church-based Center for Indigenous Rights (CEDIAC) followed CNPI into the fray, because, as one PRI-affiliated leader put it, "if we didn't we were going to get left behind when all the land was taken." In the space of a few weeks the landscape of Chilón began to change as invaders burned pastures or spread herbicide over them to make room for corn. One letter to landowners read: "We are informing you that we have . . . declared ourselves owners of the land that we have possessed since February 13, 1994. . . . We give you seventy-three hours starting today to remove your cattle, and if you don't, we will divide them among members of the CNPI because they are damaging our crops and it is urgent that we plant the fields your cattle are occupying."[14]

This letter evokes sweeping changes in Chilón's landscape and a potent new vision of indigenous territoriality. Cattle, once the mainstay of the region's estate agriculture, were now an invasive species on indigenous soil. Through 1994 and in the years that followed, pastures became cornfields, indigenous settlements and schools spread across the agricultural landscape, and signs reading "Rancho las Delicias" or "Finca el Carmen" were replaced by ones reading "Community in Rebellion" or "Emiliano Zapata." What lay at the heart of this transformation of space? Indigenous groups, of course, unanimously heralded the changes as restitution of ancient land rights and the return of land to the people who tilled it. I argue, however, rather than being simple racial restitutions, the events of 1994–1998 arose from and expressed multiple, often competing territorial projects.

For many peasants, invasions were indeed a source of desperately needed land. Despite the vast extensions of land already distributed to peasants through land reform, the insufficiency of peasant landholdings in Chiapas is widely recognized.[15] With an aging ejido population — half of rights holders are over fifty years old — the social-sector land base must also sustain thousands of young families descended from rights holders but without their own legal claim to land. In a state with limited nonagricultural sources of employment, children and grandchildren of ejidatarios swell the ranks of the landless and land-poor. With the eastern lowland agricultural frontier already parceled out or enclosed in nature preserves (Leyva and Ascencio 1996) and nearly all estates larger than established landholding limits already redistributed or broken into smaller legal parcels, invasions provided one of the few remaining ways to bring additional land into the agrarian reform process.

On the surface, then, the invasions seem to fit Jeffrey Paige's (1975: 42–43) classic definition of a "land rush," which occurs "when a landed upper class has been critically weakened . . . [allowing a] simultaneous land rush by thousands of peasants bent on obtaining land that they may legally regard as theirs. . . . [It is] a short intense movement aimed at seizing land but lacking long-run political objectives." Yet land invasions have long served not only as a means of accessing scarce land but also as a critical and versatile tactic of rural politics. Invasions have stood at the center of efforts to break up large landholdings and light fires under moribund bureaucrats in the SRA, but they have also played essential roles in diverse contests among peasant organizations, political parties, rival leaders, and ethnic groups.

Land seizures frequently provided a means for political parties and peasant organizations to consolidate constituencies and compete against rivals. In the late 1970s and early 1980s, for example, more than 400 land invasions carried out by independent peasant organizations forced Chiapas's landowner-dominated government to step up redistribution. In 1983 Governor Absalón Castellanos Domínguez unveiled the Rural Restitution Program (PRA). As we have seen, this program granted ejido status to well-established land occupiers whose claims had not been resolved by the SRA and provided them money to purchase land from private owners. With more than 80,000 hectares at stake, the PRA quickly deteriorated into a power struggle between independent organizations and Mexico's leading government-aligned peasant organization, the National Peasant Confederation (CNC). Already facing declining legitimacy due to its inability to resolve backlogged land reform demands and fearing that the PRA would fortify its rivals, the CNC promulgated a series of violent invasions of land that had already been invaded in an attempt to maintain its political control over peasant organizing (N. Harvey 1998:153). Through these reinvasions, peasants loyal to the CNC drove independent groups from their land claims and brokered separate deals with the government to channel redistributed land through the CNC (N. Harvey 1998, Reyes 1992). In this manner, most land distributed through the PRA ended up in the hands of CNC members, generating even more resentment among opposition groups in the countryside. The dynamics were similar in 1994 as competing groups staked claims to the same pieces of land, with pro-government organizations reinvading land occupied by opposition groups (or vice versa).[16]

Land invasions also played key roles in the increasingly high-stakes struggle for control of municipal governments and in broader terms were critical to ongoing struggles to democratize those governments. In the 1980s and early 1990s, efforts to decentralize government in Mexico transformed municipal governments from passive coordinators of state and federal projects to the key administrators of public works, agricultural credit, and other development assistance programs. Municipal budgets skyrocketed, more than doubling in real terms throughout Chiapas between 1983 and 1987 alone, luring new contenders for local power (INEGI 1990:329).[17]

In March 1994, Manuel Jiménez Navarro, the leader of Chilón's most important group of land invaders, used land invasions as a springboard in his campaign to force the resignation of the ladino landowner who served as municipal president. Two years later, the left-opposition PRD's support for land takeovers facilitated *its* candidate's victory over Jiménez Navarro. On numerous occasions both in Chilón and throughout the state, these politically motivated land invasions were brief affairs; the invaders (who typically already owned some property elsewhere) drifted away from the invaded parcel after they had made their political statement. Indeed, Daniel Villafuerte (pers. comm., May 12, 2000), a close observer of the invasions and accords, notes that in numerous cases the original peasant claimants could not be found once the government agreed to purchase the invaded land.

Not surprisingly, once in office, peasant leaders channeled significant state resources to their constituencies. Municipal records show the PRD administration, for example, providing assistance for its members who wished to build houses on invaded properties.[18] These policies provoked reactions from rival peasant organizations, played out in part on the terrain of land invasion. In this case, for example, the Chinchulines, a PRI-aligned indigenous paramilitary group, launched an assault against the new PRD municipal administration and its peasant supporters.[19] The Chinchulines criticized the new administration's channeling of resources to its supporters, and demanded the diversion of resources to their own members: "From the beginning of his term the municipal mayor Manuel Gómez Moreno has acted with bias. That is to say, benefiting only the group that helped him assume power and not taking into account the needs of other groups that lack the necessary resources for their subsistence" (quoted in CDHFBLC and CEDIAC 1996:7). In April 1996, Chinchulines militants seized Chilón's administrative offices and drove the PRD mayor into exile in Tuxtla Gutiérrez (*La Jornada*, July 12, 1996). As a result of these and other violent actions, including attacks on PRD land invaders, the Chinchulines won from the state a 200,000-peso credit for coffee cultivation and control over lucrative transportation concessions.[20]

On an even more mercenary level, invasion fever provided ample opportunities for individual greed. Crooked resolution of land disputes allowed some well-placed landowners to line their pockets. Others, wanting the government's cash settlement to pay off debts or invest in other areas, arranged the invasions of their own properties by cooperative peasant groups. Indigenous peasant leaders also bent invasions to their benefit. In at least two cases in Chilón, peasant leaders mustered peasants who already owned land elsewhere to invade properties that the leader could then resell after the fictive group returned home. A low-level indigenous functionary explained to me: "I know some leaders—friends of mine, even—who already had land and just took advantage of the movement to invade more land that they could sell later. . . . They invaded and then left the land abandoned until they could [illegally] sell little lots to other people who needed land."

Finally, particularly in regions with large indigenous populations like Chilón, the invasions formed part of a larger struggle over the racial character of space and politics. Over several centuries in uprising after uprising, indigenous communities have attempted to wrest control of territory from ladinos. Some twenty years before the most recent invasions, territorial struggles reached a new level when communities scattered throughout Chiapas began to expel ladinos. In the early 1970s, despite interventions by the Mexican army in favor of ladino landowners, Tzotzils from San Andrés Larráinzar waged a successful campaign to banish nonindigenous residents from the municipio. From San Andrés, confrontations between indígenas and ladinos spread to Simojovel, Teopisca, Venustiano Carranza, Chalchihuitán, Mitontic, and Chenalhó (Nash 2001:99). The history of this racial "revindication" is largely unwritten, but the results are tangible. Highland communities such as Larráinzar, Zinacantán, Chalchihuitán, Tenejapa, and Huixtán gradually "cleansed" themselves of ladinos. To the north, Bachajón and Petalcingo also expelled ladinos in the late 1970s because, as an indigenous member of Chilón's municipal government explained to me, "we didn't want to see them on our streets anymore." Other areas experienced partial expulsions (e.g., Tila, Tumbalá) or unsuccessful attempts (e.g., Chilón, Yajalón). The 1994–1998 mobilizations continued this struggle over space: in some municipios such as Chilón and Simojovel the invasions effectively drove ladinos from the countryside and into the relative safety of towns, while in remote Sitalá even the safety of town could not prevent intimidation of ladinos after 1994.[21] In other areas, such as Palenque and Yajalón, organized ladinos held their ground, but in either case the invasions represent a piece of an ongoing struggle for the "indigenous reconquest" of territory.

To Manuel Jiménez Navarro, whether or not indigenous invaders needed land appeared almost irrelevant. Tzeltals were the "authentic owners" of the land, which was part of an "original indigenous territory."[22] Thus invasions often had displacing ladinos as their first goal, as another indigenous leader declared: "The invasions weren't about production, making the land produce. They were about *restitution* of land to the indígenas, about a right to land that had been taken away. They were carried out so that the indígenas could have the land, to produce on it or not."

Struggles to define the ethnicity of territory were profoundly material as well. Ernesto Monterrosa declared, "We won the first stage when we got the land. Taking political power is the next step." In Chilón the invasions triggered an epochal transformation in the racial makeup of local politics. There indigenous leaders closely involved with land invasions forced the resignations of ladino municipal presidents. In March 1994 the CNPI leader Manuel Jiménez Navarro ousted Chilón's municipal president, Roberto Trujillo, the leader of a powerful ladino landowning family closely tied to then-governor Elmar Setzer and son of a multiterm municipal president and founder of the AGL. One of Jiménez Navarro's former municipal officials explained, "We didn't have a problem with Roberto [Trujillo], we just wanted to see what an *indigenous* government could do for a change." Since 1994, three indígenas, all linked in some way to land invasions, have served consecutive terms as municipal president in Chilón and ladino landowners and merchants have been pushed to the edges of the PRI and the municipal government they dominated for more than sixty years. In the runup to the 2000 elections, prominent ladinos fled the indígena-dominated local PRI entirely, shifting their support to the region's embryonic PAN. Neighboring Sitalá, long a citadel of highly repressive ladino rule, went through a similar shift in the ethnicity of politics, with indigenous leaders competing in and sweeping local elections.[23] Ladinos throughout the rain forest and northern Chiapas complain bitterly about the new indigenous administrations, emphasizing the officials' low educational levels and energetic corruption. Indeed, like their ladino predecessors, the new indigenous governments contain their own repressive authoritarian elements and probably do engage in corruption.[24] Nevertheless, ladinos' complaints also reflect the ways the shifting ethnic makeup of municipal politics has redirected flows of state resources and patronage. Most observers agree that the indigenous administrations have shifted funding away from largely ladino towns to their own clientele in ejidos and the countryside.

Speaking at an international symposium on agrarian reform, Arturo Luna, a former leader of the CIOAC who became a state official, reminded listeners that while the outcome of the 1994–1998 invasions of 1994–1998 were "the greatest land reform [in Chiapas] in the last half century," without policies that "integrated land and production" and enabled peasants to support themselves on the land, the reforms would fail (Luna 2001). In October 2002 a report by the SRA's special representative for Chiapas seemed to confirm Luna's prophecy (*La Jornada*, Oct. 28, 2002). At least 40 percent of all land granted through the Agrarian Accords had been abandoned by its original recipients. The special representative denounced corrupt peasants who invaded land "but didn't really need it." Her explanations evoke some of the multiple territorial projects wrapped up in land invasions. But another explanation for the widespread abandonment of land is possible, one that is closer to Luna's claim. Particularly since the massive collapse of coffee prices in 2000, invaded land lies uncultivated because peasant farmers lack the basic resources necessary to make their property produce. Reports of escalating migration out of the Chiapas countryside to the United States raise the question whether the accords simply accelerated processes, at work throughout Mexico, of transforming the countryside into a refuge for migrant laborers and their families (de Janvry et al. 1997).

While the long-term impacts of the 1994–1998 mobilizations on peasant livelihoods remain to be seen, the events of those years carried immediate consequences for the broader trajectories of agrarian change in Chiapas. After 1992, many analysts feared that changes to Article 27 of the Constitution allowing for the privatization and free sale of social-sector land would usher in a return to the prerevolutionary era of vast haciendas and plantations. Subsequent events proved that the opposite was also possible. Today in much of Chiapas, *minifundización*—the fragmentation of peasant holdings into unviable units—represents a far more serious threat to the livelihoods of the rural poor than the monopolization of land by a few owners.[25] Deterred by the fickle and highly politicized nature of property rights, investors have preferred indirect exploitation of the countryside. Rather than accumulating land in a few corporate hands, dozens of new agribusiness investors have pursued short-term contracts and other flexible arrangements with smallholders (Pólito Barrios 2000).

Over a century ago Karl Kautsky observed that the rural sector's "political significance is in inverse proportion to its economic significance" (1899:312). Today Chiapan peasants—whose economic contribution to the Mexican economy has dwindled — have shattered images of a politically stable Mexico geared to join the ranks of "developed" nations. The Zapatista uprising and subsequent peasant mobilizations touched multiple nerves: not only did they contradict the optimistic image of Mexico projected internationally by the country's technocratic leadership, they exposed the bankruptcy of "social liberalism," Carlos Salinas's much-lauded efforts to meld orthodox neoliberal economic reforms with social programs aimed at extending single-party rule (Cornelius, Craig, and Fox 1994; Dresser 1991). More than a decade of economic liberalization had battered the indigenous peoples and the countryside particularly hard and betrayed the ideals of social justice, paternalism, and agrarian populism, on which the PRI discursively constructed its rule. What's more, rebellion in Chiapas — a state in which rural populations had overwhelmingly favored the PRI in decades of elections — threatened the fragile, rural-dependent electoral dominance of the ruling party. In many ways, the PRI's efforts to stem the spread of agrarian unrest and electoral defection through the Agrarian Accords reproduced long-standing patronage politics by rewarding loyal constituents: together, the staunchly pro-PRI groups SOCAMA (Solidaridad Campesina Magisterial, or Peasant-Teacher Solidarity) and CNC received almost 30 percent of the land allocated to more than 250 peasant organizations through the accords (SIC 1998). This should not come as a surprise to anyone familiar with Mexican politics. What is remarkable about this case, however, is the extent to which the mobilizations forced the state to extend its bounty to fiercely independent, even hostile groups. CIOAC and other opposition groups that participated in negotiations bore the brunt of evictions and repression, but also leveraged tens of thousands of hectares for their members.[26] Some observers cynically labeled land redistribution programs "the key component of the low-intensity war to which indigenous communities are subjected" (López 2000:143). But they might also be framed as part of the ongoing "paradox of [the Mexican] revolution" (Middlebrook 1995). In Mexico, state actors exercise authoritarian control over the population but face the unintended consequences of consolidating state power around the legitimating ideals of agrarian revolution. In this context, social movements retain considerable ability to resist state rule and win substantial material benefits for themselves. Indigenous groups wielded considerable power after 1994, leveraging unprecedented land redistribution and furthering multiple territorial projects — but what about landowners?

As invasions spread across Chilón in February 1994, shocked ranchers watched the invasions from a distance, intervened to save livestock, and organized emergency meetings of the AGL. One month later, the ladino municipal government under Roberto Trujillo resigned under duress and was replaced by the CNPI leader, Manuel Jiménez Navarro. On March 15 the AGL sent its first major written statement of demands to President Salinas, the Chiapas state legislature, and the secretaries of defense and agrarian reform. In this document, landowners exhorted the government to immediately evict all invaded properties; separate the Bachajón ejido from Chilón, thereby creating two municipios, one indigenous and the other ladino; install a military checkpoint in Bachajón, and construct a bypass road around Bachajón "to avoid the constant danger of kidnapping and torture faced by . . . people . . . who unfortunately need to pass through on the only main street of this LAWLESS TOWN." If these demands were not met, landowners fumed, they would act unilaterally to "rescue" their properties and threatened that "if the authorities turn their backs on us today, WE WILL NOT VOTE IN THE NEXT FEDERAL, STATE, AND MUNICIPAL ELECTIONS."[27]

Landowners pressed for evictions and threatened violence into the summer of 1994, but their demands went largely unheeded, as the federal and state governments distanced themselves from landowners. Not one of the Chiloneros' four original demands was ever met. In April an agreement signed between the state government and peasant organizations established a program of subsidized buyouts of invaded properties, but only authorized evictions of properties invaded after the program went into effect. That summer, when landowners from across Chiapas held a massive protest in the state capital, Chiloneros once again held out hope for evictions. Many believed that their protests had secured the government's commitment to immediate action. When evictions were "postponed" by a federal mediator and a written response to landowners' demands reinforced the state's uncooperative attitude, Chiloneros began to moderate their position.[28] In August the AGL upped its offer of properties for sale to thirty-four (2,183 hectares) and strategically limited its demands for eviction to fifteen farms (991 hectares) invaded by *opposition* peasant groups.[29] The AGL's final offer, faxed to state officials in December 1994, called for only eleven evictions and tendered thirty-six properties for sale (2,225 hectares).[30]

Ultimately, according to government records, only one property was evicted by landowners or police in Chilón, and the state committed itself to the purchase of thousands of hectares of land.[31] Formally transferring ownership of invaded farms proved more complicated. In Chilón both peasants and landowners obstructed the buyout program for different reasons,[32] but the buyouts were hampered most of all by the generalized confusion and corruption that has always plagued property rights in Chiapas: of nineteen problem properties reported by the Secretariat of Rural Development, the owners of record of six of them were not the actual owners (some were deceased), and four properties were simply not registered with any authority.[33]

Accounting for Cooperation

Between February and December 1994, according to Mexican Treasury documents disclosed in *La Jornada*, the government issued 455 checks totaling 221 million pesos for the purchase of 39,049 hectares (*La Jornada*, June 2, 1995). Recipients of these early and lucrative payments were an elite group of high-ranking officials, including the coordinator of agrarian affairs and the relatives of several former governors. This kind of high-level corruption had historical precedent: compensation for properties affected by land reform in the 1980s, for example, was notoriously profitable for well-placed landowners. Even the AGL denounced landowner abuses, calling the governor's attention to ranchers who had invaded themselves in order to claim payments.[34] Not surprisingly, the image of fat landowners laughing all the way to the bank dominated popular conceptions of the invasion buyouts, but most landowners in Chilón had quite different experiences.

When and at what level landowners received payment was a test of their political clout and capacity for negotiating with state officials. The Martínez family, for example, received quick and substantial compensation for their San Francisco el Duraznal estate, thanks to a connection to the PRI's presidential candidate, but more commonly, landowners waited three to five years for checks. Delio Ballinas del Carpio, owner of two farms (23 and 40 hectares), claims that his paperwork "just sat there" because he "didn't have the money needed to grease the wheels."

While some landowners almost certainly reaped windfall profits in the wake of land invasions, evidence suggests that compensation — decried by landowners as abysmal and by peasant leaders as a way to get rich — may have been fairly reasonable. By December 2000, land-owners in Chilón had received some 32 million pesos for 101 proper-ties covering 7,312 hectares, with payments ranging between 2,800 and 6,800 pesos per hectare, as determined by a federal appraiser.[35] Determining whether this substantial sum was enough to send land-owners laughing all the way to the bank proves quite difficult, how-ever. Because of a substantial transfer tax on all sales of private land, landowners dramatically underreport the real value of land trans-actions. In one case a landowner who officially declared a 2-million-peso sales price for his ranch sent a letter to the property registrar complaining that the buyer still owed him 5.5 million pesos on the 9-million-peso deal![36] That said, publicly reported sales prices on cat-tle and coffee farms in the years immediately preceding 1994 ranged between 1,000 and 5,000 pesos per hectare,[37] suggesting that if the pre-1994 sales prices truly reflected underreporting, government pay-ments of 2,800–6,800 pesos compensated landowners at either near or below market value. One high-ranking official and former land ap-praiser in the Yajalón offices of the national development bank (Ban-rural), whose admitted political sympathies lean away from local land-owners, reflected that "land [value] was holding steady before the invasions, but declined dramatically after 1994." The bank official spec-ulated that in the spring of 2001, coffee groves sold for around 20,000 pesos per hectare while good pastures sold for around 9,000 pesos.[38] Interestingly, when these figures are adjusted for inflation, they re-flect almost exactly the range paid by government officials after 1994: approximately 2,800–6,300 (1994) pesos. Checks issued by the state government, however, did not compensate landowners for animals lost in the course of the invasions or capital investments such as cor-rals, milking equipment, and other ranch infrastructure.

The value of farmland, however, cannot be separated from expecta-tions of future profitability. More than one aggregate indicator sug-gested that the view from 1994 should have seemed quite dim to landowners, with neoliberal economic restructuring badly impacting both the cattle and coffee sectors. But economic crisis alone fails to account for the diversity and complexity of factors underlying land-owners' quiescence, as we shall see.

Import-Substitution Dreaming

Producing Landowners' Place in the Nation

> Tell me what you see vanishing
> and I
> Will tell you who you are.
> — W. S. Merwin, "For Now"

This chapter examines the cultural production of "production," and how this meaningful field defined landowners' understandings of their options and strategic position in the face of land invasions. After 1994, the changes in the way landowners both positioned themselves and were positioned in relation to the larger nation through debates over the meaning of production generated a strong sense of limits on the use of violence.

For landowners, production extends beyond the realm of work into almost every aspect of life. It is a critical framework for understanding the world. The cultural field of production represents what Michael Omi and Howard Winant (1994:56) call a "racial project": "simultaneously an interpretation, representation, or explanation of racial dynamics and an effort to reorganize and redistribute resources along particular racial lines." It is also a territorial project, interpreting and representing particular configurations of space in order to naturalize existing social-spatial relations and make normative claims about how space should be ordered.

Production, as a localized axis of race and class difference, conditioned landowners' attempts to position themselves in the pantheon of national development. By the late 1980s and particularly after the Zapatista uprising, shifting balances of Mexican political economy undermined landowners' ability to leverage state support for their defense of territory. Landowners experienced this shift, worked out through the cultural field of "production," as a complete upending of the way the world worked, with strong implications for their calculations of the limits and possibilities of violent action. For decades the discourse of production lay at the heart of landowners' confidence that their work had great value to the entire nation, value that would be rewarded with political and economic support. But by 1994 that social order did not seem so certain or secure.

Producing Landowners

For landowners in Chilón, the story of 1994 is written on the landscape, as clear as grass and corn. Brown scabs of pasture denuded by herbicide await planting. Young corn shoots compete with tangles of tropical fodder. Pine board houses rise in fields where cattle once grazed, and at night the blue smoke of cooking fires and the smell of corn tortillas hang over what were once Chilón's most productive pastures. The 1994–1998 invasions affected coffee and cattle land more or less equally, but for landowners, occupied pasture tells the saddest story. While coffee groves lay far from major roads in steep terrain shrouded by shade trees, Chilón's pastureland cleaves to roads for easy access to transportation—much of it lying in a conspicuous ring around the edge of town. Thus it is here that the effects of invasion are most visible.

For landowners the changing landscape crystallizes the losses of 1994 and the madness of events since then. In chapter 2 I recalled how Don Roberto, observing a hillside that before 1994 had belonged to Elí Rodríguez, Chilón's most prominent cattleman, commented: "That used to be one of the most productive pastures in Chilón. You'd look over there and just see the green filled with brown dots—with cattle. Then [in February 1994] indígenas from Piquinteel—on the other side of the hill—invaded it. Now look at it. It has a handful of milpas over there on one side and the rest of it is just overgrown with weeds." "Once the whole road from Bachajón to Chilón was all cattle, as far as you could see," Ofelia Jiménez observed bitterly. "Now there's nothing there."

Of course, there *is* something there. Wild overgrown pasture, to be sure, but also scattered indigenous settlements, ramshackle schools, a handful of livestock, and scores of cornfields. It is the lived landscape

The idealized landscape of ladino production. *(Photo by author.)*

of peasant livelihood. What is missing is *production*, a particular, racialized understanding of the meaning of production. For landowners, production was deeply rooted in the transformation of nature and the accumulation of capital through agriculture; it meant more than a livelihood.

The word "production" comes into both Spanish and English through the Latin roots "to lead" and "forward," and this etymology comes close to signifying the meaning of production for Chilón's ladino landowners. Ultimately, production is a broad field of meaning and practice concerned with practices of responsible husbandry ("leading forward") in multiple arenas of life, from the construction of masculinity to the definition of landowners' relations with the Mexican state. By exploring the meaning of production, we can see how landowners understand themselves and their relations with each other, their indigenous neighbors, and the nation.

For ladinos, one of the most incomprehensible actions of indigenous invaders was the seemingly irrational destruction of capital improvements to the land—the very stuff of production. As Ruperto Monterossa fumed, "When they invaded, they knocked down the coffee-processing equipment, the milking sheds, the tick bath. . . . If

An indigenous settlement and *milpas* rise out of invaded cattle pastures. *(Photo by author.)*

they were going to take the land, why didn't they at least *do* something with all that equipment?" Words like this, echoed by nearly every rancher I spoke with, attest to landowners' collective sense of the irresponsibility and Otherness of indigenous insurgents. Tactically, this discourse counters the antilandowner rhetoric of indigenous social movements as well as the more abstract, but no less palpably felt, critique of landed interests expressed in political economic theory. The discourse of production inverts charges of unproductive "rent seeking" typically leveled at the landed classes, magically converting rentier landlords into active transformers of nature. Indigenous peasants, landowners argue, are the real parasites, living off the natural bounty of land — land that was originally made productive through landowners' sweat and sacrifice.

Yet, when pushed, some ladinos admit that the tragedy they see written on the landscape is not that the land is producing nothing but that "it's not producing what it *should*. . . . It's not that the indígenas aren't producing, just that they're obtaining a product without *working* the land." Ladinos, Rodolfo Domínguez tells me, invest in production with the goal of creating profit, while the indígenas "grow their crops for household consumption, not productivity." Or, as Miguel Utrilla clarifies, "The indígenas only work for necessity — to buy things they need at the moment — and then they quit." Thus what I call landowners' discourse of production refers not to the generative act of agriculture itself but rather to the creation of particular kinds of social and economic value through particular kinds of physical and emotional exertion — a vocation of accumulation.

The Vocation of Accumulation

Through the discursive practices of production, landowners construct their sense of self on shaky ground riddled with contradictions. It is a mistake, however, to reduce the fabric of landowner identity to the simple mechanics of ideological mystification. Deep roots grow in shaky ground.

Early in our acquaintance, the cattleman Eulalio Hernández insisted, "Agriculture is honorable work . . . agriculture is a labor of love, something you must give your whole self to. . . . It's about progress, about getting ahead [*superación*] through enormous effort . . . it's my *vocation*. . . . When [the government] asked me, 'What's your ranch worth?' I said, 'What's your eye worth?'" Behind the bluster, Eulalio's outburst expresses the essence of the producer's life: a deep romantic attachment to land, a morally charged belief in the connection between hard work and progress, and a strong sense of vocation or purpose rooted in agriculture. For Eulalio, who immediately and without hesitation reinvested money paid for his invaded ranch in a new piece of land, being an agricultural producer is his everyday work, as his cracked hands and sun-blackened face attest. But for the many landowners in Chilón who lost their land to invaders, production is inextricably wrapped up in a nostalgic longing for the return of a mythical world — a world that made sense.

After the invasion of El Carmen Tzajalá, Roberto Trujillo's bohemian brother Fausto wrote a novel in an attempt to come to grips with his family's loss. *El sacrificio de Isac* (The sacrifice of Isaac) is, as Michael Kammen (1991:688) wrote of nostalgia, "history without guilt" — an elaborate protestation of the landowner's innocence in the face of invasion.[1] More importantly, it is a lamentation for the passing of a particular gendered and racialized identity, an elegy to production.

The novel begins and ends with the violence of invasion and landowners' defense of their property, but the remainder takes place during a bucolic interlude leading up to the conflict. At the heart of this pastoral is a creepily asymmetrical romance between the landowner Ulysses and his childlike indigenous servant, Nymph.[2] As the story unfolds, Ulysses and Nymph spend their days walking through lush forests, catching crawfish in streams, erotically bathing in cool mountain pools, and losing themselves in a haven of shady coffee groves. Young Nymph ably serves Ulysses, picking sticky sweet fruit and cooking for him, bringing him coffee, cutting his toenails, and listening eagerly as he dispenses lessons about life. In return, Ulysses instructs Nymph in the twin arts of "man's" relation to nature: the rational administration of agriculture and the romantic-intellectual appreciation of nature's splendors.

All is right in this Gauguin-tinted fantasy. Indigenous workers are respectful, docile, and erotic on command. The land is bountiful and well ordered under the owner's guidance. Beyond the clear images of romantic attachment to the land and "proper" race and gender roles, however, *El sacrificio de Isac* hides another key element of landowners' nostalgia: longing for a lost sense of purpose. Ulysses takes pride in his identity as progenitor. His sense of purpose and identity come from his role as a benevolent shaper of female nature, vegetal nature, and indigenous nature, all blurred together. As the novel ends, Ulysses stands in the ruins of his estate, contemplating this loss of purpose and searching for another source of meaning: "There was nothing to hope for, nothing to begin. He had to go on, of course, because it had all begun many years before when his ancestors had come to establish themselves in these lands, which were still forests of solitude then. . . . No, Ulysses could not turn his back on the voyage through history . . . he had to allow the wind to take his boat, and not necessarily to Ithaca, his island would be whichever one the sea led him to, because he could struggle against the minotaur, but he couldn't struggle against destiny." The novel ends with bittersweet optimism. Ulysses has been forcibly stripped of the meaning of his life—carrying on the generational legacy of production—but he at least can find a new, more existential sense of purpose in simply continuing on.

Real landowners were not always that lucky. Many, by necessity, found new careers, new attachments outside of agriculture, tracing their grandparents' footsteps in reverse: out of Chilón, back to Tuxtla Gutiérrez or San Cristóbal and back to commerce or professional jobs. For many, this path opened up new opportunities and sources of fulfillment, but others chafe at the inactivity and sterility of professional life. One former rancher, who requested that these comments remain anonymous, used money from the sale of his invasion-threatened property to buy a pickup truck and a commercial transport concession. Now he earns his living hauling people and cargo along the route between two towns, but he pines for the active life of ranch work. The man gives off a forceful, almost violent physical energy that it is difficult to imagine confined to a pickup cab. Although still strapped with muscles as thick as cables, his body has begun to decline, as much from anger and frustration as from inactivity. His back and shoulder ache constantly, making it difficult even to work in the small urban garden he bought "to keep [his] hands in the dirt."

Unlike many of his friends who recall a sanitized romanticized past, he is wry and self-reflexive, laughing heartily about his ancestors' involvement in the contraband liquor trade and his own attempts to defend his property against land reformers. Nevertheless, stories of the past still ground his life in a sense of heritage and a continuum of progress savagely broken in 1994. His family started with nothing, he says, "claiming land in the middle of the wilds in a place with nobody there," and slowly building something out of nothing through sheer determination (and a bit of smuggling). He carefully guards a beautifully inked deed map from 1873 as a tangible reminder of this past, of which, he sadly reminds me, "there's nothing left anymore."

Nowhere is the psychic dislocation of decline clearer than in its impacts on landowners' bodies. Just as the anonymous rancher connects his back and shoulder pain to land invasions, Chiloneros attribute dozens of deaths and disabilities since 1994 to *coraje* — the fury that fills older men faced with the loss of land, livelihood, and purpose. While it is difficult to know whether the rash of heart attacks, diabetes, cancer, strokes, and nervous breakdowns attributed to coraje is truly inconsistent with what one might expect in an aging male population, it is clearly experienced by Chiloneros as a socially produced epidemic. "Everywhere you look people just filled up with coraje and died," Delio Ballinas tells me, quickly naming a half-dozen landowners who succumbed to ailments after 1994. Delio's own life has been cursed with loss: land invasions forced him to abandon a series of estates in the 1970s, 1980s, and 1990s. After each successive loss, he purchased another ranch in another region. "I've had such a hard life that most men would have put a bullet in their head or strung themselves up. First we were driven out of Simojovel, then we started over in Pantelhó, and I finally came to have seven ranches there. Real success. And

I lost those ranches [to indigenous invaders] and came to Chilón and here I had two good ranches, but then I lost those [to indigenous invaders]. My family, which was so accustomed to living the good life and spending lots of money, began to crumble and they threw me out once I no longer had money. So here I am in these rooms, trying to start over again, but you have to look forward. You can't change the past."

Despite Delio's positive outlook, it is not clear to me what he is starting over "in these rooms," a decrepit adobe house rented from a friend that crumbles around us as we sit talking. Even more inexplicable: Why would he purchase another farm? From his office in Villahermosa, Tabasco, Jorge Martínez—whose own bulging carotids hint at the way *he* has wrestled with coraje—explains why someone would keep reinvesting in land through decades of loss, and why that loss was felt at such a corporeal level: "You're dealing here with people who grew up on ranches, whose whole life has been ranches, who thought they would die on ranches, but now are thrown off with nothing left to do."

In the seventeenth century Swiss doctors prescribed leeches, opium, and a trip to the Alps as a cure for life-threatening bouts of nostalgia (Boym 2001). Many Chiloneros try hobby farming instead. These mostly older, semiretired men ground their longing for an enchanted past in the present by maintaining their link to land and purpose on small plots where they plant coffee, vegetables, and fruit trees. Unlike younger former landowners who must still provide for families, these men farm as a way of keeping active in their old age. Indeed, many argue that, given the insecurity of land tenure and the violent political climate, agriculture should be left to the old. Almost no landowners or former landowners over the age of forty wished a rancher's life for their children. Eighty-one-year-old Hermenegildo Vera, whose love of rural life is so intense that he sneaked out of a hospital days after heart surgery to go horseback riding, breaks out in tears of pride when he tells me that all his children are professionals: a doctor, a veterinarian, and a teacher. "I spent my whole life on horseback," he tells me, but "education is the greatest inheritance I can leave my children." Ofelia Jiménez puts things more bluntly when I ask her if her children will carry on as ranchers. "No way!" she blurts out. "Anything but ranchers. Even if it's only as a teacher, anything but *ranchero*. . . . It's too scary with all the indígenas now, there are too many risks. It's better to be a merchant."

Most of Chilón's young ladinos have heeded this message. A few, such as Samuel Rodríguez Jr., have returned to farming after receiving an education, often as a veterinarian or agronomist, but even Samuel has his doubts: "There are very few of us who want to continue [as ranchers]. [Just] my cousins and me. For those of us who grew up with this life — we were three years old when we started going to the ranch — it's hard to stop, but other people have left or found different kinds of jobs. Many people leave [Chilón]. . . . Love of the land didn't take hold with them. Most of them also grew up on their ranches but see them only as places to have a good time. . . . No, I don't think Chilón will rise up again, for two reasons: First, there are no more properties. They all belong to the ejidatarios now. And second, there's no one left to work the ranches."

Others, such as Oscar Cruz, who did not receive a professional education, desperately wish they could return to ranching: "[After the invasion] I felt disillusioned. . . . I had no schooling, no degree, nothing to fall back on. Since then, I've worked at little jobs in different government offices. Now I earn my money teaching music at the municipal community center."

Samuel's and Oscar's boyhood friend Juan Trujillo (Don Roberto's youngest son) is more typical of twenty- and thirty-something Chiloneros. Educated as a dentist in Oaxaca, he has returned to Chilón to practice. Along with Samuel, Juan devotes considerable energy to reviving Chilón's charro, or rodeo, association, but has no desire to be a "producer." Seeing me walking back from an interview with a former landowner displaced by land invaders, Juan clowned, "I was affected by the invasions too, you know. Because now I don't have anyplace to go have fun."[3]

Even the younger generation's gravitation away from the land confirms the value of production for Chiloneros. As Hermenegildo Vera suggests, older landowners feel that their hard work and sacrifice allowed them to pass a rich legacy of education and new opportunities on to their children — a way around the harsh and insecure life they led. Paco Vera, Hermenegildo's veterinarian son, claims that he does love the land, but he is pragmatic about the future: "Mestizos have left the countryside. It belongs to the indígenas now." For both father and son, Paco's ability to find a place for himself in this new context is the triumph of his father's production ethic.

Production is not just the stuff of personal achievement, however.

As I have suggested, it also connects landowners to a noble past. When ladinos first arrived in Chilón, halfway through the nineteenth century, Miguel Utrilla tells me over coffee, the region had lost most of its indigenous population and "lay vacant and unproductive." Ladinos were poor, "maybe had one or two mules and worked transporting coffee for German-owned estates." They watched the Germans, studied their methods, and finally, like Prometheus stealing fire, a few ladinos "began to pocket a few coffee beans, taking them to try to plant the magical bush." Over time the ladinos learned, struggled to better themselves, and gradually took over the coffee trade from waning German estates. Soon other ladinos appeared—tradesmen, merchants, and professionals selling goods and services to the new estates. But eventually they succumbed to the lure of landed production. In many ways, Utrilla's narrative of ladino settlement parallels many more scholarly accounts (see chapter 4) as well as archival evidence, but like any historical narrative, it navigates a terrain of tactical omission.

Midway through the nineteenth century, Chilón, of course, was not exactly an "enormous empty forest . . . so unpopulated that [ladinos] had to bring labor from as far away as Yucatán," as Carlos Setzer put it, or a place where ladinos could "claim land in the middle of the wilds in a place with nobody there," as Alejandro Díaz insisted. Evidence in colonial archives and secondary sources suggests that Chilón, Bachajón, and Yajalón were in fact populated both by indigenous residents with deep roots in the region and by more recent indigenous settlers interned there by Spanish friars in the sixteenth century. Combined, these indigenous communities controlled large stretches of land that were taken over by ladinos in the nineteenth century.

Clearly, then, the large-scale appropriation of land by ladino settlers was not as inoffensive as their contemporary descendants claim, and the contradictions of their position are evident to many landowners. It is difficult, for example, to maintain the fiction that no indígenas lived in the region before the nineteenth century, particularly when everyone knows that the indigenous communities of Bachajón, Chilón, and Yajalón hatched a dramatic and well-studied uprising in 1712—a rebellion that lives on in ladinos' memories as a time when blood ran "seven millimeters deep across the whole church floor" after the massacre of most of Chilón's ladino population during a religious festival.[4]

It is when landowners are confronted with contradictions like this that the true stripes of their origin myths and their relation to contemporary discourses of production come clear. Landowners' guiltless origin myth is not just about an unwillingness to confront a history of appropriation but also about articulating a particular understanding of what it means to occupy a territory. There were no indígenas there before the ladinos came, they say, because the indígenas did not fully occupy the territory through production. Their claims to land are meaningless, because they did not "use" the land. Whether or not the indígenas' use of the land before the nineteenth century was as inefficient as landowners claim, one thing is clear: behind the intricate meanings of "real" production lies a simple formula. For ladino landowners, production is "what we do" and indígenas don't—a framework for knowing oneself through comparison with the Other.

Producing the Other

Despite the fact that in many ways the solid category of "landowner" disintegrates in the face of the group's complex internal divisions, "production" transcends sectoral differences and class positions, serving as a broad divide between indígena and ladino. On one hand, landowners use production to distinguish themselves from other landowners, even competing for the claim to be the most authentic producer. Delio Ballinas, for example, who at one time owned seven properties, leaps to distance himself from the derogatory label *latifundista*. "There aren't any more latifundistas, except for some politicians who have thousands of hectares. We get the blame for taking land away from the indígenas, but [latifundistas] have thousands of hectares . . . and they don't produce on the land, either. It's just for outings [*paseos*]. In Chiapas, only someone like Castellanos Domínguez [a former governor] would fit into this category."

Similarly, *finqueros* such as Carlos Setzer, Miguel Utrilla, and Roberto Trujillo, who share a historical connection to coffee estates defined by their antiquity and size, do not count as producers in the eyes of many smaller ranchers. As one explained to me, "Rancheros live on the ranch . . . and work the land with their own hands, while finqueros just have a ranch and don't invest in it." Yet this notion is certainly up for debate, and some finqueros reverse the charge of parasitism.

One man usually identified as a finquero, a man known for both hard work and fearsome drinking, speaks disdainfully of smaller-scale ladino ranchers, calling them lazy, drunken, and unproductive. Indeed, this finquero's tattered greasy work clothes and enormous cracked hands testify to the enthusiasm with which he throws himself into the physical labor of farming. Similarly confusing, numerous landowners concur that people can be producers even if they earn most of their money from commerce. "For example, Carlos Setzer is a producer," Paco Vera confirms, "even though most of his income comes from buying and selling other people's coffee." Sometimes these blurry boundaries can be quite humorous. Roberto Abarca, an indisputably wealthy merchant, regales me with stories of sacrifice and hard work on his family's estate, finishing with the landowners' favorite saying: "A rancher lives poor but dies rich." As I sit in his well-appointed living room, though, I am confronted by a framed print of another saying hanging on the wall behind him: "A merchant lives rich and dies poor."

Ultimately, then, the one coherent thread that runs through the inconsistencies in landowners' discourse of production is the idea that production is something that ladinos do and indígenas don't. As much as it charts class differences within the community of landowners, it also marks a racial divide.

As we sip coffee after breakfast in the weedy portico of Carlos Setzer's run-down casa grande, he explains: "Aaron, it's like the difference between African bees and European bees. European bees work very hard, constantly working to build up supplies for the winter season. African bees, on the other hand, because of the climate, don't think about the future. They work very hard, but only for the day. They don't produce for the future. The indígenas are like African bees: they don't accumulate for themselves or for the country."

As the descendent of German immigrants, Carlos Setzer occupies a privileged position in this racialized hierarchy of production. Ladino landowners, on the other hand, locate themselves at the uneasy midpoint between the indigenous Other ("completely lacking in a culture of production") and "more *chingón*" (tough and capable) Europeans. Even Miguel Utrilla's ladino origin myth reflects this anxiety. According to Utrilla, a culture of production did not come naturally to Chilón's ladinos. As Utrilla explained, the primogenital coffee bean — stolen along with a lesson in production from German planters — transformed the nature of ladino work: "Instead of working the land, [the first ladinos] planted for household consumption, until they got the first tiny plants of coffee. . . . [That's where we got that] sense of working to fulfill a responsibility. I don't think that's something that even the Spanish have. It's something we got from you [northern Europeans]."

According to this logic, the traces of European blood running in ladinos' veins gave them at least some chance of developing a "culture of production." Indigenous peasants had no chance at all. Despite evidence of the overwhelmingly commercial orientation of peasant agriculture and the skyrocketing influence of dynamic indigenous businesses in the region, ladinos steadfastly hold to the idea that indígenas cannot "produce." Miguel Utrilla continues: "The indígenas have a more contemplative style of working. It's a racial characteristic. Because of this style the indígenas worked only out of necessity — to buy things they needed at the moment and then they'd quit. There isn't a sense of needing to fulfill a work responsibility."

When I ask Utrilla about the rise of prosperous indigenous merchants in Bachajón, which seems to clash with his theory of racial determinism, he halts in the tracks of his broken narrative and searches for an explanation. Finally he responds by attributing indígenas' commercial success to the easy profits of the drug trade rather than hard work: "You'll see big houses and fancy pickup trucks in Bachajón now, but where did they get the original capital? There are fields of marijuana and poppies all over the area." If this were true — and it may well be true on a small scale — then the rise of indigenous business elites would parallel that of Utrilla's family much more closely than he would ever admit. Despite stories of production and sacrifice, the Utrillas' original capital flowed from the tap of a liquor still. Utrilla remembers his grandfather's store in Yajalón as a "modest" one, but it had an excellent supply of aguardiente, and he remembers "indígenas lining up to buy it every Saturday." When I tried later to probe this contradiction more deeply, Utrilla became distant and perfunctory, signaling the awkward close to a relationship that had begun with a shared enthusiasm for local history.

Indeed, prying into cracks and contradictions in the discourse of production was one of the most incendiary lines of questioning I could follow, often producing even more emotionally strident reactions than tough questions about landowners' involvement in agrarian violence. Ultimately, I believe, the reason that the image of landowners as uniquely productive is sacrosanct lies in the support it provides to so many other sustaining beliefs, from landowners' sense of connection to a noble past to their understanding of the architecture of racial order. It was also central to landowners' understanding of their place in the nation and their ability to use that position to leverage crucial economic and political support.

Shedding Latifundio: Landowners and the Nation

After the triumph of the Mexican Revolution, Chiloneros not only confronted new challenges to their control over land and political power, they also faced a surprising fall from grace. In the decades of Porfirian liberalism — the golden age of landed production that preceded the Revolution — estate agriculture fitted neatly into the broader national project of liberal development. While agribusiness elites in Chiapas's central valleys may have criticized Chiloneros' labor practices as "obstacles to the progressive development of agriculture,"[5] these critiques amounted to little more than the "narcissism of minor difference." Landed property was still privileged and protected, and the goal of liberal elites was not to destroy estate-based agriculture but to improve it. In the wake of the Revolution, however, vast estates took on a sinister aura, as even the most counterrevolutionary administrations won popular endorsement by juxtaposing themselves against the image of an abusive Porfirian landed aristocracy. In this context, Chilón's landed elites would have to adapt, not just by physically defending their property against peasants' claims to it but also by symbolically reworking their place in national taxonomies of property. Tarred with the brush of latifundio, Chiloneros worked to define a new place for themselves in the "small property" sector, enshrined in the 1917 Constitution as the most privileged and desired category of land tenure in the nation (Ibarra 1989:110).

This symbolic struggle took place on many fronts, but the rise of cattle ranching in tandem with nationalist policies of import-substitution industrialization beginning in the 1940s opened a serendipitous niche in the new polity — a new leverage point in the ongoing hegemonic struggle between landowners, indigenous peasants, and the state. Cattle production not only offered landowners a new economic basis for landed production, it rescued them from their ignoble past and gave them a new role in national development. By the 1980s, however, this niche had begun to narrow as broad changes in Mexico's political economy once again shifted the relationship between landowners, indigenous peasants, and the state. Today, despite its seemingly irrational and racist trappings, landowners' production discourse cogently reflects deep apprehension about these changes.

Producing for the Nation

> The provisioning of meat has been a constant preoccupation of every country in the world, because [meat] is the most basic and fundamental food of man, and in Mexico today, meat consumption is so low . . . that production must be quintupled if [meat] is . . . to reach every household in the country. — Secretaría de Educación Pública, *Enciclopedia Popular*, 1946

Throughout most of the postrevolutionary period, national agricultural policy has followed a two-track system, balancing an economic project — ensuring adequate food supplies by supporting agribusiness producers — and a political project — buttressing the ejido sector as a critical political constituency (Fox 1994a). To this end, a privileged stratum of commercial farmers received a disproportionate amount of financial support geared toward boosting production, while Mexico's vast peasant sector received subsidies and favorable treatment from state agencies not because it could produce food for the nation but because it could be relied on to produce votes for the ruling party. This two-track system derived from the exigencies of another Janus-faced challenge faced by the Mexican regime. Since 1940, with rapid rural out-migration, massive urbanization, and booming industrialization achieved through policies of import substitution, national food policy has been one of the most important arenas of Mexican politics (Ochoa 2000, Fox 1993, Austin and Esteva 1987). The PRI's ability to maintain legitimacy turned fundamentally on its ability to burn the fiscal candle at both ends: subsidizing industrial wages and winning support of the new urban working class with cheap food while securing an adequate supply of food and rural peace through agricultural subsidies and price supports (Ochoa 2000).

Feeding Mexico's new urban population required a massive reorientation of the production of basic grains. State support facilitated the rapid industrialization and modernization of wheat and corn production, green revolution technologies spread from their birthplace in northern Mexico through the whole country, and an elaborate network of parastatal marketing boards and food retailers emerged to provision the cities. Much has been written on the role of modernizing basic grain production in Mexican industrialization efforts (e.g., Hewitt de Alcántara 1978) as well as on the role of export-oriented cattle production in northern Mexico in generating foreign exchange for import-substitution industrialization (e.g., Sanderson 1986), but the trajectories of tropical beef production in Mexico after World War II speak to another dynamic. Feeding Mexico's booming urban population meant cheap basic grains, but feeding urban Mexico in a style befitting its new modern industrial self-image meant something else. It meant meat.

As we saw in chapter 6, the new emphasis on beef production for the domestic market gave landowners in Chilón privileged access to lucrative subsidies and political supports. Less tangibly but no less important, it also offered landowners a way to position themselves as vital actors in postrevolutionary constructions of the Mexican nation. Thus, even as coffee continued to play a central role in the economies of estates, Chiloneros took on the role of rancher, swapping the planter's white suit for blue jeans and boots, Indian porters for pickup trucks. In remaking themselves as cowboys, landowners staked out firm footing in the national pantheon, shedding their connection to Porfirian latifundios. The days of serfs and masters, company stores, and slavelike conditions could not be denied, but now they could always be said to have existed in the distant past and on someone else's estate. Now landowners were producing and accumulating for the nation.

Neoliberalism and the Betrayal of Production

By the early 1980s, the political and economic space for landowners' claims to privilege based on their status as producers began to shrink for reasons connected to large-scale shifts in Mexico's national development strategies. With the onset of the debt crisis in 1982 and the subsequent rise of neoliberal technocrats, severely constricted credit, trade liberalization, and the dismantling of input subsidies and price controls plunged the cattle sector into a massive contraction. Seven years later, neoliberal restructuring combined with an unprecedented collapse in international coffee prices compounded landowners' difficulties by sending the coffee sector into precipitous decline. Nevertheless, it would be overly simple and economistic to conclude that landowners' quiescence in the face of the 1994–1998 land invasions was merely a calculated response to economic crisis. Indeed, rather than wallowing in stagnation and gradually distancing themselves from agriculture in the years leading up to 1994, ladino landowners believed that they were experiencing something of a locally specific rural renaissance. Particularly in the livestock sector, it appeared that Chiloneros had found a way to shift from politically unviable extensive ranching to more intensive dairy production. Thus it was not solely economic logic that inhibited landowners' willingness and ability to defend their property against land invaders; political dynamics stemming from the rise of neoliberalism played a key role. As landowners are always quick to observe, "Agriculture has lots of problems and risks. If it rains too much, or not at all. If there are plant diseases. But all that passes. Only the uncertainty of land tenure stays with us forever."

Coffee, Cattle, and Crisis in Chilón

Since the early 1980s, ranchers have experienced a marked withdrawal of economic subsidies as a result of restructuring in state support for agriculture. The most significant change in ranchers' relationship with the state stems from the privatization and cutback of credit services. For decades the livestock sector enjoyed privileged access to subsidized loans at interest rates far below the open market rate. The 1989 restructuring of Mexico's national development bank, Banrural, left most ranchers ineligible for subsidized credit and forced them to seek loans at much higher interest rates from private banks. At the same time, beginning in the early 1990s, Mexico began to import beef from the United States. Since Mexican tariffs on U.S. beef exports were phased out with the implementation of the North American Free Trade Agreement (NAFTA) in 1994, imports have steadily grown (except for a brief respite after the devaluation of the peso in 1995). Ranchers in Chiapas, producing almost exclusively for domestic consumption, have watched their traditional markets disappear, saturated by less expensive imported beef (Chauvet 1999).

Similarly, after decades of strong support from the state, cutbacks in the late 1980s battered coffee producers of all sizes (Hernández and Célis 1994). Paired with five years of historic price declines (1989–1993), restructuring of the coffee sector resulted in a general decapitalization and technological regression in the industry. The 1989 coffee crash devastated landowners in Chilón. Carlos Setzer, one of the region's largest coffee producers and traders, recalls that when the 1989 catastrophe struck, he had 45,000 quintals of coffee, purchased from smaller growers or produced on his estate, stored in his warehouse. He had hoped to net almost $200,000 after paying off the substantial loans with which he purchased and produced this coffee. Instead he lost thousands. Before 1989, he says, "everyone had credit, but it was manageable, you paid it off at harvesttime." Like many other producers, after the crisis Setzer struggled to stay afloat by securing more and more credit from various sources, including dollar credits from a major German coffee import firm. When I met Setzer in 1998, he had just given up his family home in Tuxtla Gutiérrez and was finalizing the sale of a coffee warehouse and processing facility he had acquired in better times.

Despite this strong aggregate picture of crisis, fieldwork provided an important lesson in the dependence of large-scale economic trends on context. From the start of my fieldwork, landowners had insisted that their economic prospects were improving before 1994. At first I dismissed this insistence as nostalgia, or more likely an effort to make the loss of land seem even worse than it was. Slowly, however, I began to consider the possibility that landowners were right. From the vantage of grand narratives about neoliberal development, landowners may not have had many objective reasons to believe in the possibility of an agricultural renaissance before 1994, but it was clear that they did.

In 1990, after a decade of slumping cattle production, the AGL optimistically revived the long-dormant tradition of holding an annual livestock exhibition in Chilón. The fair, held from 1990 to 1993, celebrated a growing trend toward the intensification and use of technology on the region's ranches. Five or six major producers led this movement, implementing artificial insemination, careful breeding programs, more intensive land management, and improvement of pastures; and others were following. Ragged herds of creole and zebu cattle were slowly being replaced by European milk cows imported from dairies in northern Mexico. La Esperanza, the Rodríguez family's ranch just outside the town of Chilón, had even earned a national reputation for its breeding program and prize-winning Swiss brown cows. These changes had certainly not altered the overwhelmingly extensive nature of cattle production in Chilón: by 1993, only 11 percent of the municipio's herd was managed semi-intensively (up from nearly zero in previous years) and most of the new dairy ranchers got less than four liters of milk per day from their cows.[6] Less than half of all ranchers kept accounts of their income and expenses, and the profitability of cattle was still closely correlated with the amount of land available for grazing (Vera 1998). Nevertheless, through a process of innovation and imitation, ranching in Chilón was undergoing a fitful transformation.

Four context-specific factors powered this unlikely intensification in a time of crisis: First, crisis itself drove intensification. Since the 1950s, cattle and coffee have formed two halves of a resilient complementary pairing, with cattle constituting a source of year-round liquidity and coffee providing an annual bonanza (which was frequently reinvested in livestock). Cattle production effectively stabilized coffee planters' cash-starved yearly cycles and helped sustain landowners' incomes during coffee's long-run cycles of boom and bust.[7] Thus, faced with the catastrophic decline of coffee prices in 1989, landowners began to rethink their low-intensity cattle businesses, channeling money (typically from commerce and professional employment) into their herds.

Second, in 1992 the Nestlé corporation, responding to a request by ranchers, opened a milk-collection center in Chilón, providing producers with a guaranteed market, short-term credits, and technical assistance. Nestlé's expansion into the region, although still on a minuscule scale, provided ranchers with a reason for hope, and by 1994 they had stepped up production to supply the new collection site with 1,600 liters of milk per day (on top of 500–700 liters already sold to local cheese manufacturers).[8]

Third, in the early 1990s the government made new subsidized credits available to landowners in an effort to rescue the country's failing cattle industry.[9]

Finally and perhaps most importantly, after five years of losses and accumulating debts, in 1994 landowners also had reasons to be optimistic about their coffee harvests. From the eve of the Zapatista uprising to the summer and fall of 1994, when landowners had to decide how to respond to the invasions, coffee prices shot up unexpectedly. Driven by coordinated export limitations around the world (1993) and an outbreak of coffee blight in Brazil (1994), the world price soared nearly fourfold between January and July 1994. As landowners struggled to respond to land invasions, this dramatic spike dangled the possibility of escape from debt. "If we had only been able to harvest that year . . ." Wenceslao López groaned years later, his voice trailing off into thoughts of bankruptcy. Some landowners struck deals with agreeable invaders, offering them uncontested rights to estate land in return for permission to harvest the last bonanza crop. In most cases, however, indigenous peasants reaped the windfall harvest of 1994.

In short, while it goes too far to say that landed elites in Chilón avoided the buffets of agricultural crisis, they were not uniformly devastated. While landowners responded to the invasions with despair and resignation in near unison, their economic prospects varied widely. At least in some cases, signs of recovery—rising coffee prices, prize-winning cattle, and multinational investment—cast a glow over landed elites' visions of the future.

In the chaos and insecurity after 1994 land values dropped sharply in Chilón, loan defaults skyrocketed, milk and beef production plummeted, Nestlé closed its collection center, and desperate producers searched for alternative sources of income. But reference to economic crisis alone fails to account for the diversity and complexity of factors underlying landowners' quiescence. Their hopes for a renaissance were dashed against the harsh political realities of intensified indigenous activism and a neoliberal state no longer interested in "producers."

Politics and the Landowner in a Neoliberal Age

After the outbreak of invasions in February 1994, Chiloneros rushed to Tuxtla Gutiérrez, expecting immediate succor from old allies in the state. What they encountered instead haunts them to this day. Wenceslao López's first stop in Tuxtla was the office of the state agrarian prosecutor. "We got there at eight in the morning, but they made us wait like beggars on the sidewalk until three in the afternoon. When we got inside the office, we saw the invaders and their leaders sitting in a row next to the official's desk. As soon as we entered, the official excused himself to make a phone call. While the official was on the phone, the leader stood up and sat right on the official's desk and put his feet up on his chair. He told one of the others to give him a cigarette, and right at that moment I thought to myself that we were not going to be able to accomplish anything there."

What gave indigenous leaders not just a place at the table but a place for their feet *on* the table in post-1994 Chiapas?

Mexico, like most of the world, has undergone widespread economic and political restructuring along neoliberal lines over the past twenty years.[10] Since 1988, when efforts to implement rapid orthodox market liberalization, privatization, fiscal austerity, and cutbacks in social programs by President Miguel de la Madrid (1982–1988) ended in near-calamity for the PRI, neoliberal restructuring has been heterodox and unconventional. Following de la Madrid in office, Carlos Salinas rapidly reoriented government policy toward a combination of neoliberal restructuring and politically motivated social programs. Harking back to nineteenth-century formulations of Mexican liberalism, Salinas dubbed this platform "social liberalism." During Salinas's term, social liberalism proved a highly effective framework for simultaneously diffusing social unrest, rebuilding support for the PRI, and implementing a massive wave of liberalization and privatization that touched almost every sector of the Mexican economy.[11] Social liberalism's flagship enterprise, the Programa Nacional de Solidaridad (PRONASOL, or National Solidarity Program), poured millions of dollars into locally defined self-help projects in every corner of the country.[12] Brought into existence to "repair the tattered social safety net . . . inherited from the economic crisis and austerity measures of the 1982–1988 period" (Dresser 1994:4), PRONASOL was both a continuation of the age-old politics of patronage in Mexico and something quite different. Centrally, PRONASOL represented a major move away from the hierarchical, nested sectoral mediation of corporatism toward direct mediation between individual communities and the president (Dresser 1994).[13] More importantly PRONASOL and its farm-focused companion program, PROCAMPO (Programa de Apoyos Directos al Campo, or Program of Direct Aid to the Countryside), articulated a new view of the countryside:[14] social liberal policies had radically shifted support for agricultural production away from traditional sectors (i.e., corn, coffee, and cattle) toward the promotion of nontraditional exports (e.g., melons, mangoes, and macadamia nuts) and reliance on imported food. In this context, traditional producers such as Chilón's indigenous peasants received state support only in the form of politically necessary *welfare* programs like PROCAMPO, designed to buy calm in the countryside amidst devastating neoliberal restructuring. Chilón's landowners — neither peasants (eligible for welfare support) nor part of the privileged caste of nontraditional agricultural export producers favored by neoliberal policies — found themselves without a clear place in national development and increasingly cut off from state support. They experienced this marginalization as a phenomenal betrayal of "production." In Samuel Rodríguez Sr.'s words,

"The government isn't interested in production anymore, it's interested in politics."

Many works chronicle the effects of neoliberal restructuring on Chiapas's peasantry (e.g., Collier 2005, Nash 2001, N. Harvey 1998), but only the political scientist Richard Snyder (2001) has systematically addressed the high-level construction of neoliberalism in Chiapas and its effects on the state's traditional landed oligarchy. Snyder traces the undoing of Chiapas's "crony capitalist" system in which state officials protected local cattle and coffee elites. As Snyder concludes, this undoing resulted directly from the rise of neoliberal technocrats in state and federal government and the increasing militancy of peasant social movements confronted with neoliberal restructuring of the countryside. Landed elites, he suggests, served as convenient sacrificial lambs as these two factions worked out their differences and formed an uneasy alliance.

Snyder begins his story in 1988 with the election of Governor Patrocinio González Blanco, a Chiapas native who spent most of his life in the high-level circles of Mexico City's technocratic elite and was a close friend of Carlos Salinas. After serving in several important posts, including head of Banamex (the national bank), González returned to Chiapas as governor with the goal of "reconciling a [neoliberal] economic strategy that benefited a narrow segment of the population with the imperative of mobilizing political support and preserving stability in order to maintain the momentum of his career trajectory" (203). Ultimately, this contradictory imperative would constitute his political death sentence as well as the logic behind the immolation of landholders' interests.

As governor, González promoted a neoliberal economic agenda in Chiapas, facilitating the expansion of large-scale transnational agribusiness expansion in the Soconusco, pushing new exports such as flowers, melons, and macadamia nuts, and championing tourism as a new foundation for the state's economy. At the same time, while cultivating a favorable investment climate, González also worked to provide the peasant sector with a (minimal) buffer against the worst impacts of neoliberal restructuring. Corn, the peasants' lifeblood, was dismissed as "the crop of failure" (quoted in Snyder 2001:209), but Chiapas's poorest *could* be incorporated as contract farmers, hired hands, and hotel help in the state's "new economy." These efforts to include peasants in the neoliberal project met with dismal results, Snyder concludes, but, more importantly for our purposes, they also produced few benefits for landed elites, despite González's pro-landowner rhetoric.

In 1992 Carlos Salinas appointed González minister of the interior and named Chilón's favorite son, Elmar Setzer, interim governor. Elmar Setzer (Carlos Setzer's brother) had gone further and higher in national politics than any previous member of Chilón's landed elite, and Chiloneros' eyes were upon him as he took the sash of office. In the short run, Chiloneros hoped, Setzer would restore much-deserved support to coffee and cattle production, and in the long run might represent Chiloneros' interests at an even higher level. Roberto Trujillo explained that, as head of the powerful Interior Ministry, González was presidential timber (*presidenciable*), and consequently his confederate Setzer "might one day have been a minister himself, maybe even minister of agriculture!" During his brief term, Setzer did initiate a failed program to steer the benefits of economic restructuring of the coffee sector toward the traditional landed oligarchy, but the Zapatista uprising decisively extinguished both the careers of González and Setzer and Chiloneros' hopes for a return to "production." Within months of the uprising both politicians resigned in disgrace (despite the fact that they had warned Salinas of the danger of a guerrilla offensive in southern Mexico). By the summer of 1994 it was clear that the careers of González and Setzer would not be the only casualties of the Zapatista uprising. In the face of widespread invasions and rural unrest, coffee growers and cattle ranchers would provide the land needed to restore calm to the countryside. "Maybe Setzer would have used an iron fist against the invaders, but the new guy . . ." Roberto Trujillo mused, "nothing!"

In the years following 1994, the two-pronged strategy of social liberalism took even stronger hold. On one hand, the conflict increased the flow of money in Chiapas intended to purchase rural peace. These projects, like the 1997 Agricultural Development Program launched in northern Chiapas and Chilón, which strove to "ensure food self-sufficiency through the cultivation of corn, beans, and backyard animals" (Governor Ruiz Ferro quoted in *La Jornada*, Sept. 20, 1997), targeted sagging peasant production, but rarely included larger landowners in their benefits. On the other hand, successive governors strove to forge a new economy for the state, one that was based on neither peasants' "crops of failure" nor landowners' crony capitalism. Fondo Chiapas, inaugurated in 1994, for example, backed by a who's who list of Mexico's most powerful financial and industrial elite, drew investment into the state's tourism, timber, and bioprospecting industries (Pólito Barrios 2000). The Cancún-based hotel magnate Enrique Molina, a backer of Fondo Chiapas, expressed the will of these neoliberal power brokers: "The Chiapas conflict has become more and more of an obstacle to the takeoff of the Mexican economic project. . . . For that reason, we businessmen and investors have decided to participate in the Fondo Chiapas and act in cooperation with the federal and local governments to pose development against instability and belligerence" (quoted in Pólito Barrios 2000:66). While the Fondo Chiapas itself may have fallen short of expectations,[15] landowners' fall from grace was complete. No longer forces of production, they represent simply another contributor to Chiapas's deep-seated instability and belligerence — not engines of national development but obstacles to it.

Explaining the Betrayal of Production

For Chilón's landowners, the challenge posed by these remarkable changes in Chiapan politics was not to understand shifting class alliances and other abstract questions of political science but rather to grapple with the immediate betrayal of production as it infiltrated all aspects of life. Seen through the lens of production, the agricultural practices that indígenas introduced to former estates seemed irrational. The swidden landscape of rotating milpas and scrub looked like an empty wasteland. Even stranger, after seizing ladino properties, indigenous land invaders were said to have destroyed the very stuff of production. Ruperto Monterrosa was not the only ladino who could not understand why the invaders destroyed the equipment they found on the land they invaded.

Landowners could easily fit indigenous behavior into old racial arguments about "cultures of production," but the government's actions after 1994, although clearly related to the politics of appeasement, were harder to pin down. "The system doesn't want progressive agriculture anymore," Eulalio Hernández argued. "If it did, it would have protected us — the people who *really produce.*" Carlos Cañas lamented, "There's no support for improving production anymore. Any government production program exists just to calm the [peasants] down." Naturally, in landowners' accounts, the state's politicized welfare approach articulated with the inherent idleness of indígenas: "Once the indígenas get their [government] check, they get in line to buy Maseca [a brand of ready-made cornmeal] instead of producing it themselves." With this unhappy combination of state paternalism and indigenous indolence, the wholesale abandonment of the project of national production and food self-sufficiency was complete. For landowners, the state chose politics over production, and the erosion of security and support represented the collateral damage of this ill-conceived decision.

As landowners struggled to understand the reasons behind this seemingly nonsensical shift in state policy away from "real producers," many of them turned to conspiracy theories to explain the incomprehensible. Narcotics and strategic mineral reserves populated these stories, serving as proxies for the transition from an agricultural economy based on traditional products (coffee and cattle) to a new, less easily defined "neoliberal" economy. Carlos Setzer, for one, began with shadowy "international financial interests" and Chiapas's rich petroleum and uranium reserves: "Of course Ruiz [the radical Catholic bishop of San Cristóbal] is in league with international financial interests. Together they provoked the Zapatista uprising to destabilize Chiapas enough so it would want to secede from Mexico. When it was a little country of its own, the mineral rights wouldn't belong to Mexico and it would be much easier for foreigners to come in and take them."

Then his story changed course: "Actually another factor is that the drug traffickers needed a halfway point between Colombia and the United States to refuel their planes, and the Lacandón jungle was the perfect place. You know a plane once whisked Raúl Salinas from Tuxtla to the jungle. What was that all about? And another time a plane crashed in the jungle and guess whose it was? The bald guy's [Carlos Salinas's] sister. You put the rest together."

Both forks of Setzer's story deployed plot elements common throughout Mexican popular culture, including the specter of imperialism and high-level collaboration between federal officials and drug traffickers. Yet, by highlighting the shift from "real" production to the shadowy interests of transnational actors, Setzer has grasped something critical about neoliberal restructuring in Mexico, but in a way that has important consequences: in his effort to explain the conflict of 1994 without admitting his own involvement in it or conceding that he may not be all that important to the nation as a producer, Setzer painted the conflict as something larger than he, something far beyond his control. This sense that the conflict was too big, its real sources too difficult to understand or control, echoed through most Chiloneros' discussions of their response to invasions. "Before the nineties we *would* defend our land," Paco Vera told me. "In 1994 the conflict was too big. . . . We didn't defend our land . . . because . . . the conflict was something bigger than us."

In short, after 1994 landowners found themselves positioned in the nation in new ways by a new imaginary of national development. Shifts in state policy meant that once-reliable support for landowner territoriality would not be forthcoming. This was more than a tactical lapse. Worked through the complex field of production, these changes left landowners flailing for new ways to position themselves in the nation and deeply convinced that the conflict was not manageable and that resistance was doomed to failure. Landowners' changing understandings of their relations with their indigenous neighbors reinforced this drift toward resignation and quiescence.

Geographies of Fear,
Spaces of Quiescence

The men had the drawn look that comes of protecting an over-extended acreage. — Bruce Chatwin, *In Patagonia*

Imaginative geographies cannot be understood as the . . . fully coherent projections of all-knowing subjects. It is necessary to find ways to interrogate the unconscious and to explore the multiple spatialities inscribed within the geographical imaginary; these inclusions created analytical openings for the contradictions that are contained within (often contained by) dominant constellations of power, knowledge, and geography. — Derek Gregory, "Imaginative Geographies"

In 1848, during an abortive indigenous uprising, thirty ladino families fled Chilón for the relative safety of Palenque. In a poem written later that year, the landowner José Maríano Arévalo mocked those who fled:

> . . . poor little ladinos
> who, for fear of *indios,*
> go carrying their children
> crying along the roads . . .[1]

In disparaging the refugees' fears, Arévalo expressed one of the central axes of uncertainty in landowner identity: the tension between a deep-seated image of themselves as bearers of paternal authority and macho fearlessness and an equally entrenched awareness of existing as a small racial minority surrounded and outnumbered by a rapidly growing and frequently hostile indigenous population. This ontological sense of siege was ultimately spatial. It was a geographical imaginary of fear that, in tension with other forces and imaginaries, shaped landowners' calculations of the risks of violent action. Landowners' geographical imaginary of fear — always present but usually managed and tamed — took on a formative role after 1994.

Imaginative geographies, as I conceive of them, are not mental maps or environmental perceptions, but rather the concrete entanglements of knowledge (representations of space) and power (Gregory 1995, Said 1978). That is, my use of geographical imaginaries highlights the dialectical connections between representation of space and the workings of hegemony. In the particular circumstances in which landowners found themselves, their attempts to place the savage Other on a grid of geographic legibility, rather than reducing the indígenas to humble docility in the face of their power, produced fear, uncertainty, and contradictions.

Connections between capitalist exploitation on estates and subaltern terror are both intuitively obvious and well studied (Gordillo 2002b; Edelman 1994; Taussig 1986, 1980). That relatively powerful agents of capitalist exploitation may also experience collective fear of those they dominate is perhaps less obvious, but the phenomenon has not gone unnoticed (Stoler 1995a, Orlove 1994, Taussig 1984). This collective experience of fear is deeply rooted in the production of space. Chiloneros' fear of indigenous violence after 1994 arose out of particular historical representations of geography, and in turn played a key role in remaking the spaces of landed production.[2]

For more than a century, landowners' fears of indigenous "savagery" — fears that reflected particular configurations of space and were themselves inscribed in space — formed part of their taken-for-granted experience of the world. This habitual unease took on new shapes and meanings and authorized different practices as historical conditions changed, but it was always present in landowners' lives. For most of the twentieth century, paternalistic social relations on estates — understood as ways of knowing and controlling indigenous workers — created physical and mental spaces of safety in a world of hostile Indians. For landowners, indígenas' displays of respect served as embodied proof of the existence of these spaces of safety. Thus the end of indigenous respect, as perceived by landowners after 1994, represented a critical transgression of the intimate and safe spaces of estate geography. After 1994, that geography of danger radiated out from the indigenous town of Bachajón to the roads that landowners used to reach their estates, into communities of once-loyal workers, and into landowners' own bodies. Ultimately, this geography of danger shaped landowners' calculations of the costs and benefits of resisting agrarian conflict through two articulations: first, in a context of declining state support, fear shaped landowners' calculations of the economic viability of estate agriculture; and second, fear shaped the patterns and trajectories of generational change in Chilón. Together these articulations between fear, economic crisis, and generational change made violent responses to land invasions seem impossible and pointless.

Constructions of Indigenous Savagery

You don't look back along time but down through it like water. Sometimes this comes to the surface, sometimes that, sometimes nothing. Nothing goes away. — Margaret Atwood, *Cat's Eye*

Near the edge of Chilón, in a rough adobe building on the bank of the Río Chanoa, Ofelia Jiménez runs a small dry goods store. The daughter of Isidro Jiménez, a landowner and politician, Doña Ofelia remained closely connected to Las Delicias, the family's estate, until invaders seized it in 1994. Today her shop, with its stock of candles, soap, fabric, and staple foods, caters mainly to indigenous peasants — occasionally even the same people who now till her family's land. Twice during our conversation, Doña Ofelia's husband speaks Tzeltal as he attends customers. He greets each one with a combination of familiarity and distance, laughing and joking, but holding tightly to a core of condescension and disapproval. The peasants shuffle and smile with downcast eyes that flicker between self-deprecation and hate. They are intimate enemies, grown comfortable with each other's presence, but always watching, always wary.

Doña Ofelia's words resonate with this tension as well. She refers to the invaders as *la indiada*[3] — an antique moniker, evoking eighteenth- and nineteenth-century uprisings, which lumps indígenas in an indistinguishable and overtly threatening mass. Yet she also reveals that the invaders were resident workers, descendants of her childhood playmates, families bound to the Jiménez family by decades of service and ties of compadrazgo.

> Bobrow-Strain: What organization were the invaders from?
>
> Jiménez: Well, I don't know really . . . it was la indiada.
>
> Bobrow-Strain: But did you know them? Where were they from?
>
> Jiménez: They were the same people who worked on the ranch for years, had their milpas on the ranch. They were good people. They took off their hats to let us pass [when we walked by], but then they became aggressive. Before they were friendly, they had respect for the patrón, they asked him for a little piece of land for milpas and he gave it to them because they did him service. . . . Then they changed.
>
> Bobrow-Strain: How did they change?
>
> Jiménez: It had to be that they changed, because my brother gave the same treatment as my father had, all the same benefits. There's no respect now.
>
> Bobrow-Strain: How do they show their lack of respect?
>
> Jiménez: It's their attitude, the way they raise their voices [to us]. Point guns at us.

For Doña Ofelia this transformation of respectful indígenas into a gun-wielding indiada was sudden, accomplished in the instant of invasion. Like most Chiloneros, she believed, up to the very moment when the news of invasion reached her through a still-loyal worker, that invasions happened to other people — people who lacked good relations with "their Indians." A long historical view contradicts at every turn this cardinal principle of ladino discourse. Changes *were* sudden — the terrains of respect and paternal authority gave way in a terrifying and seismic manner in 1994 — but slow tectonic shifts over the years had made that cataclysm possible. I do, however, take seriously the subjective experience of being blindsided by rapid and incomprehensible change. If we are to understand this experience of a world turned upside down, we must first explore the categories and practices through which the "old" ordered world was constructed.

A Most Unbaptized People

"You've heard the saying '*Bachajontecos* are born killers,' haven't you? Well, it's true," the man says, shaking his head to emphasize the horrors conjured by his words. I *had* heard the saying. Sayings and stories about the violent nature of Tzeltals from Bachajón circulate widely in the region. Don Roberto once joked, "If there was Olympic fencing with machetes, the Bachajontecos would win. They have so much practice they can take a head off with one stroke. Sometimes they can make it fly off into the air!"

So the man's comment came as no surprise. What caught my attention was that this time the story was told by a Jesuit priest based in Bachajón who was a tireless champion of indígenas in their struggles against ladinos. Unlike Don Roberto, whose exoticization of Bachajontecos' violence stresses the line that divides the civilized ladinos and the barbaric indígenas, the priest turned his understanding of indigenous violence into a lesson on resistance to injustice. "Because Bachajontecos are so fierce," he continued, "finqueros in Chilón managed to establish fincas only around the edges of the ejido; they couldn't completely take the land away."

The Tzeltal political boss Manuel Jiménez Navarro also evoked images of Bachajontecos' supposed savagery, this time to connect contemporary mobilizations with a primordial warrior tradition: "In order to understand the struggles here in Chilón today, we should begin five hundred years ago, when this was *Mayan* land," he began, shifting to the edge of his chair.

> In those days there were two groups of indígenas here, the Reds and the Whites. The names were not because of the color of their bodies, those are simply the names they had. But the Reds and the Whites began to fight because the Reds ate the Whites' children if they caught them. And they couldn't live like that losing children all the time. That was when Bachajón received its name. Before that it was called Muk'ulum, "Big town." [But then] the people said, "Let's fight! Let's fight!" and the other people said, "Who am I? Am I not a man? Can I not fight?" and the other people said, "Who am I? Am I not a man? Can I not fight?" And that's where the name Bachajón came from: "Who am I?" "¿Machajón?" in Tzeltal was what they said before they fought. When the Spanish came they changed it to Bachajón.

In Chilón, as these examples suggest, the ingrained violence of Bachajontecos is a taken-for-granted notion that articulates with and shapes multiple political projects, bobbing up and down in the sea of history. We can trace one thread of this discourse — ladinos' historical constructions of indigenous savagery — by watching its importance to ladinos' constructions of self and Other rise and fall with changes in social, political, and economic conditions.

One afternoon in 2001, Don Roberto and I were passing time over coffee discussing rumors of a possible attempt by indigenous peasants to forcefully expel ladinos from the town of Sitalá. Eventually our conversation turned to Chilón, where, despite ladinos' strong grip on municipal authority, they have also faced recurring fears of being driven out by indígenas. As recently as the late 1970s, indígenas expelled ladinos from numerous towns, including Bachajón. During this period, ladinos across north-central Chiapas spent many nights holding nervous armed vigils against possible attack. At one point in his account of that fear-ridden period, Don Roberto looked at me gravely through a haze of cigarette smoke: "You know there was even a time when the indígenas came and slaughtered all the mestizos in Chilón while they were in church. They say there was blood seven millimeters deep across the whole church floor that time." Stunned, I managed to blurt out, "When was that?" Nothing in my research thus far had turned up an event like this during the 1970s. Don Roberto clarified, "Oh, that was during the 1770s or sometime around then."

In fact, the year was 1712, during the feast of the Santísima Trinidad, when hundreds of enraged Tzeltals descended on Chilón, killing most of its nonindigenous residents. Colonial accounts of the massacre—an early incident in a broader uprising that eventually spread through most of north-central Chiapas (Viqueira 1997, Gosner 1992)—describe the scene in dry, almost clinical language.[4] By the late nineteenth century, however, ladinos had transformed the events into a bloody melodrama. Writing in the wake of the caste war that inflamed Chiapas in 1868, Vicente Pineda (1888:6) used the 1712 massacre to graphically illustrate his call for civilizing Chiapas's indigenous population to "avoid forever the disturbances, irreparable evils, and barbaric horrors that accompany race wars." Pineda, whose nephew Alberto would lead landowners' violent campaigns against indigenous communities during the Revolution, offered a vivid account of the day laced with gore and pathos: mothers beg futilely for their children's lives and worshipers die clutching the altar before the Tzeltals turn to looting and drinking.

With ladinos' settlements in the region increasingly pressing against Bachajón's communal lands, the town also figures in accounts written by foreign travelers, including John Stephens in the 1830s (1996 [1843]) and Frans Blom in the 1920s (Blom and La Farge 1926–1927). These accounts provide evidence that as early as the mid–nineteenth century, tales of the Bachajontecos' violent nature circulated through north-central Chiapas. Neither Stephens nor Blom spent much time in Bachajón, yet both formed remarkably strong opinions about the character of the town and its people. Thus, while no proof is available, one suspects that the two foreign writers formed their images of Bachajón largely in conversation with ladinos in Ocosingo before passing through the town, or while resting afterward with the few "intelligent white men" of Chilón. These memoirs and literary examples are offered, then, as a proxy for ladino constructions of "the Bachajonteco."

While John Stephens must have experienced numerous harrowing moments during his trek through some of nineteenth-century Mesoamerica's most remote landscapes, he makes particular note of the "notoriously bad character" of Indians between Ocosingo and Chilón. After a seven-hour march from Ocosingo, Stephens and his company (which "had no dragoons . . . upon whom we could rely") nervously entered Bachajón:

> At three o'clock, moving in a north-northwest direction, we entered the village of [Bachajón], standing in an open situation surrounded by mountains, and peopled entirely by Indians, wilder and more savage that any we had yet seen. The men were without hats, but wore their long black hair reaching to their shoulders; and the old men and women, with harsh and haggard features and dark rolling eyes, had a most unbaptized appearance. They gave us no greetings, and their wild but steady glare made us feel a little nervous. . . . We had some misgivings when we put the village behind us, and felt ourselves enclosed in the country of wild Indians. We stopped an hour near a stream, and at half past six arrived at Chilón where, to our surprise and pleasure, we found a sub-prefect, a white man, and intelligent, who had traveled to San Salvador and knew General Morazán. (Stephens 1996:221–222)

Some eighty years later, Frans Blom and his companions, marching in the opposite direction, were also reluctant to stray from the civilized zones of Chilón. In a cliffhanger ending to Volume 1 of the expedition's report, Blom contemplated the journey that lay ahead: "Reluctantly we left our friendly host [in Chilón]. . . . Ahead of us lay the mountains, valleys, rivers, and bad trails. The road led right through the country of the Bachajón, feared by most Mexicans in these parts of the world" (Blom and La Farge 1926–1927, 1:237).

When the group finally reached the infamous village, the experienced Chiapas explorer-scholar Blom reported that the Indians of Bachajón were "by far the least pleasant Indians with whom we had to deal. They are drunken, revengeful, and murderous. The murders, usually sudden outbursts of a long-nursed feud, are sometimes so appallingly brutal that one would think them committed by an abnormal or degenerate people" (2:329). In the end, however, Blom, who passed more time observing and photographing the Bachajontecos than the itinerant Stephens had done, developed a more nuanced impression of the town's character. He concludes that despite their murderous outbursts and ill treatment of travelers, the Bachajontecos "are not a cruel people" (2:330), and even begins to contextualize their attitudes in light of harsh treatment by ladinos. Nevertheless, Blom's and Stephens's accounts share an important element. Both heighten their evocation of fear by mapping the Bachajontecos' savagery on a spatial grid. Bachajón serves as a physical barrier between civilization and barbarism, a space through which ladinos must pass physically in order to reach the rest of Chiapas and mentally in order to maintain domination.

Reforming Indians, Taming Terror

By the 1960s, the short run of *Horizontes* (a regional newspaper written and published by young ladino merchants and landowners, including Miguel Utrilla) provides evidence of another current of ladino discourse on indigenous savagery. Once again focused on Bachajontecos, this current emerged out of a very different place than its predecessor; not out of fear but from a relaxed and confident space of paternal authority. Stitching together elements of Mexican *indigenismo* with the easy manner of those accustomed to dealing with subordinates, *Horizontes*'s reporting on Bachajón simultaneously exoticizes Bachajontecos and expresses paternal concern about indígenas' violence. Descriptions of decapitated corpses, organs pulled from living bodies, and mysterious multiple homicides in Bachajón pepper *Horizontes*'s pages, but unlike Stephens or Blom, these writers express little concern for their own safety. Linked to witchcraft, internecine feuds, and rampant alcoholism, violence in Bachajón was constructed outside the realm of ladinos' immediate concern — a pathology native to and contained in Bachajón.[5] For the most part, despite a few strong statements about bloodthirsty killings, violence in "the ejidos without laws" was largely represented as a pitiable thing, evoking the question: What should *we* do to save our peasants from themselves? Jesuit priests from the mission at Bachajón were ladinos' chief ally in this effort to discipline the wild Bachajontecos.[6]

In a special issue of *Horizontes* celebrating the Jesuit mission's tenth anniversary in 1969, Miguel Utrilla and the newspaper's staff praised the priests for their noble work of "elevating the indígenas" through a transformation of consciousness that lifted them "out of the darkness of an immense forgetting": "As is well known, Bachajón used to be one of those towns that remain forgotten, home to only poverty and age-old rancor among the Aboriginals. . . . [The missionaries'] efforts, however, have in large part changed the attitudes of the humble indigenous inhabitants of this region" (*Horizontes*, March 10, 1969).

A front-page photo of Fr. Mardonio Morales and a smiling peasant illustrated this change. Its caption read: "The Jesuit attends a native peasant of Bachajón who, with his white clothing and hat and confident smile, is irrefutable evidence of a healthy race firmly directed toward the road to progress." Bachajontecos were not yet on the road to progress, but at least, under the benevolent Jesuits' guidance, they were headed in the right direction. Unlike those aggressive Bachajontecos of legend, the man in this photo wears a white hat, thanks to the Jesuits' efforts. Through literacy, libraries, coffee cooperatives, and Bible study, ladinos believed, the Jesuits would smooth the Bachajontecos' rough edges. In a sense, then, what the *Horizontes* writings on the Jesuit mission present is a transfer of paternal burdens from patrones to padres. In language that reflects the increasing influence of indigenista ideology, Utrilla and his colleagues present the mission as a modernizing force, molding indigenous subjects into respectable citizens, divesting them of their "unbaptized" and violent heritage and trying to incorporate them into the life of the nation.[7]

In 1969 the Jesuits of Bachajón may have echoed this outlook, albeit with more emphasis on Christian faith, but fateful changes in the mission's theology were beginning to emerge. Fr. Mardonio Morales marks 1971 — two years after the mission's tenth anniversary celebration — as the watershed moment in his work. As we saw in chapter 6, in 1971, under the influence of liberation theology and with the support of an increasingly progressive diocese, the Jesuits began to train indigenous lay teachers (*catequistas*) who would spread political activism as well as the Gospel throughout the region. Explicitly addressing the concerns of debt-bound estate workers, the Jesuits translated Mexico's Agrarian Law into Tzeltal, and several years later indigenous representatives from the municipio of Chilón played a major role in organizing the pivotal Indigenous Congress of 1974, where Tzeltals affiliated with the mission forcefully denounced landowners' abusive treatment, exploitation, and expropriation of indigenous land.

What *Horizontes* heralded on March 10, 1969, as the Jesuits' "miracle in the jungle" was quickly taking on a decidedly sinister edge in the minds of ladino supporters. The Jesuits' efforts, along with the changing contours of Mexican politics, did more than transform indígenas' consciousness; they also challenged the carefully defended boundaries of estate social relations, and shook ladinos' confidence in the power of paternalism to contain agrarian conflict. Through the late 1970s ladinos' fear grew to fever pitch. Feeding off incidences of systematic expulsion of ladinos from neighboring towns and inflamed by peasant unrest at home, ladinos began to fear imminent assaults on both Chilón and Yajalón. Telegraph wires connecting Chilón and Tuxtla Gutiérrez buzzed with alarm: "NO POLICE COMPETENT TO PREVENT DISORDERS HERE IMPLORE YOU SEND PUBLIC SECURITY DETACHMENT" and "URGENT PLEA FOR MILITARY INTERVENTION AT THIS LOCATION."[8] As José López Arévalo recalled, "There were expulsions of ladinos in Petalcingo and Bachajón. I remember that the townspeople in Yajalón were terrified. They'd post guards all over town. It was an armed fortress, and you had to give secret knocks to get into people's houses. They were all barricaded inside with guns. People thought an ethnic war was inevitable."

Ultimately, neither Chilón nor Yajalón came under attack in the late 1970s and early 1980s, but as we saw in chapter 6, these struggles and the ways the Mexican state responded to them set the stage for the eventual undoing of landed production in 1994. Indigenous militants shook ladinos to the core in the 1970s and 1980s; invading not just the ladinos' lands but also their minds and sense of security. To many observers the image of heavily armed ladinos standing guard at the entrances to their town and the doors of their homes confirmed a conception of landowners as powerful and violent. Yet the scene may also be understood as evidence of indigenous people's ongoing ability to produce "chords of exotic terror . . . in the chit-chat of a jungle night" (Taussig 1984:491). Most importantly, however, the scares of the late 1970s and early 1980s brought material changes in landowners' lives. In particular, growing insecurity in the countryside prompted many landowners to move into the relative safety of towns. Thus landowners' fears played a formative role in shaping the trajectories of economic change and remaking the spaces of landed production in Chilón, initiating a gradual disengagement from agricultural production that would intensify after 1994, when chords of exotic terror sounded ominously once again.

Respeto and the Spaces of Safety

Despite the dangerous spirits that have plagued Chiloneros' imaginations, most managed to prosper and maintain a fairly strong grip on both their fears and "their Indians." As we have seen, assassinations, lynchings, house burnings, and beatings played key roles in maintaining landowners' hegemony. Wielding political and legal authority along with increasingly sophisticated weaponry, ladinos defended their towns, homes, and estates against assault by indígenas. When necessary, they lobbied for and often won state support for their heavy-handed efforts. But hegemony also worked through the more subtle practices of estate social relations. Through ritual gift giving, rolling debt, corporal punishment, spatial isolation, financial incentives, liquor, baptismal parties, and mutual protection in times of conflict, landowners and peasants forged forms of knowledge and subjectivity through which the ladinos' domination operated. Estate social relations constituted sovereign *patrones* and docile *peones* as mutually intelligible subjects bound by ties of asymmetrical reciprocity. These intimate relations not only underpinned the economics of estate agriculture but also constructed a zone of material and symbolic safety for landowners.

Landowners' understandings of the respect accorded them by indígenas are central to both the constructions and transgressions of this cognitive safety zone. For landowners, the practice of respeto — shuffling feet, downcast eyes, submissive tones, and expressions of gratitude for landowners' largesse — stood as the primary outward manifestation of the natural order of the universe, both confirmation and affirmation of proper social relations.

In Fausto Trujillo's novel *El sacrificio de Isac,* Agar, an elderly indigenous woman, gives voice to ladinos' nostalgia for this natural order in an impassioned speech to her patrón:

"Before, at religious services we would pray aloud for the Lord to protect the Patrón, to give him strength, health, and prosperity, because our strength, health, and prosperity depend on his. . . . As long as the Patrón was happy, we were happy; poor but happy; we had work, food, a little clothing, and even some little parties. . . . You are a good Patrón and we have to give thanks to God for that every day. You give us good land for our milpas, you give us work, you take care of us when we're sick or take us to the hospital, you advance us money when we need it. Us? What do we give you? . . . Our worries don't go past being able to provide food for our three children, but you have to worry about twenty families that depend on this ranch."

This passage is a fantasy, but it is a fantasy that for generations provided a coherent framework — a dyad of patrón and peón, parent and child — through which ladinos and to some extent their indigenous workers could understand each other. According to this framework, landowners shouldered the heavy burden of providing land, livelihood, and security for their Indians. As Delio Ballinas complained, "Having peones involved a lot of responsibility. If they got sick you had to take them to the doctor and pay for medicines. When a woman got pregnant, which seemed like about twice a year, more medical expenses."

In return, landowners received the respect due them: grateful peons (like Trujillo's fictional Agar) acted out their subordination with their shuffling feet, downcast eyes, doffed hats, and ritual gifts of produce placed at the landowner's doorstep. They were the "good people" Ofelia Jiménez so fondly remembered, the ones who "took off their hats and let us pass."

Loyal peasants also quite literally provided safety for the landowner, as Fausto remembers from his childhood: "The indígenas guarded the patrón and his possessions." And stories of landowners saved from violence by loyal peasants circulate widely in Chilón, providing critical "evidence" of good relations between ladinos and their indigenous neighbors. Fausto's sister Eugenia says her "father always treated them well. Never treated them harshly or used bad words. When he had to get them to do something, he asked nicely. So the workers protected him and they protected all of us because we were his children. . . . They would warn him if there were rumors of trouble. Tell him not to go out to the ranch that day because something bad could happen." During my time in Chilón, I saw this early-warning system in action when former residents of Benjamin Trujillo's estate walked to town to alert Don Roberto of the possible invasion of his ranch.

Loyal peasants were expected not only to warn their patrón of impending conflict but even to repel invaders. As early as 1933, land reform documents noted that estate workers in Chilón "defended [estate land] as if it were their own,"[9] and loyal peasants were beaten or threatened when they defended properties during the invasions of 1994–1998. Thus, one of the most unsettling aspects of the invasions of 1994 for landowners was the widespread failure of this trusted system. In ladinos' stories, the failure of loyal peasants to warn landowners of danger and to respect their masters' property serves as a critical marker of the difference between current troubles and older conflicts. During the invasions of the 1980s, Carlos Cañas explained, most invaders came from other estates, and even those peasants who dared to invade their own workplace "still had quite a bit of respect for property owners. They didn't come anywhere near the *casco* [the center of the estate where the owner's house and outbuildings were located]. They stayed respectfully on the edges. [But] in the 1990s, they attacked the casco itself, turning out the landowner, destroying property."

Indeed, no question pushed landowners into more mental contortions than that of why, after 1994, supposedly loyal workers would betray their benefactors. When Eugenia Trujillo praised her workers' long connection to her family, I asked her whether she knew any of the invaders and whether she had spoken with them about why they had invaded her family's property. "I did," she responded, "and they told me they were forced to do it by troublemakers from Bachajón; that if they didn't take part in the invasion, they'd lose their own land. I told them that no one could do that to them because they had all their papers in order. But they thought they had no choice."

Eugenia Trujillo took this betrayal in stride, largely because most of her workers' aggression was directed at her neighbor Carlos Setzer, not at her. Another former landowner was less sanguine:

> Anonymous landowner: We still see [the invaders here in town] and I want to strangle them when I see them. Some of them act like nothing happened and say, "Good morning, Don ——," but it's very hard to forget what they did to us. Sometimes they even come into the pharmacy to ask for medicine and I tell them, "We don't have that," even if we do.

Bobrow-Strain: It sounds like these are people you knew well.

Anonymous landowner: Some were even my godchildren, and they still come by the house saying, "Hello, Godfather," like nothing happened, but I can't forget what they did.

Fausto Trujillo tells a story that for him crystallizes the tragic shift from respect to aggression: Sometime in the early 1990s, he attended a party thrown by estate workers. In the course of a night of drinking and dancing he took off his jacket and laid it aside. As the party was winding down, he could not find his jacket. Someone had taken it. "That would never have happened before," he lamented. "The indígenas guarded the patrón's body and his possessions." In the past, he said, after he had attended a party as an honored guest, "a long procession of indigenous workers would lead me home, to make sure I got home OK. The night my jacket got stolen, I was left to find my own way home in the dark. It was subtle changes like that that I noticed. . . . Gradually the distance between us grew until finally, in 1994, we [ladinos] were the enemy."

In conversation after conversation, ladinos reflected on the unraveling of respect: the indígenas don't ask ladinos to act as godparents anymore, they no longer trust employers' informal records of debts and wages. An old intimacy founded on inequality has broken down. Ofelia Jiménez complained, "Now they think they're equal and want to be the owners of the land and the town. . . . Now there are indígenas I know who come into town and won't even talk to me."

Regardless of how landowners attempt to explain and rationalize the behavior of land invaders, at the core of their efforts is a realization that old assumptions about the nature of indigenous people no longer hold. And always when indígenas come unmoored from frameworks of knowledge that tame and domesticate them, the specter of savagery looms. And the danger was not just the loss of a favorite jacket. The sudden unraveling of respeto after 1994 represented more than a shift in the social order; it signified the violent unraveling of rentier territoriality. "Before, the people were humble, they had respect," Gabino Vera mourned, caricaturing peasant posture by bowing his head and shuffling. "Now they go around threatening people with their machetes."

How did this perceived shift from familiar docile peons to an incomprehensible and aggressive mob shape ladinos' responses to agrarian conflict? How did fear shape the contours of quiescence?

Generations of Fear, Economies of Terror:
The Making of Agrarian Change in Chilón

The Tzeltal town of Bachajón had always cut off Chilón from the rest of the state, symbolically and sometimes physically limiting landowners' passage through the region. After 1994, this geography of danger overflowed the bounds of Bachajón and penetrated the intimate spaces of landowners' highways, estates, and homes.

Calvary of a Landowner

Wenceslao López remembered February 1994 as a time of waiting, a time of watching, as one by one his friends' properties succumbed to invaders. He remembered a night spent with rifle and pistol on his lap, listening to the sounds of invaders drifting across his pastures as they celebrated their occupation of a neighboring ranch. When invaders finally came to López's property, his wife, Deyanira, was doing laundry. She took over the story:

> I was all alone on the ranch, with just one boy [servant]. He saw the invaders coming down below and came running, yelling, "Nana, Nana, here come the invaders!" I had been washing clothes that morning. Down the hill, I saw that the invaders had put up some kind of white flag and a sign that said something like "No trespassing. This ranch is invaded and the government will support us." Something like that that conveyed the idea that the ranch was now theirs. My husband came back from Yajalón around ten or eleven [a.m.] and walked up to the house, followed by all of them with their rifles and machetes. He said, "Why don't you come in and talk?" and they said, "No, we have this paper that shows the ranch is ours, we've taken over the ranch."

Later that week, López returned to the ranch with an escort of loyal workers armed with machetes, hoping to salvage cattle and equipment. As they neared the ranch, Wenceslao says, the son of another loyal worker warned them that they were walking into an ambush. López turned back and shortly thereafter received a message at his house in Yajalón, saying "that if we ever came back to the ranch, they'd kill us."

López took the threat seriously. Earlier that month, invaders kidnapped and tortured López's nearest neighbor, Efraín Vera:

They first made Efraín carry sand and rocks up a steep hill on his ranch to where they had made their camp as a punishment. They hit him with sticks as he went up the hill until he got to a post they had stuck in the ground. They took off his clothes, cut off his hair, and then tied him to the post. One after another, the men took turns urinating on him. After he had been under the sun for hours he asked for water and the leader said, "Wouldn't you rather have *pozol?*" and Efraín said he would. So then the leader took pozol and mixed it with water in a dirty boot and Efraín said he wouldn't drink the pozol. After he said that, the men forced the pozol down his throat, using sticks to hold his mouth open. Then they said, "So you want water," and untied him from the pole. They tied his hands and feet like a pig, and told him to crawl to the river, which was a few hundred yards away. At the edge of the river they shoved him in and he started to drown because his hands and feet were tied. Finally they pulled him out. Some people who had seen all of this happening told Efraín's son, who came to get his father. The invaders demanded 2,000 pesos, which the son got from the bank in Yajalón, and they released Efraín.

Efraín Vera's own account of the kidnapping was more restrained. He spoke about the events hesitantly and with great difficulty: "They grabbed me because I knocked down a house they'd built on the ranch and they were mad about that. They took me to [another landowner's invaded property] and held me there for a day, tied up on the patio." Eventually he confessed that the invaders forced him to carry wooden planks up a steep road and that his son paid 200 pesos for his release. Mostly, though, he remained distant, quietly repeating: "I felt death there."

I didn't press Vera for a detailed account or seek his captors' version; in the end, there is no such thing as a "true" war story. Whether Vera's son paid a ransom of 200 or 2,000 pesos or whether Vera really was forced to drink pozol from a dirty boot mattered less to me than the ways his story circulated and the ways it shaped other Chiloneros' practices.

Nearly every Chilonero I met mentioned Vera's trials. While the accounts of the kidnapping varied somewhat, they all retained two common elements. First, they had the narrative structure of the Calvary story: a man is stripped of clothing and forced to carry his own cross up a hill. And second, they all share a fascination with themes of shoes and shoelessness. Efraín Vera's friend Hermenegildo Vera, for example, placed great emphasis on shoelessness in his account: "They made him take off his *shoes*. It was horrible. He had to take off his shoes and carry rocks from one place to another." These two themes suggest that Vera's story exerted a powerful influence over Chiloneros, not simply because it evoked the threat of physical abuse but because it evoked the threat of a *particular kind of abuse* laden with class-charged meanings. As the anthropologist Mercedes Olivera, who worked with estate laborers in north-central Chiapas as a researcher and activist in the 1970s, pointed out, the tortures inflicted on landowners through-out the region after 1994 mirrored punishments and burdensome tasks doled out by generations of estate owners. In Tumbalá, Olivera re-called, invaders forced a barefoot landowner to haul stones needed to repair a road to the estate—echoing one of the most common unpaid tasks estate workers were obliged to perform on Saturdays. Chilón's landowners got the reference: a barefoot landowner forced to haul timber along a stony path was subjected not just to physical strains and abrasions but also to a complete inversion of race and class order. In a world in which shoes serve as a powerful marker of civilization, only peons and savages walk barefoot. Vera's story, as told by Chiloneros, reflects not just scarring physical violence against one of their own but also violence against the entire order of society.

Anxious Spaces

The word "fear," etymologically related to both "pirate" and "am-bush," has its origins in the Indo-European root *per*, meaning "to push forward," "to pass through." This deep affinity between fear and passage, terror and transit, is retained in Chiloneros' dread of the open road.

During the weeks that followed the first wave of land invasions in the spring of 1994, enraged members of Chilón's AGL drafted a list of bellicose demands. Not surprisingly, the letter, addressed to President Salinas and copied to seven other institutions, including the SRA, the Ministry of Defense, and the Supreme Court, demanded immediate evictions of all occupied properties, accusing Chilón's invaders of be-ing subversive opposition forces and "pseudo-PRIistas." Perhaps less surprisingly—especially given Chiapan landed elites' formidable repu-tation as the *agents* of rural violence—four of five of the AGL's de-mands reflected fears of violence against its members. The AGL called for (1) guaranteed security for every landowner, (2) "separation of the Bachajón ejidos from the municipio of Chilón, converting [Bachajón] into a free municipio and letting indigenous towns be governed by indigenous people," (3) "construction of a bypass around the town of Bachajón to avoid the danger of kidnappings and tortures of [people] who unfortunately have to pass through the only main street in that LAWLESS TOWN," and (4) installation of a military checkpoint in Bachajón.

Armed with a historical perspective on the genealogies of racial fear in Chilón, we cannot be surprised by the particular emphases of the AGL's demands. Bachajón had long stood as a material and symbolic barrier dividing Chilón's ladinos from the rest of Chiapas. One can easily imagine John Stephens pining for a road that would bypass Bachajón or a military checkpoint "in the country of wild Indians." But Bachajón's physical location was only one source of fear, as the geography of danger spilled out from the "lawless town" into the pores of ladino Chilón.

The AGL's demands rang hollow in the corridors of the state and federal governments. No bypass or checkpoint was ever established in Bachajón, and, far from administratively separating the two towns, authorities allowed indigenous elites from Bachajón to take the helm of Chilón's municipal government. Chiloneros' fears swelled, and in the months and years that followed, they repeatedly requested police and military protection from their indigenous neighbors. By 2000, with the passage of time and the restoration of relative calm in the countryside around Chilón, the hard edge of landowners' fear had softened somewhat. In 1998, however, fear was a constant undercurrent in Chiloneros' words and actions. "I have to carry a pistol now, there's no other option," one aging landowner told me in 1998. Then, mustering a bit of bravado, he said, "At least this way, when they take me, I'll take some of them with me. We all go armed here because it's not safe."

This fear was particularly evident in Chiloneros' discussions of travel. After surviving an attempted ambush in March 1994, Roberto Trujillo told me, he became convinced that defending the territoriality of landed production extended beyond the bounds of the estate and onto the rugged roads that connect estates to towns: "What good is it to evict invaders," he asked, "if you can never get to your farm safely?" Even worse, once-loyal workers no longer knew their place. Workers' transgressions of the boundaries of estate social relations struck at the core of landed production.

Landowner after landowner complained that this undermining of social-spatial order began "when the priests started to sow hatred among the indígenas."[10] Enrique Díaz Cancino, for example, directly connected church organizing, declining respeto, and widespread crime: "There was more respect before. Now the *naturales* think they're our equals because of the priests, who teach them to throw us out. But we're not responsible for what Hernán Cortés did, are we? Before there were no robberies, no vandalism like now. I even know of two indígenas who stole money from their own mothers — that's how bad things have gotten."

Like many landowners, Enrique Díaz credits priests with undermining the natural order of things, and, as Zygmunt Bauman cogently suggests, when people speak of order — particularly when they pine for lost order — they are referring not to "things as they are [but rather to] the ways of managing them; to the *capacity* of ordering . . . the disappearance of the means and know-how to *put things in order* and keep them there" (quoted in Spark 2001:56). Ultimately, landowners' explanations for the origins of indígenas' aggression provided little comfort on this front, inflaming rather than soothing landowners' awareness of the extent to which Chiapas's agrarian conflicts had exceeded their capacity to put things in order.

For Wenceslao López, this realization came when he watched the leader of the group that invaded his ranch smoking a cigarette with his feet propped up on the desk of the SRA official charged with negotiating a settlement. Samuel Rodríguez Sr. had a similar realization when he took his complaints of illegal invasion to a friend in the regional court. The friend told him, "I'll take your complaints because that's my job, but I'm also going to tell you as a friend not to have any illusions. I'm not going to follow through with these complaints at all." The friend, Rodríguez explained, "had received orders from high up: bury the complaints [*darles el carpetazo*]. Orders from higher up."

When the threat of violence looms, one's inability to put things in order and the increasing incomprehensibility of one's adversaries take on urgency and begin to shape actions. Thus, for many other landowners, the threat of indigenous violence weighed heavily on their response to invasion. One landowner, who admits that his family did evict invaders with the help of state police officers, complains that the effort was for nothing: The invaders — affiliated with the Aguilares paramilitary organization — were driven off the ranch, but they still keep close watch on the property. "One time," the young ex-rancher tells me, "[my father] went against everyone's advice and tried to harvest coffee [on the evicted property]. He barely escaped with his life from an ambush. . . . We can't go back to the ranch and we never will be able to."

When I asked landowners why they did not defend their properties against invasion, many of them expressed both age-old fear of indigenous savagery and new awareness of the futility of violent action:

> We started to buy arms, and we were ready. We had a much higher-caliber arsenal than the indígenas, who hardly had anything. The problem with them is that they come in huge groups. . . . The indígenas have no birth control so their numbers just keep on growing.

> Alfredo, Chamber, Efraín, all of them did try to defend themselves by scaring the indígenas, but there were too many. I told them that if they killed two or three, they still couldn't do anything against that swarm of fire ants.

> They attacked and tied up any workers that we sent to harvest coffee or work in the coffee groves. . . . We decided it wasn't worth the danger [to us] or to the workers, so we decided to sell.

> Before the nineties we *would* defend our land. In the Asociación [Ganadera] when we heard about an invasion that was about to happen, we'd all go together and defend that land. . . . In '94 no one got together to defend their ranches. The conflict was too big, and like anyone, we were afraid of bullets and death.

> We couldn't defend ourselves. There were too many. We would have been massacred. When you kill one indígena, a thousand more come.

Of course, many Chiloneros also pointed to economic decline and generational changes to justify their participation in government buyout programs. These factors played a formative role — some would suggest a determining role — in shaping landowners' responses to invasions. From this perspective, landowners' palpable fear and sense of futility could simply represent post hoc rationalizations for actions taken in response to threats to their economic interest. But economic viability and generational change cannot be separated from the experience of fear.

The Economy of Terror

In many cases participation in the land-purchase programs of 1994–1998 did suit landowners' economic interests, particularly given the declining profitability of agriculture and the waning interest of the younger generation in a life on the land. Nevertheless, it is a mistake — economism of the worst kind — to think that the true thread of class interest can be winnowed out from mystifications and social externalities. Rather, fear and the economic viability of estates constitute each other in important ways.

This can be most clearly seen in the articulations between insecurity and investment. Early in my fieldwork, I visited Paco Jiménez, a young landowner who raised cattle and feed crops in Palenque, some forty kilometers northeast of Chilón. As we turned off the highway into a neat 90-hectare sorghum field, Paco slumped at the wheel of his pickup. In the corner of the field, a handful of indigenous families were cutting down drought-burned plants and erecting small houses from scavenged lumber. Paco was young, educated at Mexico's elite Ibero-American University, and brimming with innovative ideas about modernizing his production. His quarter of this sorghum field was part of that plan. Now, as we approached the occupiers, he wavered between fury and despair. After a brief discussion with the new arrivals while I waited in the truck, Paco returned. For now, he told me, his investment was safe, but he was clearly shaken. They had initiated a land reform claim on a section of the field owned by a partner of Paco's who had agreed to sell. Paco's words echoed those of every other rancher I spoke with: "No one is going to invest in land with all the invasions. If they see your land nicely planted and taken care of, they'll decide to take it."

In Chilón, landowners' sense of suffering under a state of siege was even more palpable, and so are its effects on agriculture. Seemingly endless insecurity in the form of land invasions and more prosaic "weapons of the weak" (J. Scott 1985) deflated many ranchers' will to invest in production. In a context of agrarian struggle and the recognition that, in the last instance, property rights may be manipulated by the state for political reasons, a kind of cadastral anxiety — an underlying ontological awareness of the insecurity of private property — flourished among ranchers.[11] Alfredo Pinto, connecting respeto, fear, state support, and agrarian change, fumed that before 1994 "there was *security* and respect — respect for property. People had security for their investments and were improving their ranches. Nestlé had just established a center in Chilón for gathering the region's milk. People were finally getting high-quality cattle breeds and they were putting in new types of coffee. . . . There was always agrarian conflict, but not like in 1994 — not complete invasions that forced us out, death threats, horrible things. And before, the government intervened quickly to restore the properties [to their owners]."

Many landowners, such as Samuel Rodríguez's brother Elí, gave up on Chiapas after the invasions and moved their operations to the relative tranquility of Tabasco or Quintana Roo. Most ranchers, however, diversify into more stable businesses and hope for better times. Roberto Abarca and Hans Setzer discussed the future: "I'm waiting for the next [president] to see what happens. If we don't get support then, I'll turn in my land and do something else." "We need a dictator, like what happened in Chile with Allende. We need to bring Don Porfirio [Díaz] back to life."

Generations of Fear

The gradual abandonment of agriculture and the countryside by younger Chiloneros also weighed heavily on landowners' decisions after 1994. One landowner put it plainly: "We accepted the purchase price [for our land], even though we didn't like it, because none of my children were ranchers." Generational changes are also credited with shifting landowners' responses to invasions away from violence, as César Trujillo suggested in a remarkable account of deliberations at the AGL:

[One of the key things that prevented violence in 1994] was the changing culture of [landowners'] children. Our parents were born on the ranch, grew up on the ranch, learned to talk and play on the ranch. The ranch was their life. But our parents also worked to get their children off the ranch — out to study, to get degrees and careers. This gave the children a whole new outlook. . . . I remember after 1994 there was a meeting at the [AGL] at which many people were speaking out for violence. I remember one guy saying, "I'll provide the machine guns. If we need an airplane, I'll get it," and then one of the sons stood up and said no, that wasn't the right way to go about things. That we should leave it up to the law. I think this was an important change. If this had been in earlier years, it would have been resolved with guns, like in

Sitalá [in the 1980s]. . . . The younger man who spoke out was Samuel Rodríguez [Jr.], one of the people who stood to lose the most from the invasions.

It is important, however, to resist the temptation to assume that these generational shifts are simply the automatic outcome of a modernizing logic in which rational capital-intensive agribusiness steadily displaced thuggish old-guard feudal landowners, or, more prosaically, that the glamour and ease of urban life inevitably pulled young people away from rough ranch life. Picking up on Cesar's words, the critical question is: Why did parents for whom "the ranch was their life" work so hard to ensure that their children would leave agriculture? While most landowners would simply explain this effort in terms of a "strong will to get ahead," awareness of the instability and danger inherent in ranching often formed a constant subtext, as Hans Setzer recognized: "My grandparents lived through the Revolution. My parents lived through the era of Cárdenas [who oversaw a massive redistribution of land]. My generation gets to live through this [the Zapatistas and invasions]. My children won't have to suffer anything because they'll be in the cities with good jobs."

Thus older landowners' emphasis on securing education for their children is, at least in part, a response to the constant threat of agrarian conflict. Jorge Martínez remembers that as early as the 1960s, "our father always told us that our time was limited. There was always a sense that it was only a matter of time before the indígenas would take the land away from us." And when I asked Ofelia Jiménez whether her children will be ranchers, she gasps, "No way! Anything but ranchers! Even if it's only as a teacher, anything but a rancher. . . . It's too scary with all the indígenas now, there are too many risks. It's better to be a merchant."

In the end, fear, generational change, and the economic prospects of estate agriculture in an age of neoliberal restructuring blur together in ladinos' minds. Their explanations for quiescence at once look back to the past, to the age-old fear of savage indígenas, then tack to a present marked by unprecedented indigenous aggression, and then move forward to their children's futures.

The Space of Death

> The space of death [is] an ever-present place in the colonial imagination. — Michael Taussig

The "space of death," as Michael Taussig suggests, is deeply etched in the colonial imagination. It is also inscribed in space. Fear shapes space, or, more accurately, representations of fear and violence are among the many social-spatial practices through which space is produced. The "space of death" is not just a spatial metaphor; it *is* spatial.

Chiloneros' geographical imaginary of fear, developed through long turbulent years, played a central role in defining landowners' efforts to know, discipline, and control the region's large indigenous population. By 1994 the constellation of strategies and techniques that landowners deployed to know, discipline, and control indigenous "savagery," had begun to lose coherence. For decades landowners' relations with indígenas constructed a web of spaces that they thought of as safe, known, and governable — material and symbolic boundaries that reassured ladinos that life in the midst of seemingly savage Indians was possible, was safe. In the face of indígenas' multiple transgressions of Chilón's partitioned geographies, landowners' everyday fear became formative. Worked through understandings of state support, economic crisis, and generational change, fear produced quiescence.

10

The Agrarian Spiral

We have seen that over the course of more than a century, landowners' ability to defend the spaces of estate agriculture rested on diverse material and discursive practices that positioned landowners as the sole nexus between peasants and the state, the countryside, and the nation. The emergence of multiple forms of territoriality through the twentieth century slowly displaced landowners from this position, in the process reshaping the spaces of landed production. Thus, when peasants began to invade the estates in 1994, landowners had already seen the unstable equilibria of hegemony shift against them.

In this context of shifting hegemony, landowners struggled to calculate the costs and benefits of using force to defend their estates. These were not the disembodied rational calculations of *Homo economicus*, but rather painful struggles over identity in which uncertain landowners grappled with the upending of the once reliable categories of nature, race, development, good government, and masculinity. Two interrelated struggles over meanings played pivotal roles in these calculations. First, landowners wrestled with the meaning of production as a framework for understanding the self, the Other, and their changing places in the terrain of national development and state rule. Ultimately this produced a widespread perception of limits and constraints on the use of violence. Second, engaging in a decades-old conversation about the meanings of indigenous "savagery," landowners came to see themselves as caught in a dangerous and indefinite siege by forces they could not vanquish. Worked through landowners' understandings of investment security and generational change, this sense of siege pushed landowners decisively away from violence.

Almost a decade later, the spatial and social reordering that emerged from this intense moment of struggle seems to have shifted from the terrain of the conjunctural to the terrain of the structural. "The countryside belongs to the indígenas now," Paco Vera reflected in 2000. "What will the mestizos do?"

In July 2005 I returned to reconnect with Don Roberto and other Chiloneros. A few days into my visit, I sat in on a biannual meeting of the AGL. Membership in the association had fallen to eighteen and only eleven members showed up that day, scraping folding chairs into a small circle in their echoing hall. Before Carlos Setzer, once again serving as the group's president, could call the meeting to order, a man I had met only in passing launched into a speech. He spoke passionately, sweat beading on his forehead: "Look around. Hardly any of us own cattle anymore, even though this is the Cattlemen's Association. We have to revive ranching, revive this association. Couldn't we start a community bank? Couldn't we get new support from the government? We *have* to save the association. It's the last bastion of ladinos in Chilón!"

The man's speech elicited equally passionate statements from the assembly. Ideas circulated, calls for energetic change were made. I remembered this kind of talk from my previous visits. During my earlier visits many landowners still held out hope that recent outbreaks of turmoil were more conjunctural than structural, and they pinned these hopes on political transition — on faith that the state would finally regain its senses and restore support for landed property and production. "I'm holding out for one more *sexenio,*" Roberto Abarca assured me in 1998. "If there isn't more security for investment after that, I'm moving somewhere else."

By 2000 many landowners had switched their political affiliation to the opposition PAN after years of intimate association with the ruling PRI. The reasons for this surprising shift were clear. After 1994, indigenous land invaders had slowly come to dominate Chilón's PRI machine, which now stood as a bold symbol of both landowners' abandonment by the state and the consequent unhinging of social order. "Perhaps if there were a PAN governor," one landowner observed, "he could impose a hardhanded solution." By necessity, however, supporting the PAN in 2000 also meant throwing one's lot in with an alliance between the left-leaning PRD and the PAN — the Alianza por Chiapas, headed by the gubernatorial candidate Pablo Salazar Mendiguchía. Throughout his campaign, Salazar skillfully appealed to both the left and right, indigenous groups and ladino landowners. After meeting with Salazar during a campaign visit to Chilón, for example, indige-

Local Cattlemen's Association meeting, June 2005. Carlos Setzer sits on the far right; Samuel Rodríguez Sr. is to his left. *(Photo by author.)*

nous leaders told me they were confident that the candidate supported continued land reform, while ladinos assured me that, once elected, he would immediately begin evicting invaders. Whether these contradictory perceptions arose from wishful thinking or the candidate's actual message, many landowners enthusiastically supported the Alianza. Roberto Trujillo, whose son César chaired the PAN and Alianza campaigns in Chilón, even turned over part of his property near Chilón's plaza for Alianza headquarters, and prominently advocated political change.

In June 2000, both Salazar and PAN's presidential candidate, Vicente Fox, defeated the deeply entrenched PRI in truly historic elections. In the end, however, Salazar's victory produced neither the wave of new land redistribution some indigenous leaders hoped for nor satisfied landowners' hunger for evictions and "order." Returning from Salazar's grand inauguration celebration in Tuxtla Gutiérrez, Don Roberto was quiet, almost crestfallen. Salazar's speech had catered largely to the left, with substantial concessions made to the Zapatistas. In the municipal elections several months later, only indigenous leaders stood as candidates for the victorious PRI, and the one

PAN candidate garnered little support outside the ladino-dominated municipal seat.

So by July 2005, landowners' "next sexenio" had come and almost gone with no sign of improvement. In this context, the passion AGL members expressed for reviving their association at the last meeting I attended was passion pro forma, a sort of automatic reflex that quickly subsided once Carlos Setzer scolded members, saying that their problem was not credit or cooperation; it was the lack of security. "If we're all done with speechifying," he grinned impatiently, "perhaps we can turn to the business at hand."

There was only one item on the biannual meeting's agenda. The association had lost control of a small piece of roadside property strategically situated at the entrance to town. Before 1994, the property served as a livestock-processing center for the association. In a small corral, Agriculture Department officials and the association secretary would check brands and paperwork on cattle moving in and out of town. Nestlé placed its dairy-collection equipment on the site, and a water tank mural proclaimed, "Cattlemen Welcome You to Chilón." In other words, before 1994, this lot on the edge of town was the central focus of what landowners hoped would be a region-wide renaissance of ladino landed production.

Then in 1994, with the cattle and dairy trade paralyzed by invasions, the association lent the strategic site to the municipal government for a police substation and checkpoint. The post was to serve — very literally, in the minds of association members — as the last bastion between indigenous Bachajón and ladino Chilón. The mayor erected a two-story blockhouse on the lot, but for political reasons never staffed it with police. Several years later, indigenous truck and taxi drivers from Bachajón, backed by the PRI, occupied the site and turned the guardhouse into their cooperative's office. Chilón's mayor allowed the drivers to remain, apparently hoping to avoid conflict. But now the AGL wanted its land back — or at least monthly rent from the drivers, who ran a bustling business shuttling goods and people between Chilón and Bachajón from the site.

The meeting wore on into the hot morning as eleven members debated the best strategy for reclaiming their lot. When no coherent plan emerged from the tangle of voices, my mind began to wander. First I imagined the hall not water-stained, empty, and aging, as it was in 2005, but filled to capacity and ringing with the urgent voices of the more than eighty members it had had in the spring of 1994. By all accounts, during those spring meetings the hall swelled with calls to arms, with talk of helicopters, mercenaries, and the alphabet of war: AK-47, M-16, R-15. This call to arms was never heeded, for reasons that should be clear by now. Back in the present, the talk was far less heated, and my mind continued to stray, this time to the taxi stand on the edge of town that lay at the heart of the dispute. A few days earlier, arriving in Chilón on the back of a pickup, I had noticed that the sign reading "Cattlemen Welcome You to Chilón" had become so over-grown that it was barely noticeable from the road. It was a graphic vision of the town's changing landscape.

Finally Enoch Guirao, an elderly rancher, drew my wandering mind back to the hall. Although diabetes-ridden and hobbled with age, Guirao still commanded attention, and his bitter words hung in the air: "Chilón isn't a ladino town anymore. It's a Tzeltal town now. None of our children are here. The only people with degrees and education in this town now are Tzeltals."

He was right, if a bit hyperbolic. The change in the town was palpable. During my absence, Tzeltal merchants had begun to spread their wares assertively on sidewalks downtown, converting Chilón's main street into a space of indigenous commerce in competition with ladino stores. Walking through town earlier that week, I had reflected that these street vendors had appropriated the same sidewalks that, not too long ago indígenas would have been expected to cede to any strolling ladino who came their way. I also noticed that the whole soundscape of the town had shifted from Spanish to Tzeltal during the years I'd been away — even in the town hall. A former landowner point-edly observed, "Now we've even had to listen to the mayor's [annual] state of the municipio speech given in Tzeltal." Eating my meals with Don Roberto and Doña Gloria, I even sensed a shift in the Restaurant Susy's clientele. There were more indigenous clients than I remem-bered, and there was something else, just at the edge of perception. Was it my imagination, or had a tiny ritual of subordination faded? That brief caesura in the doorway; that almost imperceptible moment when, with downcast eyes and an uncomfortable shuffle, indigenous clients seemed to ask permission before crossing into the ladino space of the restaurant. As I ate my first meal, a pair of Tzeltal men, fresh from business at the town hall, strode in, boldly taking up their space in the restaurant like good actors owning a stage. It was a subtle, striking performance of re-indigenization; a whole racial history em-bodied in gesture and motion.

Indigenous merchants and transport trucks on Chilón's main street.
(Photo by author.)

In 2005 the town of Chilón was in many ways a space reclaimed —
or more accurately, a space undergoing a profound set of racial re-
orderings. Ladinos had by no means disappeared from Chilón. An
incongruously stylish and distinctly ladino cybercafé had even been
opened on the central plaza by a man from central Mexico who had
married into the Vera clan. But ladino landed production, as I had
come to understand it, seemed a thing of the past, and ladino hegemony in town seemed to be following on its heels. Paco Vera's question filled my thoughts: if the countryside (and now perhaps the
town) belongs to the indígenas now, what will the mestizos do?

As I looked around the AGL meeting, the future was clear. Only
three of the eleven members present were under fifty and the majority
were well over sixty. Although some of these aging men and one
woman continue to produce coffee or raise cattle on a small scale
(what they sometimes jokingly refer to as "hobby farming"), their
children are searching for new horizons elsewhere or trying to recon-
figure their places in and around agriculture.

Four years earlier, one scene had crystallized for me young ladinos'
struggle to define their place in Chilón. I had rounded the corner of

the central plaza and found Juan Trujillo and Sam Rodríguez Jr. deep in conversation. Hoping I could get them to talk about the future of young ladinos in Chilón, I joined them, leaning on Sam's pickup truck. They were deeply engrossed in the subject of teeth, or rather of Sam's mother's broken bridge. Juan, who at thirty had just finished dental school, inspected the cracked acrylic teeth. They couldn't be saved, he concluded, but the metal armature could be reused. Sam pocketed the bridge and the two of them turned to a more pressing topic: repairing Chilón's *lienzo charro* (rodeo arena), where they hope to revive the town's charro festival (on hiatus since 1994). We never got to my question about the future of young ladinos, but Juan and Sam were actively engaged in making that future, one by abandoning agriculture for a professional career and the other by searching for a new material and symbolic footing for agricultural production.

Sam, who returned to Chilón after earning a bachelor's degree in veterinary medicine, had stood at the forefront of landowners' attempts to shift from the politically unviable model of extensive cattle ranching to something more intensive. After the invasions of 1994 crushed landowners' dreams of intensive dairy production, Sam searched for a new type of production tailored to current political realities. He found it in chickens. In many ways chickens are emblematic of neoliberal Mexico in the same way that cattle epitomized the country's earlier experiments with inward-looking industrialization. If large-scale extensive beef production fueled a booming urban industrial workforce, small, flexible, and inexpensive chickens represent the perfect food for Mexico's increasingly impoverished neoliberal workforce. Even more important, they can be raised in confined, easily defended spaces. Returning in 2005, however, I learned that, while Juan had built a thriving dental practice (with a growing indigenous clientele), Sam's plans had failed. No longer a producer, he earned his living as a high school teacher in an indigenous hamlet an hour and a half away.

Many former landowners had taken another route, not back into agriculture but around it. With land firmly held by indigenous peasants, these former landowners were attempting to control the agricultural economy without directly controlling the production process. Indeed, after asking, "What will the mestizos do?" Paco Vera answered his own question: "They'll find ways to live off what the indígenas produce." Buying and selling indígena-grown corn, beans, and cattle have become a major source of income for many former landowners. These

Juan Trujillo's newly constructed home and dental office. *(Photo by author.)*

landowners-turned-*coyotes*, explained a buyer for a multinational coffee firm in Chilón, have a considerable advantage over him because "they speak Tzeltal from growing up on their ranches . . . [and because] the indígenas seek out people they already know."

Landowners have long served as merchants and commercial inter-mediaries, but since the invasions of 1994, commerce is one of the very few options left to Chiloneros without professional careers who re-main in town. Indeed, exploiting indigenous peasants through com-merce may be the only way for ladinos to reconstruct their hegemony in the current political context. This movement from landed produc-tion to commerce should not be confused with the teleological march of capitalist development. Rather it is part of what Alí Reyes aptly referred to as a politically determined "agrarian spiral," in which land-owners tack back and forth between cattle, coffee, and commerce as the precarious equilibrium of regional hegemony shifts.

Ultimately, Alí's words nicely express a central conclusion of this book. The spaces of landed production in Chilón have been constantly formed and re-formed through social struggle, and this ongoing process of transformation lies at the heart of landowners' responses to agrarian conflict. The preceding chapters traced an arc of declining property, following a system of landed production from its nineteenth-century formation through its recent ungluing in the context of rural violence and neoliberal crisis. In many ways this trajectory has confirmed Marxist forecasts of the gradual disappearance of landed production. But rather than examine the case of Chilón at this level of analysis — that is, by working from large dynamics of capitalist transformation toward their manifestation in a specific case — I have begun with the "infinitesimal mechanisms" of power operating at multiple scales — the everyday forms of knowledge and subjectivity that shape subjects and hegemony — and then tried to understand how these struggles have expressed themselves in the spaces of estate agriculture. Out of this analysis emerges a different picture of the transformation of landed production: the metamorphoses described here were not inevitable or determined; landed production is a social relation forged through contingent struggles over hegemony. This cultural politics of landed production emerged throughout the empirical material presented here. For example, we have seen how the economic logic of landed production intertwined with fear, how landowners' privileged control over labor turned on the construction of a gendered and racialized estate "family," and how disproportionate state support for landowner violence accrued, in part, because of a particular resonance between discursive constructions of landed production and larger processes of Mexican development. The economic has always and everywhere also been cultural.

Landed production is also a spatial relation. It is a constellation of social-spatial practices through which landowners, peasants, and state actors define, invest with meaning, and struggle over the intimate spaces of estate agriculture. The classification, sedimentation with meanings, surveillance, and enforcement of those spaces are critical practices through which hegemony operates. They are also unstable and constantly changing outcomes of those same struggles. Conflicts between landowners and peasants during the middle years of the twentieth century, for example, were catalyzed by a new rationale of postrevolutionary state rule, but they also reflected particular social-spatial configurations of estate relations forged at the end of the nineteenth century. These postrevolutionary struggles in turn reordered space in multiple ways. Ultimately, the new social-spatial relations produced by struggles from the 1930s through the 1980s profoundly shaped the course of conflict in the 1990s.

Seen in this way, as a social relation forged through hegemony struggles and subject formation, not as a terminally limited economic category, landed production can be a resilient form, even in a world of global capitalist competition. Landowners remade themselves and estate agriculture numerous times over the past century, blending landed production with commerce and profession employment in a variety of ways. Each successive configuration of landed production profoundly shaped the dynamics of domination and subjugation in the Chiapas countryside. Thus landowners and landed production — in their diverse forms and iterations — must be taken seriously as categories of continuing importance for the study of rural politics.

For too long, studies of rural politics have engaged in nuanced debates over the category of "peasant" while leaving the category of "landed elite" largely unquestioned. In the absence of sustained scholarly attention, this category has been filled largely with an anemic political economy; with narrow readings of Marx and Ricardo that favor typologies and teleologies over politics, power, and the specificities of history and geography. In a sense, landed elites' identities and motives are assumed to be transparent and known before study of the countryside even begins. As a result, most scholars of agrarian conflict see no real need to venture into the politically uncomfortable terrain of ethnography among landed elites. This is a loss. Just as agrarian studies now explore peasants in their multiple entanglements with factory work, transnational migration, urbanization, cosmopolitan identities, and advanced capitalist agriculture, the landed elite — or more broadly, the many awkward groups and classes that exercise deep and historical domination in rural politics around the world even as they are themselves subject to powerful forms of domination in an age of globalization — must be understood as an impure category defined by multiple changing positionings. That understanding can't come from a safe and comfortable remove.

During my last visit to Chilón, I attended a second meeting as well. This time, years after first being taken for a priest on the back of that pickup out of town, I was presenting my research to staff members of the church-based Center for Indigenous Rights (CEDIAC). Deeply engaged in indigenous land struggles and closely tied to the Jesuit mission in Bachajón, CEDIAC seemed to stand for all the social justice and social movement work that I feared my scholarly complicity with landowners might undermine. Yet there I was, discussing my book manuscript with a mixed audience of indigenous leaders and young mestizo activists. Their enthusiasm and openness to my project went a long way toward easing the fears that haunted my research. In other ways, it deepened my ambivalence. Was I now a traitor to the landowners who had confided in me?

That afternoon, over lunch, Don Roberto asked me suspiciously how my meeting with CEDIAC had gone. "In many ways," I answered without hesitation, "your understandings of what has happened here in Chilón are not so different." Don Roberto looked surprised, so I explained that both landowners and CEDIAC staffers placed the events of 1994 in the context of a historical displacement of ladino landowners as the central mediators between indigenous communities and the state. Both saw the church and other organizations as playing key roles in this process, and both recognized that those roles were to reinforce an underlying neoliberal crisis in the countryside (although only a small number of landowners actually used the term "neoliberal"). "On the other hand," I concluded, "your interpretations of whether these shifts are good or bad and how much of a role indigenous people themselves played in them are *very* different." This answer seemed to satisfy Don Roberto, or at least give him something to mull over.

Not long after my return to the United States in 2000, an activist friend who tries to mediate between cattle ranchers and environmentalists in the desert of southern Arizona commented to me on the practice of listening closely to people with whom one disagrees on many topics: "I suppose you can become friends with anyone if you sit around their kitchen table and listen to them." I found this to be true in Chiapas, and I hope I have conveyed the strong affection I feel for such ladino landowners as Roberto Trujillo and Alejandro Díaz. But my friend's kitchen-table logic presumes that one is able to sit at the table in the first place. When I was new to Chiapas I naively entertained the idea that by showing how neoliberal globalization created a crisis in the lives of both indígenas and ladinos in the countryside, I could reveal common ground between the two groups. As I explained in chapter 2, Chilón's long history of racial antagonism, complex identities, and deeply sedimented layers of domination quickly dispelled this fantasy. My work will probably not bring landowners and indigenous peasants into a common political conversation. In the end, my attempt to take the relatively powerful seriously is aimed at scholars and activists who comfortably gloss landed elites like Chilón's as the bad guys in a diverse array of rural political struggles. It is written against strategic essentialisms that mobilize politics through stark binaries of good guys and bad guys. Landed elites act not from predetermined identities but from uncertain articulations of meaning and history. In this light, landed elites' responses to agrarian conflict — whether in Mexico, Zimbabwe, South Africa, or Brazil — cannot be truly understood or judged without fine-grained and very likely uncomfortable exploration of their lived experiences.

Notes

1. Introduction

1. "Ladino" is a racial category usually defined in opposition to "indígena"; it refers to a person who speaks Spanish and does not maintain an indigenous lifestyle or follow indigenous customs. See Chapter 3 for an extended discussion.

2. A *municipio* is equivalent to a county, comprising a principal town and outlying villages and hamlets.

3. Figures for 1994–1998 are taken from "Predios desocupados 1994–2000," an unpublished chart provided to me by the Secretaría Estatal de Desarrollo Agrario, Tuxtla Gutiérrez. Data on evictions for the years leading up to 1994 come from Gómez and Kovic 1993:65.

4. "Chilón," the geographical region addressed in this study, comprises the western half of the municipio of Chilón, all of the municipio of Sitalá, and parts of Yajalón. Thus "Chilón," as used here, does not perfectly match the large (2,500 km²) and overwhelmingly Tzeltal Mayan municipio officially called Chilón. My concern is to represent the fluid and "extroverted" (Massey 1994) spaces made by ongoing struggles between landowners, indigenous peasants, and the state over the scope and contours of landed property in this part of north-central Chiapas. "Chilón" occupies an odd borderland between the traditionally construed regions of Chiapas. It lies at the nexus between Chol-, Tzeltal-, and Tzotzil-speaking Mayan groups and at the interstices of the state's northern highlands, eastern lowland rain forests, and central highlands. This construction of "Chilón" as a region reflects the historical locations of ladino landed property and the extent of landowner social networks radiating out from the *town* of Chilón. Thus it includes the municipios of Sitalá and Yajalón — both bastions of ladino landed property — but *not* the eastern half of the municipio of Chilón, dominated almost entirely by three large indigenous ejidos (San Sebastián Bachajón, San Jerónimo Bachajón, and San Jerónimo Tulijá). Although many indigenous people live in and around the town of Chilón, a real partitioned geography divides the ladino-controlled western

portion of the municipio of Chilón and the overwhelmingly indigenous eastern half. In 1990, thanks to seven decades of agrarian struggle, indigenous ejidos—particularly the large San Sebastián Bachajón and San Jerónimo Bachajón ejidos—controlled some 85 percent of agricultural land in the municipio (INEGI 1994). The remaining highly productive 15 percent was still concentrated in ladino hands around the town of Chilón. In addition to this control over land, ladino landowners and merchants maintained an unbroken grip on the governments of the municipios of Chilón, Sitalá, and Yajalón dating back to the mid–nineteenth century.

5. Neil Harvey's (1998) excellent book devotes six pages to the resurgence of agrarian struggle in Chiapas after 1994. Villafuerte Solís et al. (1999) and Reyes Ramos (1998a) are among the few Mexican scholars who have chronicled the invasions and their resolutions. Sonia Toledo's (2002) work on Simojovel, to the north of Chilón, is the only other study directly focused on landowners' experience of these land invasions.

6. "Pliego peticionario que presentan los productores agropecuarios del Municipio de Chilón . . . ," Dec. 21, 1994, in AGL.

7. Property sales brokered for peasant land claimants by the Banco de Crédito Rural del Istmo and registered in RP-Y, "Libros de Escrituras Públicas, 1994–1999," out of a total 11,107 hectares of private property greater than 5 hectares (INEGI 1994).

8. See Bernstein 2004; Bobrow-Strain 2004; Borras 2005, 2003; Deininger 2003; Ghimire 2001.

9 On Brazil see Payne 2000 and Bruno 1997. On Zimbabwe see D. Moore 2005; *Journal of Agrarian Change* 1(4) (2001, special issue); and Moyo 2000. On the Philippines see Borras 2005, 2001. Borras 2003 compares recent land reforms in Brazil, Colombia, and South Africa.

10. Notable exceptions are Rutherford 2004 on Zimbabwe, Payne 2000 on Brazil, and Paige 1997 on El Salvador.

11. "Relación de poblados que han solicitado tierras y resultados (1922–1979)" (n.d.), a publication of the Liga de Comunidades Agrarias y Sindicatos Campesinos del Estado de Chiapas, found at the INAREMAC library, San Cristóbal (document 1.9.10), offers a painful account of this kind of perpetual absurdity.

2. Honest Shadows

1. See Smith 2006, Rutherford 2004, Nader 1999, McDonogh 1986, Marcus 1983.

2. See Chapter 3 and Ascencio Franco 2002 for a more in-depth look at discourses and struggles around the meaning of "landowners" in Chiapan politics.

3. Not an uncommon trajectory. See Moguel 1994 on the integration of Mexico's moderate left into the Solidarity bureaucracy.

4. In mountainous Chiapas, forced portage of ladinos was considered one of the worst abuses of debt-bound labor.

5. Numerous academic accounts affirm landowners' analysis of the church's role in mobilizating indígenas, although, unlike landowners, they do not frame these actions as manipulation of indigenous "children." See N. Harvey 1998, chap. 3; Nash 2001:163–170.

6. In fairness, this man's attitude toward peasant poverty represents an extreme iteration of a common discourse that paints pre-1994 ethnic relations in romantic terms. See Chapters 8 and 9.

7. While Gutiérrez's story nicely captures broad historical patterns, I differ with him on a number of details. For example, the state and federal SRA, rather than the INI, provided the money to purchase invaded land in the 1980s. Similarly, the INI's presence in Chiapas long predates 1976 (see Fabregas Puig 1988). See Chapters 5 and 6 for my elaboration on these programs and events.

8. Oscar Cruz is a pseudonym at his request.

3. Landed Relations

1. Unfortunately, my one encounter with Enrique Díaz came before I was able to copy photographs in the field.

2. *Naturales* (naturals) is an archaic moniker for indigenous people still used by a handful of older ladinos. See Chapter 8 on the intertwining of race and nature in Chilón.

3. Note that they never use the term *terrateniente* (landlord) except in response to critics who have had the temerity to apply it to them. For added emphasis, Chiloneros frequently refer to themselves as *pequeños propietarios* (small landowners), further differentiating themselves from the vilified large landowners. Chapters 5 and 8 examine how landowners actively position themselves in the larger Mexican nation through these labeling practices. "Landed elite" is *my* label, derived from the field of agrarian political economy. Landowners, however, will frequently also refer to themselves as "ranchers," a term closely associated with the transition to cattle raising, described in Chapter 6. See Ascencio Franco 2002.

4. Eugenia is an exception. This research was carried out largely in the company of men. For the most part, women I spent time with referred my questions about land, agriculture, and conflict to their fathers, husbands, or brothers. There were other exceptions: Amparo Setzer, wife of Carlos Setzer; and Deyanira Vega de López, an elderly woman who played a major role in negotiations with the invaders of her family's ranch. Both women who deferred to men and women who took on roles traditionally reserved for men were centrally involved in the production of masculinity. It is this larger production of masculinity and its relation to landowners' identities that interests me.

5. See CDHFBLC 1996 for an example.

6. There are many possible reasons why landowners appear as foils for the indigenous peasantry in academic and popular discourse. A true genealogical account of this classificatory practice has yet to be written. Nevertheless, constructing landowners as a unified enemy shared by all indigenous peasants clearly does powerful cultural and ideological work. In particular, it unifies and provides a coherent collective identity for what would otherwise be a discordant mass of competing indigenous communities and organizations.

7. Thus this book forms part of ongoing debates over the future and merits of agrarian studies (D. Moore 2005, 1998; Hart 2002; Watts 2002; Bernstein and Byres 2001; Goodman and Watts 1997; Stoler 1995a).

8. For Ricardo, this meant a theory of ground rent unfurled in support of an argument about the benefits of international trade. Likewise, Marx gave landed production its most thorough examination as part of his efforts to reconcile the existence of value seemingly produced by nature (differential ground rent) with the labor theory of value (D. Harvey 1999).

9. The discussion here is highly condensed. Readers who wish an expanded analysis of the relation between rent and landed production in Chilón may consult Bobrow-Strain 2003. Key texts in the larger debates around rent and landed production include Marx 1967 and Ricardo 1919, as well as Bernstein and Byres 2001; Paige 1997, 1975; Huber and Safford 1995; Edelman 1992; Neocosmos 1986; Winson 1982; de Janvry 1981; Richards 1979; Fine 1979; and B. Moore 1966. See Guthman 2004 and Coronil 1997 for innovative applications of the concept of rent.

10. A concern with "paths" of agrarian transition developed quite early in debates about landed production from a realization that changes under way in national agricultures around the world during the late nineteenth century bore little resemblance to the classic English passage from feudalism to capitalism outlined in *Capital*. Lenin (1977), having made his argument that Russian agriculture was in fact undergoing a rapid capitalist transformation, identified two additional "main lines" of capitalist development "objectively possible" for Russian agriculture. The "American path," with its lack of landed aristocracy and proliferation of small capitalist farms, won Lenin's admiration for its dynamic ability to generate innovation and swell the domestic market. The "Junker path," in contrast, was purely "retrograde," an "internal metamorphosis of feudal landlord economy" in which "the entire agrarian system becomes capitalist and for a long time retains feudal features" (32). If these different iterations of landed production could only be classified properly, it seemed, a wide range of concrete outcomes for capitalist development (e.g., de Janvry 1981), democratization (e.g., B. Moore 1966), and revolutionary struggle (e.g., Paige 1975) would be revealed. See Bernstein and Byres 2001 for a

review and Neocosmos 1986 for a particularly lucid discussion of these wranglings.

11. See D. Moore 1998 and Stoler 1995a, Preface, for discussions of these challenges.

12. On territory and territoriality see Delaney 2005, Sack 1986, and Vandergeest and Peluso 1995.

13. This piece of my definition, in part, builds on Agnew's (2000) concise formulation.

14. Lefebvre was one of the first scholars to trace connections between hegemony and space, arguing at a high level of abstraction that different modes of production produce specific hegemonic forms of space. I am clearly more interested in the everyday micro-workings of power through which space and hegemony articulate in a particular case. I also draw inspiration from and build on the writings of historians and anthropologists on power and hegemony in modern Mexico (Joseph, Rubenstein, and Zolov 2001; Vaughan 1999, 1997; Rubin 1997; Wells and Joseph 1996; Mallon 1995; Alonso 1995; Joseph and Nugent 1994; Nugent 1993). In a compelling review of the cultural history of Mexico, Vaughan (1999:277) contends that space has been one of the central foci of work in this field. Citing the critical human geographer Edward Soja, Vaughan wrote, "Space is understood to be socially constituted and socially constituting. The ways we perceive, value, and occupy physical space are themselves shaped by our spatially organized communities . . . and sites within them that socialize us, create symbolic meanings, and articulate uneven power relations." Nevertheless, while many of the authors Vaughan cites make quite explicit their engagement with the other factors she highlights (identity, gender, discourse, ritual, and hegemony), spatial theory must be read into most of the texts after the fact. I aim here to flesh out more explicitly the connections between space, hegemony, and power.

15. The same should be said for forms of "indigenous territoriality." Indigenous territorialities have been the subject of much research from the colonial period (e.g., Viqueira 1997) to the Revolution (e.g., Rus 1994) to the present (e.g., Eber 2003, Nash 2001, Burguete 1999, Harvey 1998, Reyes et al. 1998). This research has made important moves beyond seeing indígenas' struggles for land solely in terms of agricultural production to conceiving control over land as part of larger struggles over autonomy, citizenship, and democracy. Nevertheless, it is important to avoid homogenizing, essentializing, or romanticizing indigenous territoriality. In subsequent chapters I examine its many intertwining forms, ranging from the rent-seeking behavior of indigenous political bosses to discursive efforts aimed at constructing "primordial" land rights to the "restoration" of ethnic territory through the expulsion of ladinos from some towns.

4. Children of the Magic Fruit

1. The department of Chilón sent samples of mahogany, cedar, and ash. These woods almost certainly came from the eastern lowlands — now the municipio of Ocosingo — included at that time in the Department of Chilón (not the more limited "Chilón" under examination here; see n. 4 of Chapter 1 for a discussion of my construction of "Chilón" as a region).

2. "Expediente matrimonial de Atítlano Díaz y Cristina O. Cancino," November 1896, in AHD, Chilón files, IV.D.2.a.

3. "Intestado de Mariano Constantino," in APJ, Ocosingo files, 1888–1890; and "Lista de cuidanos ladinos que satisfacen los Santo Diezmos del Año de Mil Ochocientos Cuarenta y dos," Oct. 17, 1842, in AHD, Chilón files, VI.C.8.

4. On this period see Cosío Villegas 1994, Buffington and French 2000, and González 2001.

5. Late-nineteenth-century land privatizations are — after the 1994 Zapatista uprising — probably the most widely researched aspect of Chiapan history. There is a vast literature on the topic, and, because it does not harm my overall argument, I have omitted many intricacies of the evolution of these enclosures and their multifaceted consequences for the state's indigenous population. Readers who wish more detail should examine Olivera and Palomo 2005, García de León 1998, Benjamin 1996, Wasserstrom 1983, or Jan de Vos's trilogy on the conquest of the Lacandón rain forest (2002, 1994, 1988).

6. Fr. Marciano Trejo to el Sr. Provisor y Gobernador del Obispado, July 4, 1848, in AHD, Sitalá files, III.A.2.

7. An 1851 church census of agriculture in Guaquitepec and Sitalá, which found no fincas, haciendas, or large ranches, seems to confirm the priest's observation: "Padrón general de Guaquitepec y Sitalá," July 3, 1851, in AHD, Guaquitepec files, IV.D.4.

8. Fr. Manuel Zetino to el Sr. Provisor y Gobernador del Obispado, Jan. 3, 1898, in AHD, Sitalá files, IV.C.3.4.

9. "Padrón general de Guaquitepec y Sitalá." July 3, 1851, in AHD, Guaquitepec files, IV.D.F; and Ramírez 1885.

10. The latter process has received far more scholarly attention. See Washbrook 2005 and Alejos 1999. On the former, see Wasserstrom 1983.

11. I am engaged in research on this subject; Anna Garza is also investigating the question from the point of view of a historian focused on ladinos of San Cristóbal. See Garza 2005 and Bobrow-Strain n.d.

12. "Guaquitepec: Datos de las producciones agrícolas, año de 1900," June 28, 1901, in APJ, Ocosingo files.

13. "Recibos de la tesoría municipal de Sitalá, año 1903," in AMS. These values were determined by averaging the estimated worth of estate assets from various probate cases in the 1900s.

14. "Diligencias de jurisdicción voluntaria promovidas por el señor

Samuel Pascacio en representación de don Manuel Pineda," Sept. 14, 1906, in APJ, Ocosingo files.

15. "Cuadro que manifiesta el nombre de las fincas del Departamento que tienen gravamen real, cuyos datos han sido escrupulosamente copiado de los libros de hipotecas del Registro de la Propiedad que datan del año 1872," n.d. in APJ, Ocosingo files. This multi-page chart covers the period 1872–1934. See also Bobrow-Strain n.d.

16. "Copia certificado de las diligencias de mensura y adjudicación de un terreno . . . denominado El Carmen Zaquilá adjudicado al Sr. Manuel J. Penagos," April 18, 1897, in WLT.

17. At least one German landowner (Ricardo Franz) learned his craft administering rubber production in Cameroon before purchasing Chilón's Verapaz estate.

18. "Memorando sobre el café en Chiapas," Oct. 12, 1899, in CGPD, roll 165/xxiv, no. 15132. All citations of the CGPD in this book derive from Thomas Benjamin's extensive notes. I thank him for making these notes public.

19. See López Reyes 2005 on this moment in Yajalón.

20. I am indebted to Jan Rus for this insight.

21. "Estado de Chiapas, Departamento de Chilón, Municipio de Sitalá, Padrón del Número de Contribuyentes de este Pueblo, Año de 1904" (n.d.), in AMS.

22. This portrait derives from interviews with landowners and peasants. An informal agreement between landowner and peon that, for unknown reasons, found its way into writing confirms the overall picture. In the document signed by Tulaquil's owner, José Morales Abarca, and marked with the thumbprint of Juan López Pérez, the two agreed that "Morales Abarca offers Juan López land he can farm this year without charging a single centavo of rent, as long as he fulfills his responsibility to work three days a week for [Morales] at the usual wage . . . and gives [Morales] his eight-year-old daughter, Antonia López, to take care of [Morales's] son": "Acta levantada entre José Morales Abarca y Juan López Pérez," May 11, 1962, in AMS.

23. "Juzgados," May 11, 1949, in AMCH. The recorded price for estate sales in the 1940s and 1950s hovered around 15 pesos per hectare (based on a survey of documents in RP-Y). See comments in Chapter 7 on price reporting.

24. See, for example, "Juicio intestamentario de Manuela Cruz de Navarro," May 18, 1906, or "Segunda sección del juicio intestmentario del Sr. Abraham Ramos," July 28, 1911, in APJ, Ocosingo files.

25. "Queja del indígena Diego Guzmán contra el alcalde primero de Yajalón," Jan. 30, 1889, ibid.

26. "Diligencias practicadas contra Porfirio Bautista por maltrato a Doroteo Maldonado," Nov. 29, 1897; "Contra Rodolfo Cristo por homicidio," Feb. 4, 1908; and "Contra el señor Fco. Solano por heridos a An-

tonio López," Sept. 9, 1899, all ibid. In every case of abuse I discovered, judicial officials either exonerated the alleged perpetrator or issued arrest warrants that were never carried out.

27. "Juicio por el robo de maíz," Nov. 30, 1930, ibid.

28. "Libro de comunicaciones del juzgado," Feb. 10, 1876 in APJ, Ocosingo files; "Juzgados," May 11, 1949; July 7, 1949; Aug. 27, 1951; Oct. 10, 1951; Oct. 19, 1951; Nov. 18, 1951.

29. As opposed to a system of "rent in kind," in which peasants exchange produce for access to land, and labor for themselves and labor for the lord are not separated by time nor space (Marx 1967:795).

30. For other classic discussions of debt peonage in Mexico see Nickel 1997, Knight 1986, and Katz 1976, 1974.

31. Francisco León to Porfirio Díaz, Dec. 20, 1898, in CGPD, roll 156/XXII, no. 17495. Indigenous porters, León argues, require less supervision, care, and feed than mules. Besides, if a mule dies or becomes incapacitated, the merchant loses its value, but the loss of an indígena costs the merchant nothing.

32. "Libro de Juzgados de Sitalá," May 13, 1922, in AMS; "Queja del indígena Diego Guzmán," Jan, 30, 1889; Agente Municipal in Bachajón to Agente Municipal in Sitalá, Jan. 7, 1911, and Prof. Mariano L. Domínguez to Agente del Ministerio Público, Aug. 21, 1936, both in APJ, Ocosingo files.

33. Chapter 6 has an extended discussion of these challenges to estates. Other actors, including federal rural teachers, also challenged these boundaries. This process is discussed in Chapter 5.

34. For the sake of fairness and complexity, it must be said that exceptions to this pattern exist. Roberto Trujillo, for example, sometimes pays male workers' wages directly to their wives, so that the money does not disappear into a bottle.

35. In 1949, for example, an itinerant worker was forced to work on the estate of José Arévalo until he discharged a debt of 80 pesos incurred through the purchase of food while working on two estates: "Juzgados," Aug. 13, 1949, in AMCH.

36. And perhaps their children's lives as well. Several cases indicate that children inherited their parents' debts. In one case, a landowner sent workers to compel an indigenous woman and her sister to labor in his house and estate until they discharged debts left by the woman's deceased father-in-law: Prof. Mariano L. Domínguez to Agente del Ministerio Público, Aug. 21, 1936, in APJ, Ocosingo files.

37. "Diligencias practicados en contra de los indígenas Jerónimo y Miguel Hernández por la muerte de un caballo," April 23, 1896, ibid.

38. According to Israel Gutiérrez, many of the estates profiled in later chapters, including San Antonio Bulujib, Golonchán, and Picoté, did pay with scrip redeemable only on the estate into the late 1940s. Oscar Franz confirmed that Picoté operated a tienda de rayas as late as the 1980s.

39. Ejidos are discussed in Chapter 6.

40. See García de León 1998, Benjamin 1996, Baumann 1985, and Hernández 1979.

41. León to Díaz, Dec. 20, 1898, in CGPD, roll 156/XXIII, no. 17495.

42. "Circular No. 6," Feb. 14, 1903, in AMS.

43. "Diligencias practicadas contra Manuel Molina por Resistencia a la autoridad," Jan. 29, 1901, in APJ, Ocosingo files; Félix Aguilar to [illegible] Gutiérrez, June 11, 1888, in AMS.

5. Killing Pedro Chulín

1. "Gran Partido 'Unión Obrera Chilonera' solicita su registro en este Secretaría," April 25, 1928, in AGN, document 2.312 (5).

2. *La Jornada* (Mexico City), Jan. 7, 1994, p. 1.

3. "Diligencias de averiguación de hechos dictados por el Sr. Abraham Suárez," Nov. 11, 1918, in APJ, Ocosingo files.

4. "Contra Carlos Bertoni por los delitos de robo de documentos, destrucción de cosa ajena, desobediencia y resistencia a la autoridad," Oct. 4, 1920, ibid.

5. "Dictamen del Gobernador," May 17, 1946, in RAN-TG, Ejido Guaquitepec files.

6. On this relatively progressive interlude in Chiapan state politics see Benjamin 1996, chaps. 6 and 7.

7. Comisión Agraria de Sitalá to Procurador de Comunidades Indígenas, Dec. 4, 1940, in RAN-TG, Ejido de Sitalá files.

8. "Dictamen," May 17, 1946, ibid.

9. Restitution carried a higher standard of proof and required the state's admission that the community's land rights antedated the revolutionary regime. By contrast, a land grant (*dotación*) circumvented the question of preexisting rights and made peasants direct recipients of the state's benevolence. See Nugent 1993 and Ibarra 1989.

10. Marcelo Mendoza to Delegado Agrario, Nov. 30, 1954, in RAN-TG, Ejido Guaquitepec files.

11. Certificado de Inafectabilidad de San Antonio y Anexos, in RAN-DF, document 275.1/1800.

12. Raquel F. Martínez to Agente del Ministerio Público, Oct. 22, 1960, and Juez Mixto to Comandante de la Policía Municipal, Sitalá, Oct. 15, 1960, both in AMS.

13. Héctor Gallegos to Presidente Municipal de Chilón, March 30, 1962, in AMCH.

14. Quoted in. Alberto Gutiérrez to Presidente Municipal de Chilón, April 26, 1962, ibid.

15. Lisandro Díaz C. to Humberto Martínez V., June 9 and 16, 1962, ibid.

16. "Certificacción" by Humberto Martínez V., July 31, 1963, ibid.

17. Quintín Monterrosa, Agente Municipal de Sitalá, to Alberto Hernández, July 24, 1939, in AMS. The analysis in this section arose from long interludes spent in six archives sifting through peasants' complaints dating from the 1840s to 2001. These hundreds of letters, petitions, and appeals addressed to authorities at all levels of the Mexican political system tell a remarkable story. Only sporadic demands appear until the 1940s, but by the 1980s they fill entire rooms. Some seven hundred appeals — requesting roads, schools, Mexican flags, sheet metal, bags of concrete, volleyballs, water pipes, electrical service, and resolution of legal woes — from 1980 alone survive in the chaotic archive of Chilón municipio. In fact, during the five years leading up to the Zapatista uprising, the quantity of petitions sent from Chilón to the nation's president was nearly unparalleled in Mexico (Presidencia de la República 1993). Over time the petitions grew increasingly articulate and reflected consultation with an expanding number of peasant organizations and advocacy groups. More importantly, the content of the letters changes dramatically over time. From the 1840s, when complaints first appear, through the 1940s, letters deal almost exclusively with disputes between peasants and landowners. By the 1940s, with the formation of independent peasant communities, evidence of conflicts among indigenous power brokers appears. As indigenous communities developed their own land claims and systems of political domination, internal power struggles followed: peasant invasions of other peasants' fields, internecine killings, and corruption within ejido leadership flourished. The mixture of landowner-peasant and intracommunity disputes continued into the 1970s. By the 1980s, however, petitions focused almost entirely on power struggles within indigenous communities. Finally, the actors involved in these conflicts shifted notably. From the 1930s on, formerly isolated peasants had more access to outside authority. Indigenous communities sent scores of delegations as far away as Mexico City to plead their cases with countless mediators. During the 1940s, 1950s, and 1960s, new advocates for indigenous causes make their appearance: special prosecutors for indigenous affairs, delegates for social action, federal labor inspectors, and agrarian reform officials all weighed in on conflicts between landowners and peasants, sometimes clashing with more landowner-friendly wings of the state.

18. "Oficio 896," Celedonio Constantino, Representante del Jefetura de Sectores Militares de Ocosingo, to Agente Municipal de Sitalá, Nov. 15, 1927, in AMS.

19. Owner of the 200-hectare Finca Tulaquil and municipal president of Sitalá, 1950, 1956–1958, and 1965–1967.

20. "Oficio 123," Erasto Urbina to Presidente Municipal de Sitalá, Feb. 21, 1938, in AMS.

21. Director General de Asuntos Indígenas to Presidente Municipal de Sitalá, July 22, 1954, ibid.

22. On federal teachers in Chilón see Maurer 1978; on those in Chiapas see van der Haar 1993.

23. "Campesinos de Moyos quejándose contra terratenientes," Oct. 10, 1935, in AGN, document 2.331.8(5)5181.

24. "Circular 4," April 4, 1928, and "Circular a los Dueños o Encargados de las fincas," June 13, 1934, both in AMS.

25. Secretario General de Educación Pública to Agente Municipal de Sitalá, July 21, 1927, ibid.

26. "Convocatoria," March 28, 1940, in AMS.

27. Circular from Auxiliar de la Procuraduría del Departmento de Asuntos Indígenas, May 31, 1941, ibid.

28. Not surprisingly, peasants in Chilón often transferred the forms of appeal and submissive tone of their relations with landowners to the new "father," the state. In a letter addressed to the wife of President Adolfo López Mateos, peons on the vast Golonchán estate seamlessly (perhaps even ironically) combined awareness of agrarian law with an age-old discourse of humility: "It is true that, in view of the negative ruling on the Law of Uncultivated Lands, continued litigation of this Case before the judicial authorities of this jurisdiction is indicated, but in view of our humble condition as poor indígenas who neither speak nor read Spanish, and with no one to defend us and our rights . . . , we felt obliged to occupy a small piece of Golonchán": Campesinos Indígenas de Golonchán to Eva Sámano de López Mateos, Oct. 5, 1962, in RAN-TG, Ejido Golonchán files. The presence of new mediators is obvious in this flawlessly composed and typed appeal from illiterate non-Spanish-speaking peasants.

29. "Oficio 67," March 1, 1940, in AMCH.

30. Diario Oficial de la Nación, multiple issues.

31. Secretario General de Gobierno to Presidente Municipal de Chilón, Jan. 26, 1967, in AHPL.

32. *Horizontes* (Yajalón), Sept. 15, 1967.

33. The agrarian committees of Pojcol and El Carmen, for example, clashed through the 1960s over competing claims on several estates in eastern Chilón: RAN-TG, Ejido de Pojcol files. June Nash (1967) also noted a marked shift in the nature of intracommunity violence after the 1940s in Chiapas's central highlands.

34. [Illegible] to Agente Municipal de Sitalá, n.d., and "Acta del Juez Municipal," April 14, 1942, both in AMS.

35. "Libro de Juzgados de 1942," entry of April 14, ibid.

36. Presidente del Comité Agraria de Golonchán to Presidente Municipal de Sitalá, March 18, 1940, ibid.

37. Diario Oficial de la Nación, multiple issues.

38. "Censo de Cantinas y Comercios," 1962, and Comité Agraria de Cantajal to Presidente Municipal de Chilón, Feb. 8, 1962, both in AMCH.

39. Domingo Vilchis, Sebastián López, Pascual de la Cruz, Mauro Ló-

pez, and Vicente Estrada to Governor Aranda Orsorio, Sept. 4, 1954, in AHPL.

40. Delegado Agrario to Jefe de Zona de Organizaciones Agrarias y Ejidales, Aug. 11, 1971, in RAN-TG, Ejido Guaquitepec files.

41. Carlos Bertoni to Delegado Agraria, Sept. 27, 1948, ibid.

42. Campesinos Indígenas de Golonchán to Eva Sámano de López Mateos. October 5, 1962, in RAN-TG, Ejido Golonchán files.

43. Landowners' impunity continued after 1970 and was increasingly complemented by the hard-handed assistance of state forces. On "bloody populism" see Chapter 6 and Cruz and Kovic 1993.

44. *Horizontes*, Jan. 16, 1967.

45. "Proyecto de dictamen sobre dotación de ejidos al pueblo Sitalá del Municipio de Chilón," June 20, 1933, in RAN-TG, Ejido de Sitalá files.

46, RAN-DF, Ejido Delina files, document 25/25269.

47. Certificado de Inafectabilidad de San Juan Cabtejaj, document 275.1/1302 in RAN-DF; and RAN-TG, Ejido de la Providencia files. Article 27 of the Mexican Constitution sets the following limits on landowner-ship: irrigated farmland, 100 hectares; irrigated cotton, 150 hectares; ba-nanas, sugarcane, and coffee, 300 hectares; cattle, land needed to support 500 head. Chiloneros typically described their lands as *monte* (wild); such land was counted as one-eighth of an irrigated hectare.

48. "Acta de inexistencia del poblado de Shishontonil," March 11, 1957, in RAN-TG, Ejido Shishontonil files. The official, an agricultural engineer named Abel Trujillo López, seems to have made a career of determining that groups of peasants were ineligible to receive land; he made similar rulings in regard to Golonchán, Jérico, and Jotolá.

49. In one documented case, Isaías Solórzano, a landowner and former municipal president, was released after being briefly held for the murder of a peasant (*Horizontes*, Aug. 23, 1967).

50. Adolfo R. Aguilar to Juez Municipal, Sitalá, Aug. 30, 1945, in AMS.

51. Document 2.331.8(5)5181, Oct. 10, 1935, in AGN.

52. Landowners rarely recall the equally barbarous tactics of the Pine-dista guerrillas — lynching Carranza's peasant supporters from a ceiba tree in Bachajón, for example.

53. For this landowner, the fundamental lesson of Villa's life was that "with equal rights, everyone is free to make their own future and get ahead by honest work and the desire for progress."

54. "Lista de socios de la Asociación Ganadera Local de Chilón, Chia-pas," Sept. 14, 1965, and "Relación de Socios de la Asociación Ganadera Local de Chilón, Chiapas," 1980, both in AGL. In 1965 members averaged 70 head apiece, with the largest herds topping out at 200. By 1980 the AGL claimed almost 5,000 head, and this figure did not include four of the largest ranchers in the organization, who did not provide data on their herds; the average herd had risen to 85 and the largest was reported at 409.

6. The Dead at Golonchán

The epigraph to this chapter is taken from García de León 2002.

1. Both landowners and peasant leaders involved in the incident agree that many more people were killed than the official count indicates. General Castellanos Domínguez would later serve as governor (1982–1988) and then, in 1994, be kidnapped by Zapatista fighters in retaliation for his iron-fisted rule. Castellanos Domínguez is the patriarch of a prosperous family of landowners from Ocosingo and Comitán that included the indigenista novelist Rosario Castellanos.

2. On this moment in Chiapas and Mexico see García de León 2002, Harvey 1998, Martínez Quezada et al. 1994, Gómez and Kovic 1993, Reyes 1992, Rubio 1987, Alonso 1984, Singer 1984, and Pontigo and Hernández 1981.

3. On bloody populism see Benjamin 1996:235. See also Gomez and Kovik 1993, Reyes 1992:104, and Burguete 1987.

4. "Acta del Juzgado," April 20, 1949, in AMS.

5. "Relación de todas las personas ganaderas . . . ," Oct. 10, 1947, ibid.

6. Land reform drew peasants away from Chilón's estates in two ways: by creating ejidos, as discussed in Chapter 5, and by facilitating migration to lands opened for colonization in the lowland Lacandón rain forest. On this migration see Leyva and Ascencio 1996.

7. Between 1950 and 1970 cattle production on ejidos declined steadily from 26 to 17.7 percent of the industry total. Meanwhile, private property owners' share of cattle production in the country soared from 33 to 73.3 percent (Rutsch 1984: 24).

8. San Cristóbal's powerful Pedrero family had managed to gain control over the liquor licensing board and excise police in Chiapas, and used that authority to obtain an absolute monopoly on legal production of cane liquor in the state. To enforce their monopoly, the Pedreros' excise police stepped up raids of Chilón's and Sitalá's clandestine stills and replaced locally produced liquor with 20-liter cans of their own liquor flown in weekly from San Cristóbal.

9. This saying nicely plays on the etymological links between "capital" and "cattle," now mostly lost in English with the exception of the word "livestock," or living stock. The connection between "pecuniary" and cloven hoofs is also lost in English but preserved in Spanish.

10. Coffee growers such as Carlos Setzer and Rodolfo Domínguez began to recruit labor from Guatemala for peak harvest periods.

11. In Chapter 8 I discuss the important political supports for landowner territoriality associated with the transition to cattle ranching, particularly stepped-up legal protections for landed property and the creation of new rural police forces.

12. As we saw in Chapter 5, these small properties also buffered estates

from land reform and peasant invasions. Ramiro Ramos, whose Tulaquil estate lay directly in the path of PST invaders, admits that the support of loyal peasants to whom he had given land in return for labor enabled him to avoid invasion. This strategy could backfire, however; Ruperto Monterrosa, whose El Desengaño estate was lost to invaders in 1980, told me, "We made the mistake of giving peasants small plots of land, but that just gave them a taste of ownership and made them want more land."

13. UGRCH to AGL (circular), July 18, 1965, in AGL.

14. Certificado de Inafectabilidad, San Antonio Patbaxil, in RAN-DF, document 275.1/1504. The time from first application to receipt of an exemption certificate ranged from one to ten years, but most landowners' petitions came in well under the seven-year average response time for a peasant's land reform claim.

15. Certificado de Inafectabilidad, Guadalupe Fracción Sur, documents 275.1/1945 and 275.1/2223; DAAC to Departmento de Inafectabilidad Agrícola y Ganadera, April 9, 1965; and Director General de Inafectabilidad Agrícola y Ganadera to Oficina Técnica (memo), March 1, 1965, file 23/27859 all in RAN-DF.

16. Recall the case of San Antonio Bulujib in Chapter 5, in which the Bertonis clearly fudged the requirement that their property be free of pending land claims. But also remember that political exigencies frequently caused officials to overlook the protections guaranteed by exemption.

17. Indeed, the UGRCH and AGL, both organized under the auspices of the National Cattlemen's Confederation (CNG), mirror the architecture of hierarchically organized corporatist peasant organizations—a perfect illustration of the way the PRI sought to incorporate competing sectors of the economy and order their relations.

18. AGL to DAAC, Aug. 9, 1965; Josefina Ordoñez to AGL, Oct. 8, 1965 (emphasis added), both in AGL. It is not clear from the context whether de Cosas was a land reform official or a counselor at the UGRCH.

19. UGRCH to all local cattlemen's associations, Nov. 30, 1963, in AGL (emphasis added).

20. "Informe del Gobierno Municipal," 1980, in AMCH; Presidente Municipal de Chilón to Diputado Federal, Feb. 9, 1980, in RAN-TG, Ejido de Chilón files.

21. Rodolfo Domínguez to Presidente Municipal de Chilón, June 10, 1980, in AMCH.

22. "Juzgado," Feb. 14, 1959, ibid.

23. Ovalle Muñoz 1984 is the only academic study specifically focused on conflict in Chilón during this period, although numerous authors mention or discuss the Golonchán massacre, using such spellings as "Wolonchán" and "Colonchán" (e.g., García de León 2002, Benjamin 1996, Pontigo and Hernández 1981).

24. Presidente Municipal de Chilón to Diputado González Camacho,

Jan. 21, 1975, in AHPL; Presidente Municipal de Sitalá to PRODESCH, Oct. 7, 1976, in RAN-TG, Ejido Golonchán files.

25. Presidente Municipal de Chilón to Gobernador Patrocinio González (telegram), March 25, 1980, in AMCH.

26. "Acta levantada en el poblado de Piquinteel," Oct. 10, 1980, ibid.

27. Confederación Nacional Campesina to Presidente Municipal de Chilón, Jan. 24, 1980; and Agente Municipal to Presidente Municipal de Chilón, July 8, 1980, both ibid.

28. Agente and Juez Municipal de Chilón to Juan Sabines. July 10, 1982, in AHPL.

29. In 1962, for example, Golonchán's owner burst into a meeting of the Agrarian Committee as it waited for Trujillo. According to the peasants, "Gustavo Flores shouted that the *federales* [federal troops] would come if we kept meeting to carry out the census [of qualified ejido members], and . . . we were startled and afraid of attack, so we fled, leaving only a small group of about fourteen people": Campesinos Indígenas de Golonchán to Eva Sámano de López Mateos, Oct. 5, 1962, in RAN-TG, Ejido Golonchán files.

30. "Informe de la CAM," May 2, 1963, ibid. Before a land reform claim can proceed, two legal qualifications must be established: the town (or population center) must be deemed collectively qualified by reason of its location, the length of its existence, and the number of individuals qualified for land reform residing in it; and the proposed beneficiaries of land reform in that town must meet extensive criteria to be considered qualified.

31. Campesinos de Golonchán to el Sr. Presidente López Mateos, June 1, 1963, in AMS.

32. "Informativo de la CAM," June 5, 1980, in RAN-TG, Ejido Golonchán files.

33. Jefe de la Zona Ejidal to DAAC, Jan. 19, 1972, ibid.

34. The following discussion derives from interviews with Fr. Mardonio Morales and landowners in Sitalá, as well as Ovalle Muñoz 1984, Pontigo and Hernández 1981, and the following articles in the weekly newsmagazine *Proceso:* F. Gómez. "En Chiapas, el Gobierno . . . ," June 9, 1980, pp.10–14; H. Castillo, "Organizaciones políticas gatilleras," June 9, 1980, p. 12; F. Ortega, "A tiros, la tropa evacua la finca invadida en Wolonchán . . . ," June 23, 1980, p. 26; G. Correa, "Sabines nos mandó matar . . . ," June 30, 1980, pp. 12–15; R. Millán, "Las autoridades provocaron . . . ," July 7, 1980, pp. 22–23; F. Ortiz, "Confirma el alcalde de Sitalá . . . ," July 21, 1980. p. 10; F. Ortiz, "Policía y tropas en Chiapas, al servicio de finqueros . . . ," July 21, 1980, pp. 10–13; I. Ramírez, "Los problemas de Nicaragua, El Salvador y Guatemala, juntos en Chiapas," March 22, 1982, pp. 12–17; G. Correa, "Despojos, represión y abuso oficial . . . ," March 22, 1982, pp. 14–15; and G. Correa and P. Hiriart, "Con el apoyo de Sabines . . . ," March 29, 1982, pp. 20–21; and in *Uno Más Uno*

(Mexico City), V. Avilés, "En busca de una credencial del PRI, los in-dígenas . . . ," July 2, 1980, p. 4.

35. It is generally assumed on the left that the prices paid for land in the 1980s brought fabulous windfalls to landowners. This is also the common wisdom in regard to prices in 1994–1998, an assumption that I challenge in a later chapter. Therefore, in the case of the 1980s, I take these assump-tions, suggesting that prices were ridiculously high in the 1980s or ab-surdly low in the interim period, with a grain of salt. Even among land-owners, memories of how lucrative the sales were vary greatly. Alejandro Díaz, for example, argued that the sales prices "were an excellent amount of money for the land." Oscar Franz, on the other hand, concurred with Favre. "The price was OK for the land, but we had cattle and [coffee-processing] machinery that was worth much more. Sabines just told us, 'We buy land, not houses,' and so we got no compensation for all our infrastructure." A number of landowners whose land had *not* been invaded volunteered their properties for sale, a choice that can easily be read as evidence of favorable prices. These "voluntary" sellers, however, explain their participation as a rational response to the ongoing threat of invasion. Some actual data on the sales prices can be found at the public registrar's office in Yajalón. Records for seven estates (divided into twenty-seven legal parcels) covering some 2,500 hectares show an average purchase price of 1,638 pesos per hectare. Adjusted for inflation and a change in currency denomination, the 1980s prices were similar to those offered after 1994. Ultimately, as I argue in Chapter 7, no general statement is possible regarding the value of 1994–1998 purchases. Numerous factors — level of indebtedness, generational shift, and degree of reliance on agricul-ture for a living (e.g., Delio Ballinas was highly dependent on income from his invaded properties, while Gustavo Flores had numerous other sources of income) — distort any calculations.

7. The Invasions of 1994–1998

1. "Libro de Actas de la Asociación de 1994," minutes of January assem-bly, in AGL.

2. Property sales brokered for peasant land claimants by the state Banco de Crédito Rural del Istmo and registered in "Libros de Escrituras Públi-cas, 1994–1999," in RP-Y.

3. Comunidades agrarias, like ejidos, are a category of land tenure in Mexico's agrarian reform system. A group of peasants hoping to establish a comunidad agraria must provide evidence that the land in question was both owned by their community and illegally appropriated by a land-owner prior to 1917; this is a higher legal threshold than that required for the formation of an ejido. Comunidad agraria members are typically indí-genas and own their land collectively.

4. On Salinas's Article 27 reforms see Vázquez 2004, Cornelius and Myhre 1998, de Janvry et al. 1997, Randall 1996, and DeWalt et al. 1994.

5. The federal SRA issued more than one million exemption certificates to "small" property owners in Chiapas (see Chapter 6). These certificates sheltered properties against expropriation — at least in theory. During the 1994–1998 invasions state actors ignored the certificates when they decided what land would be redistributed.

6. For numerous examples of this type of competing and overlapping claims see Liga de Comunidades Agrarias y Sindicatos Campesinos del Estado de Chiapas, "Relación de poblados que han solicitado tierras y resultados (1922–1979)," in INAREMAC library, document no. 1.9.10. This dynamic was, of course, not limited to Chiapas. For example, see Dennis 1987 on Oaxaca.

7. Treated by all actors involved as military occupations rather than land invasions, these seizures followed a different dynamic from the mobilizations to come and are not the subject of this chapter.

8. This account of the events at Liquidámbar was assembled from *El Tiempo* (San Cristóbal de Las Casas), June 16–20, 1998; SAIIC 1997; and AMDH 1995. Typical of the confusion surrounding Chiapan agrarian politics, some accounts claimed that Liquidámbar covered as much as 3,500 hectares. Newspapers listed the owner's name variously as Lawrence Hudler, Lauren Huckler, and Laurent Hutile.

9. This and subsequent quantitative claims made in this chapter were calculated from SRA 2000, CESMECA 1998, INEGI 1995, and two unpublished charts provided to me by the Secretaría Estatal de Desarrollo Agrícola, Tuxtla Gutiérrez.

10. These ten municipios experienced slightly more than their share of invasions.

11. They were members of the UCIAF, associated with Desarollo Paz y Justicia, the legal front for Paz y Justicia.

12. "Dictámen del Cuerpo Consultivo Agrario," March 8, 1990, in RANDF, San Sebastián Bachajón files.

13. "A la opinión pública," broadsheet signed by the president of Ejido San Sebastián Bachajón, n.d. (spring 1994), in AGL.

14. CNPI to Efraín Vera Arévalo and Rosemberg Molina Hidalgo, Nov. 28, 1994, ibid. See Chapter 9 for an account of what happened to Efraín Vera when he attempted to retrieve his cattle.

15. According to SRA 2000, the social-sector land base in Chiapas comprises 41 hectares per rights-holding head of household or 7 hectares per capita.

16. For example, members of CIOAC and a PRI-aligned peasant group have alternated possession of several properties in Villa Corzo since 1995 (*Cuarto Poder* [Tuxtla Gutiérrez], May 22, 2000).

17. Israel Gutiérrez explained: "Before 1984, municipal presidents received checks from Tuxtla for their office expenses and salaries, and that's

about it. Sometimes they were able to construct some public work or other. . . . This started to change in 1981, when Juan Sabines started channeling money directly to the presidents. . . . Then in 1984, with the changes to [Article 117 of the] Constitution, the president got to control his own checkbook. . . . Before, the only money the president handled was from taxes on coffee and whatever fines he could collect. Now there is a director of public works and a director of agricultural development who manage lots of money and projects. . . . This had a big impact on the town. Before no one wanted to be president, they had to practically force some landowner or merchant to take the job, now *everyone* wants to be president."

18. "Libro de Sesiones de Cabildo, 1996," minutes of Sept. 26 and Dec. 2, in AMCH.

19. The Chinchulines formed in 1988 as the United Front of Ejidatarios to fight political rivals for control over the ejido council of San Jerónimo Bachajón. Particularly at stake in these disputes were transportation concessions, control over gravel extraction, and land concentration within the ejido. Of the many press reports consulted on the Chinchulines, one stands out in particular: F. Ortiz, "Las atrocidades y la impunidad del grupo armado 'los Chinchulines,'" *Proceso*, May 13, 1996, pp. 18–23.

20. CDHFBLC and CEDIAC 1996; CONPAZ et al. 1996; interview with an anonymous former member of the Chinchulines, Chilón, Dec. 20, 2000. Despite this victory, things did not end well for the Chinchulines. During April and May 1996, disputes between the Chinchulines and rivals over control of the ejido council of San Jerónimo Bachajón grew increasingly violent. On May 4 the Chinchulines attacked a group of ejidatarios who voted against them in council elections. The next day, 200 of their opponents descended on Bachajón and carried out a "meticulous operation" (*Proceso*, May 13, 1996) to execute the Chinchulines' top leader. Three other Chinchulines leaders were killed in subsequent fighting that day. In retaliation, the leaderless Chinchulines rioted in Bachajón, burning twenty-three houses, driving scores of opponents from Bachajón, and killing two teachers. This riot received considerable attention nationally and internationally, thanks to rapid response by Jesuit human rights workers stationed in Bachajón. After allowing the Chinchulines to operate with considerable impunity for several years (for a glimpse of this history see Unión de Indígenas Tzeltales de San Jerónimo Bachajón to Presidente del Congreso del Estado, Nov. 25, 1991; testimony before the Chiapas state legislature by Víctor Ortiz del Carpio, July 15, 1993; Comisión Estatal de Derechos Humanos to Presidente Municipal de Sitalá, Sept. 11, 1995, all in AHPL), the state commission assigned to investigate the events of May 5, 1996, ruled largely in favor of the Chinchulines' opponents. The state agreed to free people arrested in conjunction with the murder of the four Chinchulines, compensated the families of the teachers murdered by the Chinchulines, and provided material assistance for the Chinchulines'

opponents whose houses and cars were burned in the riot: "Informe de la Comisión Plural para el Caso de Bachajón," May 9, 1996; "Acuerdo 00354," Congreso del Estado, LIX Legislatura, Comisión de Hacienda, Aug. 14, 1996; "Convenio del 6 de Septiembre," signed by Comisión Plural para el Caso de Bachajón, PGR, Comisión de Desplazados, and Gobierno de la República, Sept. 6, 1996, all in AHPL.

21. See Toledo 2002 on the Simojovel case.

22. See also "A la opinión pública," broadside signed by Nicolas Guzmán P., Manuel Jiménez Navarro, and other ejido authorities, n.d. (c. February 1994), and "Restitución del territorio original a los pueblos y comunidades indígenas," broadside signed by ejidatarios de San Sebastián Bachajón, CNPI, and Comité de Campesinos Pobres, Feb. 22, 1994, both in AGL.

23. Although ladinos appear to have held on to important positions in Sitalá under the indigenous municipal president.

24. In the spring of 2001 indigenous protestors drove Sitalá's municipal president into exile, accusing him of pocketing money earmarked for public works. Meanwhile, during my year in Chilón, the president constructed one of the town's most ostentatious houses, complete with 12-foot-high electric gates.

25. See Villafuerte el al. 1999. Although observers frequently blame population pressures for the problem of *minifundización*, this explanation fails to capture the complexities of land tenure in Chiapas (Bobrow-Strain 2001).

26. Calculated from CESMECA 1998 and SIC 1998.

27. Carlos Alexis Hernández Vera and Elí Rodríguez Zúñiga to Carlos Salinas de Gortari et al., March 15, 1994, in AGL.

28. See *La Jornada*, July 6 and Aug. 6, 1994, for reports of the federal moratorium on evictions; Secretario de Gobierno and Secretario de Hacienda del Estado, "Respuesta al pliego de peticiones de la coalición de propietarios rurales . . . ," n.d. (c. summer 1994), in AGL.

29. AGL to Diputado Gonzalo López Camacho, Aug. 8, 1994, ibid.

30. "Pliego peticionario que presentan los productores agropecuarios del Mpo. de Chilón . . . ," Dec. 21, 1994, ibid. The decision whether to offer a property for sale was made individually by each landowner in the context of often heated discussions within the AGL. Early drafts of the AGL's offer letter attest to this process: they are covered with scribbled and crossed-out notes saying "*X* is yes," "*Y* is out," and "*Z* is still deciding." Slowly the AGL worked toward a general consensus in favor of participation, and those landowners who waited longer to agree to participate generally encountered more difficulties in negotiations with the state.

31. The one evicted property was subsequently purchased for a pro-government peasant group. Through dozens of interviews and surveys of other data sources, I identified two or three likely evictions that did not appear in official reports. Peasants themselves often violently evicted members of rival peasant organizations and occupied the properties them-

selves, but I consider this a separate phenomenon. Many other properties were "voluntarily vacated" by invaders waiting for a purchase agreement who hoped that their cooperation would win the state's favor. In Chilón, most of these vacated properties were eventually sold to peasants, but not necessarily to the original invaders.

32. Some peasant land invaders refused to enter into negotiations with the government, preferring the informal access to land they already enjoyed over legal title and a mortgage. Similarly, several heavily indebted landowners refused to accept sales that did not cover their liens. Other landowners simply dragged their feet, frustrated by the low compensation offered for their farms.

33. "Predios ocupados, San Sebastián Bachajón que no pueden ser adquiridos," and printout of a spreadsheet prepared by Secretaría de Desarrollo Agrario, Gobierno del Estado, n.d., both in WLT.

34. Carlos A. Hernández Vera, chairman of AGL, to Artemio Rojas, governor's representative to the Comisión Ejecutiva Agraria, May 12, 1994, in AGL.

35. "Libro de Escrituras Públicas (1994–1999)," in RP-Y. As these figures indicate, most of the properties purchased in Chilón were relatively small, averaging 56 hectares. More than half of the invaded properties in the entire state were smaller than 50 hectares and only a quarter were more than 100 hectares (Villafuerte et al. 1999:136). Statewide, properties slated for purchase through the accords had a median size of just under 60 hectares (calculated from CESMECA 1998). Contrary to popular perceptions, most of the affected landowners were relatively small-scale farmers. Nevertheless, in many cases one family owned multiple divisions of a larger property. The Utrilla family, for example, sold five legally subdivided pieces of El Horizonte in Sitalá totaling 771 hectares.

36. "Fracción La Alianza," in RP-Y, "Libro de Escrituras Públicas, 1988." Sales prices for invaded properties, on the other hand, were reported directly by the Banco de Crédito Rural del Istmo, and all observers agreed that they accurately reflected sales prices.

37. Fifty percent sample of all transactions recorded in "Libro de Escrituras Públicas (1993–1999)," in RP-Y.

38. Peasants, whose participation in land markets often reflects a different economic calculus, may be willing to pay even higher prices (i.e., Chayanov 1986). In an informal conversation in July 2001, a peasant from the region reported purchasing a hectare of coffee plants for 60,000 pesos.

8. Import-Substitution Dreaming

1. My discussion of *El sacrificio de Isac* is based on an unpublished manuscript shared with me in 2000. The book was published in 2002 as a volume in Coneculta Chiapas's Biblioteca Popular series.

2. With the exception of Nymph, indigenous characters and towns carry Old Testament names (the invaders come from Sodom and Gomorrah!) — evidence of their ancient ways and stormy unpredictability. Many ladino characters and places, on the other hand, carry classical Greek names (Athena, Penélope, Ithaca), symbolic, one supposes, of rationality and civilization.

3. Landowners of all ages reflect on the loss of a place to have fun, and their nostalgic longings for the past frequently evoke childhood picnics, cool river swims, and horseback riding. What is telling about Juan's remark is that his loss is framed *exclusively* as the loss of a place to have fun.

4. See also Viqueira 1997, Gosner 1992, and the original report, "Informe sobre la sublevación de los Zendales . . ." (1714), housed at the Bancroft Library of the University of California, Berkeley (MS M-M 435).

5. Gov. León to Porfirio Díaz, Dec. 20, 1898, in CGPD, roll 156/XXIII.

6. Gobierno del Estado, "Diagnóstico Municipal 1993," in AHPL.

7. Interestingly, the literature of agrarian studies has had much to say about the landowner-merchant divide, but merchant capital played a large role in ladinos' integrated economy. Efraín Vera explained: "Right now I'm a merchant because coffee is bad. When coffee is good, it pays for our inventory here in the store. When coffee is bad, the store pays for the ranch."

8. "Informe del Secretario," July 18, 2001, in AGL.

9. Gobierno del Estado, "Diagnóstico Municipal 1993."

10. For general overviews of neoliberal restructuring in Mexico see Otero 2004, 1996; Middlebrook and Zepeda 2003; Dussel Peters 2000; Cook, Middlebrook, and Molinar 1994; and Lustig 1992. On neoliberalism in rural Mexico see Cornelius and Myhre 1998, de Janvry et al. 1997, Randall 1996, and Grammont and Tejera 1996. On Chiapas see Nash 2001, García and Villafuerte 1998, and Harvey 1998.

11. On social liberalism see Soederberg 2001; Centeno 1997; Cornelius, Craig, and Fox 1994. Considerable research has focused on social liberalism as an instrument of regime legitimation. Noting the efficient way Salinas's renewed commitment to social programs diffused dissent and delivered electoral victories for the PRI (Dresser 1994; Cornelius, Craig, and Fox 1994; Santín 2001), some scholars have reduced social liberalism to its instrumentalist bones. Writing in 2001, for example, Soederberg called social liberalism "superficial" and a "gimmick." While it is difficult to dispute her contention that social liberalism was quite explicitly designed to buttress support for the president and palliate the snowballing inequalities that resulted from market-oriented reforms, it is unwise to analyze this complex assemblage of power relations only in terms of its intended effects. My understanding of state rule stresses the need to examine its unintended outcomes. All techniques and logics of rule frame social problems and their solutions in particular ways in the service of particular interests. These framings, however, always have a wider life that transcends the intentions and interests mobilized in their making.

12. On PRONASOL see Dresser 1991; Pastor and Wise 1997; Cornelius, Craig, and Fox 1994.

13. For an exception to the rule that PRONASOL undermined corporatist organizations see Fox 1994b.

14. PROCAMPO, launched in 1993 as a rural-focused complement to PRONASOL, provided direct welfare payments to small producers of corn and other traditional crops to compensate for the negative impacts of trade liberalization. As a program to give direct payments to producers rather than price supports or other trade-distorting subsidies, PROCAMPO was designed to bring Mexican farm supports more in line with WTO rules. PROCAMPO has not received as much scholarly attention as PRONASOL, but see Klepeis and Vance 2003, Sadoulet et al. 2001, and Pastor and Wise 1997.

15. By 2004 Fondo Chiapas had generated only five projects and only U.S.$7 million in direct investment (although it helped to attract additional outside investments in its projects). Only two of its five projects are actually located in areas that experienced sustained conflict during the 1994–2000 period (www.fondochiapas.org.mx/proyectos.html).

9. Geographies of Fear

1. " . . . pobrecitos los ladinos/que por temor de los indios/ban cargando sus niñitos/llorando por los caminos . . .": *Colección de poesías de J. M. Arévalo desde 1846 hasta el presente* (1872). Photocopy in possession of Alí Reyes.

2. This chapter also adds a level of geographic depth and nuance to debates in anthropology over the formative role of violence and terror in reshaping the very social relations from which they emerge (Nordstrom 1997, Nordstrom and Robben 1995, Nordstrom and Martin 1992, Feldman 1991).

3. Literally Indians as a whole.

4. "Informe sobre la sublevación de los Zendales . . ." (1714), housed at the Bancroft Library of the University of California, Berkeley (MS M-M 435).

5. The one exception was *Horizontes*'s ongoing attacks on ladino liquor merchants in Bachajón. The paper's staff held these merchants responsible for inflaming the town's lawlessness.

6. *Horizontes* can be found at the UNAM's Hemeroteca Nacional. The passages quoted in this paragraph are from June 28, 1964, p. 7; May 3, 1967, p. 10; and Nov. 8, 1968, p. 3.

7. On June 28, 1964, *Horizontes* saluted Mexico's Instituto Nacional Indigenista for its efforts to incorporate "the Indian into our civilization."

8. Presidente Municipal de Chilón to Governor Salomon González Blanco, Jan. 16, 1978 (telegram), and Presidente Municipal de Chilón

to Governor Patrocinio González, March 25, 1980 (telegram), both in AMCH.

9. "Proyecto de dictamen sobre dotación de ejidos al pueblo Sitalá del Municipio de Chilón," June 20, 1933, in RAN-TG, Ejido de Sitalá files.

10. Interview with a landowner who wished to remain anonymous. While no priest would characterize himself as teaching hatred, the mission has fomented an oppositional attitude toward landowners. A parish priest from Chilón said to me, "Mestizos say that we've neglected them in favor of the Tzeltals, and I suppose they're right in some ways. We *have* neglected them. Most of us came here because we were interested in working with the indígenas." Another priest told me that he made an early decision to work only with the region's indigenous peasants and "never deal directly with the finqueros."

11. Even after the 1992 amendments to Article 27 of the Constitution, the state remains the ultimate owner of land within the nation, reserving the right to grant and revoke private property rights according to the dictates of "public interest." Attempts to allay the fears of private property owners by changing the wording of Article 27 in 1983 (cf. Fox and Gordillo 1989) have not assuaged this cadastral anxiety among ranchers in Chiapas, given their belief that the state has often sacrificed their property rights to restore peace during periods of agrarian upheaval.

Glossary

aguardiente cane liquor

Bachajontecos residents of the town of Bachajón

baldío resident estate worker who trades labor for access to a plot of land

cacique political and economic boss

campesino peasant

cantina bar; tavern

Carrancistas followers of the revolutionary leader Venustiano Carranza

casa grande big house; the landowner's house on an estate

casco the central core of an estate; the land and outbuildings immediately surrounding the casa grande

catequista lay teacher of Catholic doctrine

charro cowboy; a participant in Mexico's traditional rodeo festival

Chiloneros residents of the town of Chilón; used here to refer to ladino residents

científico technocratic adviser to the nineteenth-century dictator Porfirio Díaz

compadrazgo fictive kinship based on reciprocal relations between godparent and godchild

compraventista commercial intermediary

coraje fury; rage

ejidatario member of an ejido

ejido one of the central categories of land tenure in Mexico's land reform sector, characterized by a combination of common property rights and individually farmed plots

fajina (or **faena**) extra day of unpaid labor provided by estate workers

fideicomiso trust

finquero owner of an estate

ganaderización the large-scale transition from farming to cattle production

ganadero cattle rancher

hacendado owner of a hacienda

hacienda large estate

latifundio large estate; the term is typically used to imply that the property surpasses legal limits on landholding

latifundista owner of a latifundio

mestizo person of mixed indígena and European descent

milpa swidden plot typically planted in corn, beans, and squash

minifundización the fragmentation of peasant holdings into unviable units

naturales an old term for indígenas with a derogatory connotation

patrón boss

peonaje peonage

peón peon

peones acasillados debt-bound resident estate workers

Pinedistas supporters of Alberto Pineda, who led a guerrilla campaign against the revolutionary army of Venustiano Carranza

pozol corn drink

quintal hundredweight; 100 pounds (about 46 kilograms)

ranchero rancher or country folk

respeto respect

San Cristobalenses residents of San Cristóbal de Las Casas

selva rain forest

sexenio six-year presidential term of office

terreno nacional federally owned land

tienda de raya estate store; scrip store

trapiche sugar mill

Tzeltal one of the four main Mayan linguistic groups in Chiapas, concentrated in the central highlands and north-central portions of the state; also a Tzeltal-speaking indígena

Zapatistas members or supporters of the EZLN: Ejército Zapatista de Liberación Nacional (Zapatista Army of National Liberation)

Bibliography

Archival Sources

AGL   Asociación Ganadera Local (Local Cattleman's Association), Chilón

AHD   Archivo Histórico Diocesano (Historic Diocesan Archives), San Cristóbal de Las Casas

AHPL   Archivo Histórico del Poder Legislativo de Chiapas (Historical Archives of the Chiapas Congress), Tuxtla Gutiérrez

AMCH   Archivo Municipal de Chilón (Archives of the Municipio of Chilón); documents loosely organized by year

AMS   Archivo Municipal de Sitalá (Archives of the Municipio of Sitalá); documents loosely organized by year

APJ   Archivo del Poder Judicial de Chiapas (Archives of the Chiapas Judiciary), San Cristóbal de Las Casas

CGPD   Colección General Porfirio Díaz (General Porfirio Díaz Collection), Puebla

RAN-DF   Registro Agrario Nacional/Archivo General Agrario (National Agrarian Registry/General Agrarian Archive), Mexico City

RAN-TG   Registro Agrario Nacional, Delegación Tuxtla Gutiérrez (National Agrarian Registry), Tuxtla Gutiérrez

RP-Y   Registro Público (Public Registry), Yajalón

WLT   Papers of Wenceslao López Trujillo, Yajalón

Secondary Sources

Agnew, John. 2000. "Territoriality." In *The Dictionary of Human Geography*, ed. R. J. Johnston, D. Gregory, G. Pratt, and M. Watts. Oxford: Blackwell.

Alejos García, José. 1996. "Dominio extranjero en Chiapas, el desarrollo cafetalero en la Sierra Norte." *Mesoamérica* 32:283–298.

——. 1999. *Ch'ol/kaxlan: Identidades étnicas y conflicto agrario en el norte de Chiapas, 1914–1940*. Mexico City: Universidad Autónoma Metropolitana.

Alejos García, José, and Elsa Ortega Peña. 1990. *El archivo municipal de Tumbalá, Chiapas, 1920–1946*. Mexico City: UNAM.

Alonso, Ana. 1995. *Thread of Blood: Colonialism, Revolution, and Gender on Mexico's Northern Frontier.* Tucson: University of Arizona Press.

Alonso, Jorge. 1984. *Crepitar de banderas rojas: Campaña y elecciones socialistas.* Mexico City: Centro de Investigaciones y Estudios Superiores en Antropología Social.

AMDH. 1995. *Boletín Chiapas*, no. 13.

Ascencio Franco, Gabriel. 2002. "La imagen del ranchero en la literatura chiapaneca." *Pueblos y Fronteras* 4:11–30.

Aubry, Andrés. 1986. "Retrato político de Chiapas en tres sexenios y tres sexenios de desarrollo a lo Chiapaneco." INAREMAC working paper, San Cristóbal de Las Casas.

Austin, James, and Gustavo Esteva. 1987. *Food Policy in Mexico: The Search for Self-Sufficiency.* Ithaca: Cornell University Press.

Baumann, Friederike. 1985. "Terratenientes, campesinos y expansión de la agricultura capitalista en Chiapas, 1886–1916." *Mesoamérica* 5:8–61.

Becerra O'Leary, José. 1998. "Palabras de José Becerra O'Leary, Representante Especial en el Estado de Chiapas." Address delivered May 19, Casa de la Cultura, San Cristóbal de Las Casas.

Benjamin, Thomas. 1996. *A Rich Land, a Poor People: Politics and Society in Modern Chiapas.* Albuquerque: University of New Mexico Press.

Benjamin, Walter. 1969. *Illuminations.* New York: Schocken.

Bernstein, Henry. 2004. "'Changing Before Our Very Eyes': Agrarian Questions and the Politics of Land in Capitalism Today." *Journal of Agrarian Change* 4(1):190–225.

Bernstein, Henry, and Terence J. Byres. 2001. "From Peasant Studies to Agrarian Change." *Journal of Agrarian Change* 1(1):1–56.

Blom, Frans, and Oliver La Farge. 1926–1927. *Tribes and Temples: A Record of the Expedition to Middle America Conducted by the Tulane University of Louisiana in 1925.* 2 vols. New Orleans: Tulane University of Louisiana.

Bobrow-Strain, Aaron. 2001. "Between a Ranch and a Hard Place: Violence, Scarcity, and Meaning in Chiapas, Mexico." In *Violent Environments,* ed. N. Peluso and M. Watts. Ithaca: Cornell University Press.

———. 2003. "Rethinking Thuggery: Landowners, Territory, and Violence in Chiapas, Mexico." Ph.D. dissertation, University of California, Berkeley.

———. 2004. "(Dis)accords: The Politics of Market-Assisted Land Reforms in Chiapas, Mexico." *World Development* 32(6):887–903.

———. n.d. "Liquid Fincas: Land, Commerce, and Liquor in North-central Chiapas, 1820–1950." Working paper.

Borras, Saturnino. 2001. "State-Society Relations in Land Reform Implementation in the Philippines." *Development and Change* 32(3):545–575.

———. 2003. "Questioning Market-Led Agrarian Reform: Experiences from Brazil, Colombia, and South Africa." *Journal of Agrarian Change* 3(3):367–394.

———. 2005. "Can Redistributive Reform be Achieved via Market-Based Voluntary Land Transfer Schemes? Evidence and Lessons from the Philippines." *Journal of Development Studies* 41(1):90–134.

Boym, Svetlana. 2001. *The Future of Nostalgia.* New York: Basic Books.

Bruno, Regina. 1997. *Senhores da terra, senhores da guerra: A nova face política das elites agroindustriais no Brasil.* Rio de Janeiro: Forense Universitarial.

Buffington, Robert, and William French. 2000. "The Culture of Modernity." In *The Oxford History of Mexico,* ed. W. Beezley and M. Meyer. Oxford: Oxford University Press.

Burguete Cal y Mayor, Aracely. 1988. *Chiapas etnocida reciente: Represión política a los indios, 1974–1987.* Mexico City: AMDH.

———, ed. 1999. *México: Experiencias de autonomía indígena.* Copenhagen: Grupo Internacional de Trabajo sobre Asuntos Indígenas.

Carney, Judith, and Michael Watts. 1990. "Manufacturing Dissent: Work, Gender and the Politics of Meaning in a Peasant Society." *Africa* 60(2): 207–241.

Carrascosa, Manuel. 1883. *Apuntes estadísticos del estado de Chiapas.* Mexico City: Francisco Díaz de León.

———. 1889. *Memorial que presenta el C. Manuel Carrascosa como gobernador constitucional del estado de Chiapas a la legislatura,* Vol. 3. Tuxtla Gutiérrez: Secretaría de Fomento.

Centeno, Miguel Angel. 1997. *Democracy within Reason: Technocratic Revolution in Mexico.* University Park: Pennsylvania State University Press.

CDHFBLC. 1996. *Ni paz, ni justicia.* San Cristóbal de Las Casas.

CDHFBLC and CEDIAC. 1996. "Reporte sobre el contexto social e histórico del conflicto en San Gerónimo Bachajón." San Cristóbal de Las Casas.

CENCOS. 1974. *Documentos del Primer Congreso Indígena, San Cristóbal, 1974.* Mexico City.

CESMECA. 1998. "Predios invadidos, Chiapas, 1994–1998" and "Fideicomisos agrarios, Chiapas, 1994–1998." San Cristóbal de Las Casas. Printed spreadsheets.

Chanona Marín, Luis Alberto. 1952. "Perfil de la reforma agraria en el estado de Chiapas." Licenciatura en Derecho, Universidad Autónoma Metropolitana, Mexico City.

Charnay, Désiré. 1956. "San Cristóbal." *Ateneo* 6:126–148.

Chauvet, Michelle. 1999. *La ganadería bovina de carne en México: Del auge a la crisis.* Azcapotzalco: Universidad Autónoma Metropolitana.

Chayanov, A. V. 1986. *The Theory of Peasant Economy.* Madison: University of Wisconsin Press.

Collier, George, with Elizabeth Lowery Quaratielo. 2005. *Basta! Land and the Zapatista Rebellion in Chiapas.* Oakland: Food First Books.

CONPAZ, CDHFBLC, and COCD. 1996. *Militarización y violencia en Chiapas.* Mexico City: Impretei.

Cook, María Lorena, Kevin Middlebrook, and Juan Molinar Horcasitas, eds. 1994. *The Politics of Economic Restructuring: State-Society Relations and Regime Change in Mexico.* La Jolla: Center for U.S.-Mexican Studies, University of California, San Diego.

Cornelius, Wayne, Ann Craig, and Jonathan Fox, eds. 1994. *Transforming State-Society Relations in Mexico: The National Solidarity Strategy.* La Jolla: Center for U.S.-Mexican Studies, University of California, San Diego.

Cornelius, Wayne, and David Myhre, eds. 1998. *The Transformation of Rural Mexico: Reforming the Ejido Sector.* La Jolla: Center for U.S.-Mexican Studies, University of California, San Diego.

Coronil, Fernando. 1997. *The Magical State: Nature, Money, and Modernity in Venezuela.* Chicago: University of Chicago Press.

Cosío Villegas, Daniel. 1994. *Historia mínima de México.* Mexico City: Colegio de México.

Deere, Carmen Diana. 1990. *Household and Class Relations: Peasants and Landlords in Northern Peru.* Berkeley: University of California Press.

Deininger, Klaus. 2003. *Land Policies for Growth and Poverty Reduction.* Oxford: Oxford University Press.

de Janvry, Alain. 1981. *The Agrarian Question and Reformism in Latin America.* Baltimore: Johns Hopkins University Press.

de Janvry, Alain, Gustavo Gordillo, and Elisabeth Sadoulet, eds. 1997. *Mexico's Second Agrarian Reform: Household and Community Responses, 1990–1994.* La Jolla: Center for U.S.-Mexican Studies, University of California, San Diego.

de la Cadena, Marisol. 2000. *Indigenous Mestizos: The Politics of Race and Culture in Cuzco, Peru, 1919–1991.* Durham: Duke University Press.

Delaney, David. 2005. *Territory: A Short Introduction.* Malden, Mass.: Blackwell.

de la Peña, Moisés. 1951. *Chiapas económico.* 4 vols. Tuxtla Gutiérrez: Departamento de Prensa y Turismo, Sección Autográfica.

Dennis, Philip. 1987. *Intervillage Conflict in Oaxaca.* New Brunswick: Rutgers University Press.

de Vos, Jan. 1988. *La paz de Dios y del rey: La conquista de la selva lacandona, 1525–1821.* Mexico City: Fondo de Cultura Económica.

———. 1994. *Oro verde: La conquista de la selva lacandona por los madereros tabasqueños, 1822–1949.* Mexico City: Fondo de Cultura Económica.

———. 2002. *Una tierra para sembrar sueños: Historia reciente de la selva lacandona, 1950–2000.* Mexico City: Fondo de Cultura Económica.

DeWalt, Billie R., Martha W. Rees, and Arthur D. Murphy, eds. 1994. *The End of Agrarian Reform in Mexico: Past Lessons, Future Prospects.* La Jolla: Center for U.S.-Mexican Studies, University of California, San Diego.

Díaz Olivares, Jorge. n.d. "Bachajón zona de refugio en los altos de Chiapas." Master's thesis, Universidad Iberoamericana.

Dresser, Denise. 1991. *Neopopulist Solutions to Neoliberal Problems: Mexico's National Solidarity Program.* La Jolla: Center for U.S.-Mexican Studies, University of California, San Diego.

———. 1994. "Bringing the Poor Back In: National Solidarity as a Strategy of Regime Legitimation." In *Transforming State-Society Relations in Mexico: The National Solidarity Strategy,* ed. W. Cornelius, A. Craig, and J. Fox. La Jolla: Center for U.S.-Mexican Studies, University of California, San Diego.

Dussel Peters, Enrique. 2000. *Polarizing Mexico: The Impact of Liberalization Strategy.* Boulder: Lynne Rienner.

Eber, Christine. 1995. *Women and Alcohol in a Highland Maya Town: Water of Hope, Water of Sorrow.* Austin: University of Texas Press.

———. 2003. "Buscando una Nueva Vida: Liberation through Autonomy in San Pedro Chenalhó, 1970–1998." In *Mayan Lives, Mayan Utopias: The Indigenous Peoples of Chiapas and the Zapatista Rebellion*, ed. J. Rus, R. A. Hernández Castillo, and S. L. Mattiace. Lanham, Md.: Rowman and Littlefield.

Eco, Umberto. 1995. *The Island of the Day Before*. New York: Harcourt Brace.

Edelman, Marc. 1992. *The Logic of the Latifundio: The Large Estates of Northwestern Costa Rica since the Late Nineteenth Century*. Stanford: Stanford University Press.

———. 1994. Landlords and the Devil: Class, Ethnic, and Gender Dimensions of Central American Peasant Narratives. *Cultural Anthropology* 9(1):58–93.

Estado de Chiapas, Oficina de Informaciones. 1895. *Chiapas, su estado actual, su riqueza, sus ventajas para los negocios*. Tuxtla Gutiérrez.

———. 1909. *Anuario estadístico del estado de Chiapas*. Tuxtla Gutiérrez: Tipografía del Gobierno.

Executive Intelligence Report. 1994. "Surge en Chiapas 'Sendero Luminoso Norte': Avanza el complot narcoterrorista para aniquilar a las naciones de Iberoamerica." Executive Intelligence Review News Services, January.

Fabregas Puig, Andrés. 1988. *Indigenismo y cambio estructural en Chiapas: Avances y perspectivas*. Tuxtla Gutiérrez: Universidad Nacional Autónoma de Chiapas.

Favre, Henri. 1985. "El cambio socio-cultural y el nuevo indigenismo en Chiapas." *Revista Mexicana de Sociología* 47(3):161–196.

Feldman, Allen. 1991. *Formations of Violence: The Narrative of the Body and Political Terror in Northern Ireland*. Chicago: University of Chicago Press.

Ferguson, James. 1999. *Expectations of Modernity: Myths and Meanings of Urban Life on the Zambian Copperbelt*. Berkeley: University of California Press.

Fernández Ortiz, Luís M., and María Tarrío García. 1983. *Ganadería y estructura agraria en Chiapas*. Xochimilco: Universidad Autónoma Metropolitana.

Fine, Ben. 1979. "On Marx's Theory of Agricultural Rent." *Economy and Society* 8(3):241–278.

Foucault, Michel. 1990. *The History of Sexuality: An Introduction*. Vol. 1. New York: Vintage Books.

———. 2003. *Society Must Be Defended: Lectures at the Collège de France, 1975–76*. New York: Picador.

Fox, Jonathan. 1993. *The Politics of Food in Mexico: State Power and Social Mobilization*. Ithaca: Cornell University Press.

———. 1994a. "Political Change in Mexico's New Peasant Economy." In *The Politics of Economic Restructuring: State-Society Relations and Regime Change in Mexico*, ed. M. L. Cook, K. J. Middlebrook, and J. M. Horcasitas. La Jolla: Center for U.S.-Mexican Studies, University of California, San Diego.

———. 1994b. "Targeting the Poorest: The Role of the National Indigenous Institute in Mexico's Solidarity Program." In *Transforming State-Society Relations in Mexico: The National Solidarity Strategy*, ed. W. Cornelius, A. Craig, and J. Fox. La Jolla: Center for U.S.-Mexican Studies, University of California, San Diego.

Fox, J., and G. Gordillo. 1989. "Between State and Market: The Campesino's Quest for Autonomy." In *Mexico's Alternative Political Futures*, ed. W. Cornelius, J. Gentleman, and P. Smith. La Jolla: Center for U.S.-Mexican Studies, University of California, San Diego.

García, María del Carmen, and Daniel Villafuerte Solís. 1998. "Economía y sociedad en Chiapas." In *La sociedad frente al mercado*, ed. M. Tarrío and L. Concheiro. Xochimilco: Universidad Autónoma Metropolitana.

García de León, Antonio. 1978. "La guerra de los Mapaches: El bestiario de la contrarevolución en Chiapas." San Cristóbal de Las Casas: Centro de Investigaciones Ecológicas del Sureste.

———. 1998 [1985]. *Resistencia y utopía: Memorial de agravios y crónica de revueltas y profecías acaecidas en la provincia de Chiapas durante los últimos quinientos años de su historia*. Mexico City: Era.

———. 2002. *Fronteras interiores, Chiapas: Una modernidad particular*. Mexico City: Océano.

Garza Caligaris, Anna María. 2005. "Los barrios de San Cristóbal: Población y género durante el Porfiriato." *Anuario de Estudios Indígenas* 10:115–143.

Ghimire, Krishna. 2001. "Land Reform at the Turn of the Century: An Overview of Issues, Actors, and Processes." In *Land Reform and Peasant Livelihoods: The Social Dynamics of Rural Poverty and Agrarian Reform in Developing Countries*, ed. K. Ghimire. Geneva: UNRISD.

Gómez Cruz, Patricia J., and Cristina María Kovic. 1993. *Con un pueblo vivo en tierra negada*. San Cristóbal de Las Casas: CDHFBLC.

González, Luís. 2001. "El liberalismo triunfante." In *Historia general de México*. Mexico City: Colegio de México.

Goodman, David, and Michael Watts. 1997. "Agrarian Questions: Global Appetite, Local Metabolism, Nature, Culture, and Industry in *Fin-de-Siècle* Agro-Food Systems." In *Globalising Food: Agrarian Questions and Global Restructuring,* ed. D. Goodman and M. Watts. New York: Routledge.

Gordillo, Gastón. 2002a. "Locations of Hegemony: The Making of Places in the Toba's Struggle for la Comuna, 1989–99." *American Anthropologist* 104(1):262–277.

———. 2002b. "The Breath of the Devils: Memories and Places of an Experience of Terror." *American Ethnologist* 29(1):33–57.

Gosner, Kevin. 1992. *Soldiers of the Virgin: The Moral Economy of a Colonial Maya Rebellion.* Tucson: University of Arizona Press.

Gould, Jeffrey L. 1998. *To Die in This Way: Nicaraguan Indians and the Myth of Mestizaje, 1880–1965.* Durham: Duke University Press.

Grammont, Hubert, and Héctor Tejera Gaona, eds. 1996. *La sociedad rural mexicana frente al nuevo milenio.* 4 vols. Mexico City: Plaza y Valdés.

Gramsci, Antonio. 1971. *Selections from the Prison Notebooks.* New York: International Publishers.

Gregory, Derek. 1995. "Imaginative Geographies." *Progress in Human Geography* 19(4):447–485.

Gremio de Agricultores del Estado de Chiapas. 1914. *El servicio doméstico en Chiapas: Estudio económico social aprobado y mandado publicar por el gremio de agricultores del estado residentes en San Cristóbal de Las Casas.* San Cristóbal de Las Casas: Tipografía Flores.

Guha, Ranajit. 1982. *Writings on South Asian History and Society.* Delhi: Oxford University Press.

Guthman, Julie. 2004. "Back to the Land: The Paradox of Organic Food Standards." *Environment and Planning* 36(3):511–528.

Gutmann, Matthew C. 1996. *The Meanings of Macho: Being a Man in Mexico City.* Berkeley: University of California Press.

Hale, Charles. 1996. "Mestizaje, Hybridity and the Cultural Politics of Difference in Post-Revolutionary Central America." *Journal of Latin American Anthropology* 2(1):34–61.

Hall, Stuart. 1974. "Marx's Notes on Method: A 'Reading' of the '1857 Introduction.'" *Working Papers in Cultural Studies* 6:132–170.

———. 1996. "On Postmodernism and Articulation: An Interview with Stuart Hall." In *Stuart Hall: Critical Dialogues in Cultural Studies,* ed. D. Morley and C. Kuan-Hsing. London: Routledge.

———. 2002. "Race, Articulation, and Societies Structured in Dominance." In *Race Critical Theories: Text and Context,* ed. P. Essed and D. T. Goldberg. Malden, Mass.: Blackwell.

Hart, Gillian. 1991. "Engendering Everyday Resistance." *Journal of Peasant Studies* 19(1):93–121.

———. 2002. *Disabling Globalization: Places of Power In Post-Apartheid South Africa.* Berkeley: University of California Press.

Harvey, David. 1990. *The Condition of Postmodernity: An Enquiry into the Origins of Cultural Change.* Cambridge: Blackwell.

———. 1999. *The Limits to Capital.* London: Verso.

Harvey, Neil. 1998. *The Chiapas Rebellion: The Struggle for Land and Democracy.* Durham: Duke University Press.

Hernández, Luis, and Fernando Celis. 1994. "Solidarity and the New Campesino Movements: The Case of Coffee Production." In *Transforming State-Society Relations in Mexico: The National Solidarity Strategy,* ed. W. A. Cornelius, A. Craig, and J. Fox. La Jolla: Center for U.S.-Mexican Studies, University of California, San Diego.

Hernández Chávez, Alicia. 1979. "La defensa de los finqueros en Chiapas: 1914–1920." *Historia Mexicana* 28(3):335–369.

Hewitt de Alcántara, Cynthia. 1978. *La modernización de la agricultura mexicana: 1940–1970.* Mexico City: Siglo Veintiuno.

Huber, Evelyne, and Frank Safford. 1995. *Agrarian Structure and Political Power: Landlord and Peasant in the Making of Latin America.* Pittsburgh: University of Pittsburgh Press.

Human Rights Watch. 1997. "Deberes incumplidos: Responsabilidad oficial por la violencia rural en México." At http://www.hrw.org/spanish/informes/1997/deberes8.html. Accessed February 2006.

Ibarra Mendivil, Jorge L. 1989. *Propiedad agraria y sistema político en México.* Hermosillo: Colegio de Sonora.

INEGI. 1990. *Anuario estadístico del estado de Chiapas.* Aguascalientes.

———. 1994. *Chiapas, resultados definitivos, VII censo agrícola-ganadero, 1990.* Aguascalientes.

INI. 1988. *El INI hoy: 40 aniversario.* Mexico City.

Joseph, Gilbert M., and Daniel Nugent, eds. 1994. *Everyday Forms of State Formation: Revolution and the Negotiation of Rule in Modern Mexico.* Durham: Duke University Press.

Joseph, Gilbert M., Anne Rubenstein, and Eric Zolov, eds. 2001. *Fragments of a Golden Age: The Politics of Culture in Mexico since 1940.* Durham: Duke University Press.

Kammen, Michael G. 1991. *Mystic Chords of Memory: The Transformation of Tradition in American Culture.* New York: Knopf.

Katz, Friedrich. 1974. "Labor Conditions on Haciendas in Porfirian Mexico: Some Trends and Tendencies." *Hispanic American Historical Review* 54(1):1–47.

———. 1976. *La servidumbre agraria en México en la época porfiriana*. Mexico City: Secretaría de Educación Pública, Dirección General de Divulgación.

Kautsky, Karl. 1988. *The Agrarian Question*. London: Zwan.

Kay, Cristóbal. 1999. "Rural Development: From Agrarian Reform to Neoliberalism and Beyond." In *Latin America Transformed: Globalization and Modernity*, ed. R. N. Gwynne and C. Kay. London: Oxford University Press.

Keith, Michael, and Steve Pile. 1993. "The Place of Politics." In *Place and the Politics of Identity*, ed. M. Keith and S. Pile. London: Routledge.

Klepeis, Peter, and Colin Vance. 2003. "Neoliberal Policy and Deforestation in Southeastern Mexico: An Assessment of the PROCAMPO Program." *Economic Geography* 79(3):221–240.

Knight, Alan. 1986. "Mexican Peonage: What Was It and Why Was It?" *Journal of Latin American Studies* 18(1):41–74.

Krauze, Enrique. 1997. *Mexico: Biography of Power: A History of Modern Mexico, 1810–1996*. New York: Harper Collins.

Lefebvre, Henri. 1991. *The Production of Space*. Cambridge: Blackwell.

Lenin, V. I. 1977. *The Development of Capitalism in Russia*. Moscow: Progress.

Leyva Solano, Xochitl, and Gabriel Ascencio Franco. 1996. *Lacandonia al filo del agua*. Mexico City: Fondo de Cultura Económica.

Li, Tania M. 1999. "Compromising Power: Development, Culture, and Rule in Indonesia." *Cultural Anthropology* 40(3):277–309.

———. 2000. "Articulating Indigenous Identity in Indonesia: Resource Politics and the Tribal Slot." *Comparative Studies in Society and History* 42(1):149–179.

López, Adriana. 2000. "Los nuevos zapatistas y la lucha por la tierra." *Chiapas* 9:139–158.

López Reyes, Jasmina. 2005. "El café en Yajalón: Cambio social en una región cafetalera." *Anuario de Estudios Indígenas* 10:335–357.

Luna, Arturo. 2001. Address delivered at Seminario internacional: La lucha por la tierra y la reforma agraria en el nuevo mundo. San Cristóbal de Las Casas.

Lustig, Nora. 1992. *Mexico, the Remaking of an Economy*. Washington: Brookings Institution.

Mallon, Florencia. 1995. *Peasant and Nation: The Making of Postcolonial Mexico and Peru.* Berkeley: University of California Press.

——. 1996. "Constructing Mestizaje in Latin America: Authenticity, Marginality and Gender in the Claiming of Ethnic Identities." *Journal of Latin American Anthropology* 2(1):170–181.

Marcus, George. 1983. *Elites: Ethnographic Issues.* Albuquerque: University of New Mexico Press.

Martín Echeverría, Leonardo. 1960. *La gandería mexicana.* Mexico City: Banco de México.

Martínez Quezada, Álvaro, Conrado Márquez Rosano, Homelino Ovanda León, María del Carmen Legorreta, Mauricio Ortega Gutiérrez, Pablo E. Muench Navarro, and Renato Zarate Baños. 1994. *Reforma agraria y movimientos campesinos en el estado de Chiapas.* Chapingo: Universidad Autónoma.

Marx, Karl. 1967. *Capital.* Vol. 3. New York: International Publishers.

Massey, Doreen B. 1994. *Space, Place, and Gender.* Minneapolis: University of Minnesota Press.

Maurer Avalos, Eugenio. 1978. "La educación bilingüe en un poblado de Chiapas, México." Mexico City: Centro de Estudios Educativo.

——. 1983. *Los Tseltales.* Mexico City: Centro de Estudios Educativos.

McDonogh, Gary W. 1986. *Good Families of Barcelona.* Princeton: Princeton University Press.

Middlebrook, Kevin J. 1995. *The Paradox of Revolution: Labor, the State, and Authoritarianism in Mexico.* Baltimore: Johns Hopkins University Press.

Middlebrook, Kevin J., and Eduardo Zepeda. 2003. *Confronting Development: Assessing Mexico's Economic and Social Policy Challenges.* Stanford: Stanford University Press.

Moguel, Julio. 1994. "The Mexican Left and the Social Program of Salinismo." In *Transforming State-Society Relations in Mexico: The National Solidarity Strategy,* ed. W. Cornelius, A. Craig, and J. Fox. La Jolla: Center for U.S.-Mexican Studies, University of California, San Diego.

Moore, Barrington. 1966. *Social Origins of Dictatorship and Democracy: Lord and Peasant in the Making of the Modern World.* Boston: Beacon.

Moore, Donald S. 1998. "Subaltern Struggles and the Politics of Place: Remapping Resistance in Zimbabwe's Eastern Highlands." *Cultural Anthropology* 13(3):344–381.

——. 1999. "The Crucible of Cultural Politics." *American Ethnologist* 26(3):654–689.

——. 2005. *Suffering for Territory: Race, Place, and Power in Zimbabwe.* Durham: Duke University Press.

Moyo, Sam. 2000. "The Political Economy of Land Acquisition and Redistribution in Zimbabwe, 1990–1999." *Journal of Southern African Studies* 26(1):5–32.

Nader, Laura. 1999. "Up the Anthropologist: Perspectives Gained from Studying Up." In *Reinventing Anthropology,* ed. D. Hymes. Ann Arbor: Ann Arbor Paperbacks.

Nash, June C. 1967. "Death as a Way of Life: The Increasing Resort to Homicide in a Maya Indian Community." *American Anthropologist* 69(5):455–470.

———. 2001. *Mayan Visions: The Quest for Autonomy in an Age of Globalization.* New York: Routledge.

Nelson, Diane M. 1999. *A Finger in the Wound: Body Politics in Quincentennial Guatemala.* Berkeley: University of California Press.

———. 2003. " 'The More You Kill the More You Will Live': The Mayan 'Race' and Biopolitical Hopes for Peace in Guatemala." In *Race, Nature, and the Politics of Difference,* ed. D. S. Moore, A. Pandian, and J. Kosek. Durham: Duke University Press.

Neocosmos, Michael. 1986. "Marx's Third Class." *Journal of Peasant Studies* 13(3):5–44.

Nickel, Herbert J. 1997. *El peonaje en las haciendas mexicanas: Interpretaciones, fuentes, hallazgos.* Freiburg: Arnold Bergstraesser Institut.

Nordstrom, C. 1997. *A Different Kind of War Story.* Philadelphia: University of Pennsylvania Press.

Nordstrom, Carolyn, and JoAnn Martin. 1992. *The Paths to Domination, Resistance, and Terror.* Berkeley: University of California Press.

Nordstrom, Carolyn, and Antonius C. G. M. Robben. 1995. *Fieldwork under Fire: Contemporary Studies of Violence and Survival.* Berkeley: University of California Press.

Nugent, Daniel. 1993. *Spent Cartridges of Revolution: An Anthropological History of Namiquipa, Chihuahua.* Chicago: University of Chicago Press.

Nugent, Daniel, and Ana Alonso. 1994. "Multiple Selective Traditions in Agrarian Reform and Agrarian Struggle: Popular Culture and State Formation in the Ejido of Namiquipa, Chihuahua." In *Everyday Forms of State Formation: Revolution and the Negotiation of Rule in Modern Mexico,* ed. G. M. Joseph and D. Nugent. Durham: Duke University Press.

Ochoa, Enrique C. 2000. *Feeding Mexico: The Political Uses of Food since 1910.* Wilmington, Del.: Scholarly Resources.

Olivera, Mercedes. 1980. "Sobre la explotación y opresión de las mujeres acasiallados de Chiapas." In *El sur de México: Datos sobre la problemática indígena,* ed. G. Munch, D. Ryesky, M. Olivera, A. Pérez, A. M. Salazar, W. Hartwig, and V. K. Hartwig. Mexico City: UNAM.

Olivera, Mercedes, and María Dolores Palomo, eds. 2005. *Chiapas: de la Independencia a la Revolución.* Tlapan: CIESAS.

Ollman, Bertell. 1976. *Alienation: Marx's Conception of Man in Capitalist Society.* Cambridge: Cambridge University Press.

Omi, Michael, and Howard Winant. 1994. *Racial Formation in the United States: From the 1960s to the 1990s.* New York: Routledge.

Ong, Aihwa. 2000. "Graduated Sovereignty in South-East Asia." *Theory, Culture and Society* 17(4):55–75.

Orlove, Ben. 1994. "The Dead Policemen Speak: Power, Fear, and Narrative in the 1931 Molloccahua Killings (Cusco)." In *Unruly Order: Violence, Power, and Cultural Identity in the Highland Provinces of Southern Peru,* ed. D. Poole. Boulder: Westview.

Otero, Gerardo. 1996. *Neoliberalism Revisited: Economic Restructuring and Mexico's Political Future.* Boulder: Westview.

———. 2004. *Mexico in Transition: Neoliberal Globalism, the State and Civil Society.* New York: Zed.

Ovalle Muñoz, Pedro de Jesús. 1984. "Movimientos campesinos en la zona tzeltal de Chiapas." *Textual* 17:63–78.

Paige, Jeffrey. 1975. *Agrarian Revolution: Social Movements and Export Agriculture in the Underdeveloped World.* London: Free Press.

———. 1997. *Coffee and Power: Revolution and the Rise of Democracy in Central America.* Cambridge: Harvard University Press.

Pastor, Manuel, and Carol Wise. 1997. "State Policy, Distribution, and Neoliberal Reform in Mexico." *Journal of Latin American Studies* 29 (2):419–456.

Payne, Leigh A. 2000. *Uncivil Movements: The Armed Right Wing and Democracy in Latin America.* Baltimore: Johns Hopkins University Press.

Paz, Octavio. 1985. *The Labyrinth of Solitude.* New York: Grove.

Pedrero Nieto, Gloria. 1981. "El proceso de acumulación originaria en el agro chiapaneco." In *Investigaciones recientes en el área Maya, XVII Mesa Redonda, San Cristóbal* 3:31–39.

Pineda, Vicente. 1888. *Historia de las sublevaciones indígenas habidas en el Estado de Chiapas, Gramática de la lengua tzeltal que habla la generalidad de los habitantes de los pueblos que quedan al oriente y al noreste del estado. Y diccionario de la misma.* Tuxtla Gutiérrez: Tipografía del Gobierno.

Pólito Barrios, Elizabeth. 2000. "El capital extranjero y nacional en Chiapas." *Chiapas* 9:61–82.

Pontigo, J. Luís, and Gonzalo Hernández. 1981. "Poder y dominación en la zona norte de Chiapas." In *Investigaciones recientes en el área Maya, XVII Mesa Redonda, San Cristóbal.*

Presidencia de la República. 1993. *Temas nacionales en las cartas al presidente.* Mexico City.

Procuraduría General de la República. 2000. *Boletín* 569/00.

Rabasa, D. R. 1895. *Estado de Chiapas: Geografía y Estadística.* Mexico City: Tipografía del Cuerpo Especial de Estado Mayor.

Ramírez, José María. 1885. *Memoria sobre diversos ramos de la administración pública del estado de Chiapas, presentada al XIV Congreso por el gobernador constitucional José María Ramírez.* Chiapas: Imprenta del Gobierno en Palacio.

Randall, Laura ed. 1996. *Reforming Mexico's Agrarian Reform.* Armonk, N.Y.: M. E. Sharpe.

Reyes Ramos, María Eugenia. 1992. *El reparto de tierras y la política agraria en Chiapas, 1914–1988.* Mexico City: UNAM.

———. 1998a. "Los acuerdos agrarios en Chiapas: ¿Una política de contención social?" In *Espacios disputados: Transformaciones rurales en Chiapas,* ed. M. E. Reyes Ramos, R. Moguel, and G. van der Haar. Xochimilco: Universidad Autónoma Metropolitana.

———. 1998b. "Conflicto agrario en Chiapas: 1934–1964." Ph.D. dissertation, UNAM.

Reyes Ramos, María Eugenia, Reyna Moguel, and Gemma van der Haar, eds. 1998. *Espacios disputados: Transformaciones rurales en Chiapas.* Xochimilco: Universidad Autónoma Metropolitana.

Ricardo, David. 1919. *Principles of Political Economy.* Harmondsworth: Penguin.

Richards, Alan. 1979. "The Political Economy of *Gutswirtschaft.*" *Comparative Studies in Society and History* 21(4):483–518.

Robles, Rosario. 1988. "Estructura de la producción y cultivos, 1950–1960." In *Historia de la cuestión agraria mexicana,* ed. J. Moguel, R. Robles, and B. Rubio, vol. 7. Mexico City: Siglo Veintiuno.

Romano, Agustin. 2002. *Historia evaluativa del Centro Coordinador Indigenista Tzeltal-Tzotzil,* vol. 1. Mexico City: Instituto Nacional Indigenista.

Rosaldo, Renato. 1993. *Culture and Truth: The Remaking of Social Analysis.* Boston: Beacon.

Rose, Nikolas S. 1999. *Powers of Freedom: Reframing Political Thought.* Cambridge: Cambridge University Press.

Roseberry, William. 1994. "Hegemony and the Language of Contention." In *Everyday Forms of State Formation: Revolution and the Negotiation of Rule in Mexico,* ed. G. Joseph and D. Nugent. Durham: Duke University Press.

Rubin, Jeffrey W. 1997. *Decentering the Regime: Ethnicity, Radicalism, and Democracy in Juchitán, Mexico.* Durham: Duke University Press.

Rubio, Blanca. 1987. *Resistencia campesina y explotación rural en México.* Mexico City: Era.

Rus, Jan. 1994. "The 'Comunidad Revolucionaria Institucional': The Subversion of Native Government in Highland Chiapas, 1936–1968." In *Everyday Forms of State Formation: Revolution and the Negotiation of Rule in Modern Mexico,* ed. G. M. Joseph and D. Nugent. Durham: Duke University Press.

———. 1995. "Local Adaptation to Global Change: The Reordering of Native Society in Highland Chiapas, Mexico, 1974–1994." *European Review of Latin American and Caribbean Studies* 58:71–89.

———. 2005. "El café y la recolonización de los Altos de Chiapas, 1892–1910." In *Chiapas: de la independencia a la revolución,* ed. M. Olivera and M. D. Palomo. Tlapan: CIESAS.

Rutherford, Blair. 2004. "'Settlers' and Zimbabwe: Politics, Memory, and the Anthropology of Commercial Farms during a Time of Crisis." *Identities* 11(4):543–562.

Rutsch, Mechthild. 1984. *La ganadería capitalista en México.* Mexico City: Linea.

Sack, Robert David. 1986. *Human Territoriality: Its Theory and History.* Cambridge: Cambridge University Press.

Sadoulet, Elisabeth, Alain de Janvry, and Ben Davis. 2001. "Cash Transfer with Income Multiplier: PROCAMPO in Mexico." *World Development* 29(3):467–480.

Said, Edward. 1978. *Orientalism.* New York: Pantheon.

SAIIC. 1997. *South American Indigenous Information Bulletin.*

Sánchez Franco, Irene. 1999. "Teología de liberación y formación de identidad entre tzeltales de la zona norte de Chiapas." Master's thesis, CIESAS.

Sanderson, Steven E. 1986. *The Transformation of Mexican Agriculture: International Structure and the Politics of Rural Change.* Princeton: Princeton University Press.

Santín, Osvaldo. 2001. *The Political Economy of Mexico's Financial Reform.* Aldershot: Ashgate.

Sayer, Andrew. 1992. *Method in Social Science: A Realist Approach.* London: Routledge.

———. 2000. *Realism and Social Science.* London: Sage.

Scott, David Clark. 1994. "Chiapas Ranchers Vow to Take Law into Their Own Hands." *Christian Science Monitor,* April 14.

Scott, James C. 1985. *Weapons of the Weak: Everyday Forms of Peasant Resistance.* New Haven: Yale University Press.

Secretaría de Economía. 1930. *Censo Agrícola-Ganadera de 1930.* Mexico City.

Secretaría de Industria y Comercio. 1960. *Censo Agrícola-Ganadera.* Mexico City.

SIC. 1998. "Los acuerdos agrarios en Chiapas." At http://www.sic.chia pas.com/staach/informe/acuerdos.html. No longer available online. Printout available from the author.

Singer, Marie Odile Marion. 1984. *El movimiento campesino en Chiapas, 1983.* Mexico City: Centro de Estudios Históricos del Agrarismo en México.

Slack, Jennifer Daryl. 1996. "The Theory and Method of Articulation in Cultural Studies." In *Stuart Hall: Critical Dialogues in Cultural Studies,* ed. D. Morley and C. Kuan-Hsing. London: Routledge.

Smith, Gavin. 1989. *Livelihood and Resistance: Peasants and the Politics of Land in Peru.* Berkeley: University of California Press.

Smith, Katherine E. 2006. "Problematising Power Relations in 'Elite' Interviews." *Geoforum* 37:643–653.

Snyder, Richard. 2001. *Politics after Neoliberalism: Reregulation in Mexico.* Cambridge: Cambridge University Press.

Soederberg, Susanne. 2001. "From Neoliberalism to Social Liberalism: Situating the National Solidarity Program within Mexico's Passive Revolutions." *Latin American Perspectives* 28(3):104–123.

Spark, Alasdair. 2001. "Conjuring Order: The New World Order and Conspiracy Theories of Globalization." In *The Age of Anxiety: Conspiracy Theory and the Human Sciences,* ed. J. Parish and M. Parker. Oxford: Blackwell.

SRA. 2000. "Estructura Agraria de Chiapas." At http://www.sra-eservi cios.gob.mx/sra-e/dgia/fuentes/find.asp. No longer available online; printout available from author.

Stephens, John Lloyd. 1996 (1843). *Incidents of Travel in Yucatán.* Washington: Smithsonian Institution.

Stevens, Evelyn. 1973. "Marianismo: The Other Face of Machismo in

Latin America." In *Male and Female in Latin America,* ed. A. Pescatello. Pittsburgh: University of Pittsburgh Press.

Stoler, Ann Laura. 1995a. *Capitalism and Confrontation in Sumatra's Plantation Belt, 1870–1979.* 2nd ed. Ann Arbor: University of Michigan Press.

———. 1995b. *Race and the Education of Desire: Foucault's "History of Sexuality" and the Colonial Order of Things.* Durham: Duke University Press.

Taussig, Michael. 1984. "Culture of Terror—Space of Death: Roger Casement's Putumayo Report and the Explanation of Torture." *Comparative Studies in Society and History* 26(3):467–497.

———. 1986. *Shamanism, Colonialism, and the Wild Man: A Study in Terror and Healing.* Chicago: University of Chicago Press.

Tejera Gaona, Héctor. 1997. *Identidad, formación regional y conflicto político en Chiapas.* Mexico City: Instituto Nacional de Antropología e Historia.

Tenorio-Trillo, Mauricio. 1996. *Mexico at the World's Fairs: Crafting a Modern Nation.* Berkeley: University of California Press.

Toledo Tello, Sonia. 1996. *Historia del movimiento indígena en Simojovel, 1970–1989.* Serie Monografías 6. Tuxtla Gutiérrez: Instituto de Estudios Indígenas, Universidad Autónoma de Chiapas.

———. 2002. *Fincas, poder y cultura en Simojovel, Chiapas.* Mexico City: Instituto de Investigaciones Antropológicas, UNAM.

Tolstoy, Leo. 1996. *War and Peace.* New York: Norton.

Toraya, Bertha. 1985. "Origen y evolución de la tenencia de la tierra en el Soconusco, Chiapas: El caso de Santo Domingo." *Cuadernos de la Casa Chata,* no. 125, pp. 91–128.

Vandergeest, Peter, and Nancy Lee Peluso. 1995. "Territorialization and State Power in Thailand." *Theory and Society* 4(3):385–426.

van der Haar, Gemma. 1993. *Balancing on a Slack Rope: A Study of Bilingual Teachers in Chiapas, Mexico.* Wageningen: Department of Agricultural Education, University of Wageningen.

Vaughan, Mary Kay. 1997. *Cultural Politics in Revolution: Teachers, Peasants, and Schools in Mexico, 1930–1940.* Tucson: University of Arizona Press.

———. 1999. "Cultural Approaches to Peasant Politics in the Mexican Revolution." *Hispanic American Historical Review* 79(2):269–305.

Vázquez Castillo, María Teresa. 2004. *Land Privatization in Mexico: Urbanization, Formation of Regions, and Globalization in Ejidos.* New York: Routledge.

Vera Hernández, Carlos Alexis. 1998. "Situación y problemática acerca de la ganadería bovina asociado del municipio de Chilón, Chiapas." MVZ thesis, Universidad Nacional Autónoma de Chiapas.

Villafuerte Solís, Daniel, María del Carmen García Aguilar, and Salvador Meza Díaz. 1997. *La cuestión ganadera y la deforestación: Viejos y nuevos problemas en el trópico y Chiapas.* Tuxtla Gutiérrez: Universidad de Ciencias y Artes del Estado de Chiapas.

Villafuerte Solís, Daniel, Salvador Meza Díaz, Gabriel Ascencio Franco, María del Carmen García Aguilar, Carolina Rivera Farfán, Miguel Lisbona Guillén, and Jesús Morales Bermúdez. 1999. *La tierra en Chiapas, viejos problemas nuevos.* Mexico City: Plaza y Valdés.

Viqueira, Juan Pedro. 1997. *Indios rebeldes e idólatras: Dos ensayos históricos sobre la rebelión india de Canuc, Chiapas, acaecida en el año 1712.* Tlalpan: CIESAS.

Washbrook, Sarah. 2005. "Desarrollo económico y reclutamiento y control de mano de obra en el norte de Chiapas, 1876–1911." In *Chiapas: de la Independencia a la Revolución*, eds. M. Olivera and M. D. Palomo. Tlalpan: CIESAS.

Wasserstrom, Robert. 1983. *Class and Society in Central Chiapas.* Berkeley: University of California Press.

Watts, Michael. 2002. "Chronicle of a Death Foretold: Some Thoughts on Peasants and the Agrarian Question." *Österreichische Zeitschrift für Geschichtswissenschaften*, no. 4, pp. 22–51.

———. 2003. "Development and Governmentality." *Singapore Journal of Tropical Geography* 24(1):6–34.

Wells, Allen, and Gilbert M. Joseph. 1996. *Summer of Discontent, Seasons of Upheaval: Elite Politics and Rural Insurgency in Yucatán, 1876–1915.* Stanford: Stanford University Press.

Williams, Raymond. 1980. *Problems in Materialism and Culture.* London: Verso.

Winson, Anthony. 1982. The Prussian Road of Agrarian Development. *Economy and Society* 11(4):381–408.

Wolf, Eric R. 1969. *Peasant Wars of the Twentieth Century.* New York: Harper and Row.

Zedillo, Ernesto. 1998. "Palabras del presidente Ernesto Zedillo." Address delivered May 19 at Casa de la Cultura, San Cristóbal de Las Casas.

Index

Aaron Bobrow-Strain
is an assistant professor in the department
of politics at Whitman College.

Library of Congress Cataloging-in-Publication Data
Bobrow-Strain, Aaron, 1969–
Intimate enemies: landowners, power, and violence
in Chiapas / Aaron Bobrow-Strain.
p. cm.
Includes bibliographical references and index.
ISBN 978-0-8223-3987-8 (cloth : alk. paper)
ISBN 978-0-8223-4004-1 (pbk. : alk. paper)
1. Landowners — Mexico — Chiapas — History.
2. Elite (Social sciences) — Mexico — Chiapas —
History. 3. Land reform — Mexico — Chiapas —
History. 4. Social conflict — Mexico —
Chiapas — History. 5. Violence — Mexico — Chiapas —
History. 6. Chiapas (Mexico) — Social conditions.
I. Title.
HD1331.M6B63 2007
972'.75 — dc22   20070002141